About the Author

Andrew James is a former Australian soldier. During his time with the Army he served in the Special Forces and fought in the war in Afghanistan. Following his military service, Andrew continued his studies at Sydney University where he read History and English. During his degree he supported himself by working as an expedition leader on the Kokoda Track in Papua New Guinea where he first became interested in Stan's story. Andrew is twenty-six years old and resides in Sydney. *Kokoda Wallaby* is his first book.

Dedication

To Lieutenant Mick Fussell, 4RAR (Commando) and
Private Greg Sher, 2 Commando Company.

When you go home,
Tell them of us and say,

For their tomorrow,
We gave our today.

KOKODA
WALLABY

KOKODA
WALLABY

ANDREW JAMES

ALLEN&UNWIN

First published in 2011

Copyright © Andrew James 2011

All rights reserved. No part of this book may be reproduced or transmitted in any form or by any means, electronic or mechanical, including photocopying, recording or by any information storage and retrieval system, without prior permission in writing from the publisher. The Australian *Copyright Act 1968* (the Act) allows a maximum of one chapter or 10 per cent of this book, whichever is the greater, to be photocopied by any educational institution for its educational purposes provided that the educational institution (or body that administers it) has given a remuneration notice to Copyright Agency Limited (CAL) under the Act.

Allen & Unwin
Sydney, Melbourne, Auckland, London

83 Alexander Street
Crows Nest NSW 2065
Australia
Phone: (61 2) 8425 0100
Fax: (61 2) 9906 2218
Email: info@allenandunwin.com
Web: www.allenandunwin.com

Cataloguing-in-Publication details are available
from the National Library of Australia
www.trove.nla.gov.au

ISBN 978 1 74237 696 7

Internal design by DiZign, Sydney
Maps by DiZign, Sydney
Index by Puddingburn
Photo credits: ARU Archives pp. 84, 87, 89, 92, 93; Australian War Memorial pp. 259, 261; The *Daily Telegraph* p. 59; Craig Eyes, Power House pp. 36, 45; Mitchell Library pp. 69, 74, 76, 78, 80, 83. All other photos have been supplied by the Bisset family.

Set in 11.5/15 pt Bembo by Post Pre-press Group, Australia
Printed and bound in Australia by Griffin Press

10 9 8 7 6 5 4 3 2 1

The paper in this book is FSC certified. FSC promotes environmentally responsible, socially beneficial and economically viable management of the world's forests.

Contents

	Acknowledgements	viii
	Foreword	ix
	Preface	xi
	Prologue	1
1	Youth	5
2	It's Only the Game that Counts	22
3	Green and Gold	60
4	Yellow and Blue	100
5	Shifting Sands	113
6	The Bloody Track	151
7	Retreat	181
8	Run Rabbit	216
9	Captain Bisset Military Cross	242
10	Days in the Sun	257
	Epilogue	278
	Index	281

Acknowledgements

Firstly I would like to thank Stan and Gloria Bisset for the tireless help and overwhelming kindness they extended to me throughout my research for this project. The vast majority of this work comes from Stan's own recollections, as told to me through many hours of conversation in the living-room of their home in Peregian Springs on the Sunshine Coast. Without Stan's patience and willingness to assist me wherever possible, and without Gloria's kindness and wonderful hospitality, this book would never have come to fruition.

Secondly, and almost as importantly, I need to thank my father Bill. During my time overseas with the Army, Dad launched himself tirelessly into the editing of this work as well as contributing an enormous amount of his own research (as a pre-eminent expert on the 2/14th Battalion and the Kokoda Campaign, an assertion I feel confident no one would challenge) and managed to turn the text from a draft into a coherent narrative.

Additionally, I need to thank my mother Liz for her meticulous proof-reading of the final drafts, my partner Bec for her continual creative advice and support, and Peter, Diana and Sonia from DiZign for their many hours of work on the design and layout.

FOREWORD

By Patrick Lindsay

I'll never forget watching Stan Bisset as he stood in front of his beloved brother's grave at Bomana War Cemetery outside Port Moresby. It was August 1998, during what Stan and his fellow Kokoda Diggers called the Last Parade — their pilgrimage to say a final farewell to the mates they had left behind. It was the first time Stan had visited the grave since Butch had died in his arms on the Track fifty-six years earlier. He stood there silently for a long time. I could see the emotions surging through him. As always, he stood ramrod straight, but tears welled in his eyes as the memories flooded back.

There before him lay Butch, whose life was cut short by the terrible random selection of war, like that of so many others on the Track. Stan had vowed to lead a good and productive life to honour Butch's sacrifice. And he was as good as his word. He raised a fine family, forged a long and successful career and has done all in his power to keep Butch's memory and the story of Kokoda alive.

While I watched, Stan gently wiped the tears from his eyes with his powerful hands and then brought them to his side. He squared his shoulders and paused. Then he swept his right arm up in a crisp, practised salute: a homage from a warrior; a farewell from a brother.

Stan had a deep-rooted sense of duty and an unshakeable sense of honour. He had star quality: that indefinable amalgam of physical presence and character that sets the remarkable ones apart. He was a genuine sporting hero who blossomed into a military hero in the cauldron of war.

I vividly remember the first time I met him — we were interviewing veterans for a documentary we were filming. My immediate thought was that they've ordered a hero from Central Casting and they've sent the perfect specimen.

Stan's former commanding officer and lifelong friend, the late Phil Rhoden, told me that Stan had no time to grieve for Butch during the battles along the Track and it took him many years to recover from the loss. Like so many other Kokoda veterans, the campaign was one of the defining experiences of Stan's life. Somehow, Stan dealt with the blows and got on with his life.

Stan Bisset was quite simply one the finest men I have met. I have been privileged to call him a friend and a mentor for twenty years. He personified so many attributes of the Digger to me — courage (both moral and physical), compassion, selflessness, independence, loyalty, resourcefulness, devotion, coolness, and humour. He carried himself with the bearing of a natural leader and a champion sportsman. Even as he neared his century, he continued to inspire me and all those who knew him with his dogged refusal to surrender any ground to Father Time.

Stan Bisset, like this wonderful story of his life, was timeless.

Patrick Lindsay is the author of fourteen books including *The Spirit of Kokoda*, *The Essence of Kokoda* and *The Spirit of the Digger*.

Preface

So, why Stan's story? For any work of this kind it is probably worth beginning with that most basic of questions. Researching and writing a biography is a tough undertaking and the modern reader is not starved for choice in this genre, so what is it about this man's life that makes it a story worth telling?

On one level, the answer is relatively obvious. Stan Bisset might already be a familiar name for a considerable number of readers. Many Australian rugby supporters will recognise him as a member of our 1939 touring team and something of a living legend within the Australian Rugby Union fraternity. Other readers who have an interest in, or who have walked, the Kokoda Track in Papua New Guinea could recognise him as one of the most distinguished Australian officers of several key battles of the war in New Guinea — including the horrific battles of Gona and the Ramu Valley. Stan was awarded the Military Cross for leadership and courage under fire at the latter.

These achievements and experiences alone make Stan's story one worth telling, but the narrative of this one man's life also has a broader significance. In a way, Stan's story typifies that of an entire generation of Australians — born at the time of the Great War, children of the Great Depression, young adults during the horrific years of the Second World War, middle-aged parents through the socially disruptive decades of the 1950s and 60s, and finally, the elderly in the rapidly changing world of the 'information age'. It is almost inconceivable that one generation could bear witness to so much change and endure such challenges. Stan's story encapsulates all this, and more.

The war through which Stan lived and fought changed his life in every conceivable manner. He lost his brother and his closest friends. His lifestyle changed from one of leisure and glamour as an international athlete to that of a husband and father working multiple jobs as a tradesman and engineer simply to make ends meet. It is almost too easy for us, living in this privileged and sometimes disturbingly sanitised world, to empathise with the suffering and sacrifices of past generations on more than a superficial level. At school or in our lounge-room we may read that seventy-three young Australians died at the Battle of Isurava, but it is often difficult to connect with this fact as anything more than a statistic.

Our nation is, however, currently experiencing a resurgence of interest in our military history. Huge numbers of Australians now flock to the battlefields of Gallipoli every Anzac Day and every year thousands of trekkers attempt the arduous pilgrimage across the Kokoda Track.

Additionally, for the first time in four decades, Australians are beginning to understand what it really means to send our sons off to war, to kill and to die on the battlefields of some foreign land. I spent the winter of 2008 in the mountains of southern Afghanistan and when two men from my company were killed in action, we were taken aback by the outpouring of public grief at their loss. The funeral of Private Greg Sher, a close friend with whom I had served for years, was attended by over 4000 mourners — amongst them the Prime Minister, the Minister for Defence, the Leader of the Opposition, the Chief of the Defence Force, the Chief of the Army, the Chief of Special Operations and many other dignitaries. Greg's face was on the front page of every major Australian newspaper for several days, as was the face of another friend, Mick Fussell, killed in November 2008. When Trooper Mark Donaldson was awarded the Victoria Cross in the same month, it consumed

Preface

the Australian press for an entire week. Australians could scarcely believe that we were actually asking our young men to leave their families, their partners, their children, and go to some godforsaken corner of the earth to kill or be killed by other young men.

It is in this context that the sacrifices of the past are beginning to take on a whole new meaning. We have begun to realise again just how traumatic is it for a family to lose someone they love so dearly. Sending the bodies of two friends home from war was certainly the hardest thing I have ever had to do. They received the recognition they rightfully deserved, but that makes it all the more poignant to remember that the remains of another 100,000 Australian war dead lie in the fields of four continents and at the bottom of every ocean.

Stan's story is worth telling, not because his achievements as a Wallaby or as a decorated soldier make him a 'hero' (at least, not in his own eyes) but rather, because his amazing talents and achievements serve to highlight the challenges endured, and sacrifices made, by an entire generation of men and women who lived through these years with him, and whose stories remain untold.

Prologue

Papua New Guinea, 2000

The tropical sun is fierce, even at this early hour of the morning. A group of Australian trekkers makes its way up the steep, arduous trail from the Isurava Battlefield to the old resthouse clearing. On this morning, nearly sixty years after the last Australian soldier passed along the Kokoda Track, the vegetation looks startlingly different to the way it looked in August 1942. The waste and ruin of war have long disappeared. The clearing where they stand is covered by kunai grass and ringed by scarlet flowers. From the tiny native hut on the site, one can see across the valley to where the smoke is swirling up into the morning sky from the tiny villages of Abuari and Missima. On a clear day like this the ubiquitous palm oil groves of the Yodda plain are visible down the steep Eora valley and one can faintly make out the azure green of the fields just to the east of Kokoda.

The trekkers, like all those who pass this way, take a break as they reach the small clearing and collapse, exhausted, in the shade of the tiny hut. To the one native family who call this home, these foreigners make a fascinating sight. Like the several thousands of young Australians who attempt the challenging expedition across the Owen Stanley Range every year, they sport the latest in trekking gear: gortex 'wicking' shirts, lycra legging 'skins', composite Scarpa boots, camelback hydration systems and carbon-fibre trekking poles.

The hill up from Isurava is one of the toughest on the trail and these trekkers who set out earlier in the day are thoroughly spent after their climb. As they take a much-needed drink in the shade, five men emerge from the same jungle trail that the trekkers have just climbed. The trekkers are astonished to see two of the men are elderly with walking sticks and white hair. All conversation stops and jaws drop. The two elderly men are Con 'Vappy' Vafiopolous, a former medical orderly with the 2/14th Battalion, and Stan Bisset, the unit's former adjutant. They have come to Isurava by helicopter to assist historians Ross and Phil Clover and John Rennie in their research of the battlefield. This morning they have agreed to accompany the trio all the way up to the rest-house escarpment.

Throughout the decades the trees, vines and shrubs have grown, died, and re-grown. Monsoon rains have lashed the earth and scoured rivulets in the jungle hillsides. New garden tracks have been cut and old ones have become overgrown. Con and Stan look about disconcertingly, trying to recall a boulder here or a creek there, some reference point that might trigger a memory. But the second Stan sees the native hut on the cleared escarpment, he turns to Ross. 'That's exactly where the war-time rest-house stood,' he says with absolute confidence. The vegetation may have grown but the precipice beyond the grassy ledge where the hut once stood has not changed in a millennium.

As they re-enter the jungle on the high side of the clearing, Con immediately exclaims, 'Hey, I know where we are.' He turns to John and Ross and points to a diamond-shaped boulder in the centre of the track so large that trekkers can only squeeze past it. 'We set up an emergency dressing-station right here during the withdrawal,' Con begins to explain. 'The lads brought up several stretcher cases from Isurava and left them here.' He pauses, gesturing to the flat-topped rock that did, in fact, bear an uncanny resemblance to a surgeon's table. 'It was the first place we could treat them.' The rock is an immovable marker in the swirling sea of vegetation and memories.

Prologue

'In fact,' explains Con, 'I believe I amputated a boy's foot right here on the rock.' The trekkers look on, incredulous.

'They brought my brother, Hal, here,' says Stan. 'He'd been shot in the stomach. George Woodward and some of the 10 Platoon boys carried him up and Don Duffy and I got a look at him. We knew straight away that he was going to die.' The group looks on in silence. 'In fact,' Stan gazes up and down the trail, 'we only carried him just down there, not more than a hundred yards.' Stan walks briskly down the trail followed by the others, and suddenly stops again. 'Yes,' he says, 'it was definitely here. Don and I carried him into that clearing, just in there.' It doesn't look to John and Ross as if there could be any kind of clearing in the thick jungle, but as the small party pushes off the track to the west a dozen paces, they stumble into a tiny open space, only the size of a small carport. It is an impressive feat of navigation after fifty-seven years. 'Don and I laid him down, just here,' Stan continues. 'Don gave him some morphine and then had to push on. I sat with Hal and held his hand. He died in the early morning and we buried him right here.' Stan points to the centre of the tiny, dark clearing. The group is transfixed now.

'Did you talk?' asks Ross. Stan seems lost in thought.

'Oh, yes,' he replies eventually. 'We talked about home, about Mum and Dad, that sort of thing. I sang him a few songs. But mainly I just sat in the rain and held him.'

'What did you sing?' someone asks.

'Oh, I suppose I sang "Mountains of Mourne", probably some Gilbert and Sullivan, and "Danny Boy".'

'Why "Danny Boy"?' asks John. Again, Stan pauses for a moment.

'It was our favourite.'

Kokoda Wallaby

And if you come, when all the flowers are dying,
And I am dead, as dead I well may be,
You'll come and find the place where I am lying,
And kneel and say an 'Ave' there for me.

And I shall hear, tho' soft you tread above me,
And all my dreams will warmer, sweeter be,
For you shall bend, and tell me that you love me,
And I will sleep in peace until you come to me.

CHAPTER ONE

Youth

When Stanley Young Bisset first came into the world in the back room of his parent's townhouse at 73 Grosvenor Street, Balaclava, on 27 August 1912, thoughts of sporting fame and the horrors of war were hardly at the forefront of George and Olive's thoughts. Stan was the fourth of their five children. Murray and Noel were considerably older, then came Thomas Harold, known to all as 'Hal' or later as 'Butch', then Stanley followed by Jean, who was known as 'Jonnie'. Both parents were heavily involved in the family business, The House That Jack Built, a well-known and long-established drapery store and workshop on Greville Street in the prominent Melbourne shopping district of Prahran.

The House That Jack Built appears to have produced one of those exceptional circumstances in which both husband and wife brought complementary attributes to the working relationship. George Simpson Bisset had spent his life in the drapery business. Not only was he a born salesman with an intimate knowledge of the industry, but he was also genuinely dedicated to his customers. George would stop at nothing to ensure that his clients received exactly what they wanted. Behind the store was a small workshop where half a dozen seamstresses worked during the week making tailored orders for clients and general stock for the shop, and George oversaw this process. Nor was his passion for distributing good quality dresses and drapery to the public limited to the store in Prahran. There were occasions when he would travel through the tracks of rural Victoria, the Dandenongs in particular, selling clothes and dress goods from the back of a one-horse jinker.

When Stan was a little older he sometimes accompanied his father on these trips and could recall some fleeting images — manhandling the heavy carrying cases, driving through raging bushfires and blinding rains, being stuck in muddy bogs and seeing poisonous snakes flicked into the air by the turning cart wheel — images of an Australia long past. While George was the born salesman exhibiting close attention to detail and a passionate knowledge of his trade, Olive was at the 'business-end' of the Bisset family partnership. She worked tirelessly to ensure that The House That Jack Built had orderly accounts, well-kept books and a generous supply of stock flowing from the workshop.

Stan's fondness for his parents became apparent late one afternoon in 1916. Stan had been sent to spend the day with his grandparents in Greenmeadows Gardens in nearby St Kilda so that George and Olive could spend a busy day in the shop. Fed up with the lack of interesting activities at his Nanna's and Pop's, four-year-old Stan casually strolled out the front door and down the road to the Balaclava tram terminus where, unnoticed by the station guards, he hopped onto the afternoon tram to Prahran and soon presented himself on the front doorstep of his parents' shop.

All in all it was a happy and profitable family partnership. Australia had suffered a severe depression in the 1890s but by the early 1900s Melbourne was experiencing a boom and the Greville Street shop was ideally placed to benefit from this bubble of economic good fortune. Prahran was turning into a busy,

Black Rock, 1915. Stan (left) with his sister 'Jonnie'.

well-to-do shopping district for Melbourne's growing 'society' and the market for the Bissets' business was expanding rapidly. George and Olive were so dedicated that they rented a two-storey terrace near the shop where they could sleep over during periods of heavy work.

The outbreak of the First World War did not seriously impact on the business; indeed it was during this period that the Bissets decided to invest in a second home, close to the beach in the township of Black Rock. Just to the south of the bay-side suburb of Sandringham and now well and truly absorbed within metropolitan Melbourne, the Black Rock of the Great War era was a wild and largely undeveloped patch of coast. Only a handful of holiday houses were scattered amongst the tea-trees and dunes along the shore of Port Phillip Bay. The only way into Melbourne was via the single horse-drawn cable-tram that ran from Beaumaris to Sandringham and then a train to Melbourne.

The extent to which the three youngest Bisset children revelled in this wilderness environment was such that George and Olive enrolled them in Black Rock State School and took on a full-time housekeeper, Millie Pocock. While Millie and her daughter Hilda cared for the three children at Black Rock, George and Olive devoted all their energies to the business during the week. The children meanwhile led a barefoot existence, roaming free through the dunes and along the deserted beaches and seeing to the regular chores that each had to perform: mainly stripping and collecting tea-tree bark for fuel and feeding and watering the fowls housed in the backyard. Millie always rewarded these chores with big chunks of freshly baked bread coated with salty dripping, which was a common substitute for butter in those days.

Millie Pocock accompanied young Stanley on his first day of school at Black Rock, but from then on he and Hal had to make their own way. This involved a walk of several kilometres along narrow, winding tracks through the scrub. Stan and Hal found these tracks somewhat intimidating, because the scrub was a popular haunt for gangs of older boys who built themselves hideaways and would set about terrorising or 'capturing' the younger children. Some of the boys wore army-issued gas masks, giving them an even scarier appearance. Hal, in particular, a fair and somewhat sickly child, was terrified of travelling through the scrub in the dark. Stan, Hal and Jean had the added problem of also having to cross

Youth

Mrs 'Mum' Ring's bull paddock. Unless they were prepared to make a mile-long detour, the children had no alternative but to cross the field, creeping across it as inconspicuously as possible.

After-school adventures included earning pocket money by scouring the backyards of hopefully empty weekenders to retrieve empty bottles they could cash in with merchants. The family had a bathing box, a wooden shed right on the beach, and Murray taught Stan to swim in the shallow waters of the bay. Generally, they

By the Yarra River, Warrandyte, 1920. A close bond developed between Stan (left) and Hal as a result of their bushland adventures.

roamed freely, exploring the rugged cliffs and rocky foreshores of Sandringham, Half Moon Bay, Black Rock and Beaumauris. Tree and rock climbing often came at a cost. In Stan's case, it was two broken arms and one broken collarbone, but these breakages had

Grosvenor Street, Balaclava, 1921. Hal (left), Noel (sitting) and Stan, dressed and ready for Sunday school.

their compensations. It meant several weeks of convalescence in the workshop under the doting care of his adored seamstress. There, Stan learned to crochet, a favourite children's pastime in that era. Four tiny nails were inserted into the top of a wooden cotton reel, then the wool was wound around each nail and stitched in a special pattern, forming a long 'rat's tail' that emerged through the hole in the cotton reel.

George, Olive, Murray and Noel used to come down to Black Rock on weekends, and in typical Bisset fashion they would often invite staff from the shop. George and Olive were devout Presbyterians and would go out of their way to offer any kindness or hospitality they could.

In 1920 the Bissets sold the Black Rock property, much to Stan and Hal's disappointment. It was only a year, however, before they bought a new house in the bush at Warrandyte, twenty-five kilometres north-east of the city on the banks of the Yarra. Their house, which they named Glenmore, lay in a beautiful setting on an acre or so of land. There was even enough room for a tennis court.

While living at Warrandyte, Stan and Hal often spent weekends at Tremont in the Dandenongs in the family's newly acquired holiday home with its superb views overlooking Western Port Bay to the east and Port Phillip Bay to the west. The journey was all the more thrilling when they rode in the side-car of Murray's Indian motorbike. School holidays were spent at their uncle Frank's farm up at Christmas Hills, fifteen kilometres to the north-east near Yarra Glen. Stan and the boys loved to help out on the farm. More exciting still, they were allowed to go hunting and rabbiting all over the property. Stan and Hal soon became excellent shots and could fell a rabbit with a .22 rifle from a distance of fifty paces. Both boys, however, preferred the then popular practice of rabbiting with ferrets. One afternoon while waiting at a burrow entrance on a particularly steep slope with Hal and his cousin Stanton, Stan caught sight of a huge rabbit bounding up out of the burrow and through the nets. A flying leap sent Stan rolling head over heels down the long hill with his fingers clenched tightly onto the rabbit's ears and yelling back to Hal and Stanton, 'I've got him! I've got the blighter!' It was only when he reached the bottom of the hill, scratched and grazed, that he discovered that his grip was in fact fastened around the head of the dead rabbit already hanging from his belt, the prey of an earlier catch.

If Stan and Hal were unable to get away on weekends or holidays, there was no lack of activity at Warrandyte. They kept chooks, ducks and pigeons, grew strawberries and gooseberries and ate all sorts of freshly grown garden vegetables. Their backyard was the Australian bush, which may appear benign but is teaming with insects, lizards, snakes and a myriad of strange and often nocturnal native animals. The boys shared their bush adventures with a half-bred Labrador named Boy, who had been disinherited by his former owner for fighting viciously with every other dog he encountered. Boy took out his great store of aggression on the many black snakes that lurked in the undergrowth, especially during the hot, dry summers. Jonnie often joined the boys as they ducked through the rear paddock for a swim in the brisk-flowing Yarra River. The river provided a whole new world for the children. The bush may be tamed, but the river is an animate being, temperamental in character. During winter when the river was in flood, the swirling currents and eddies could sweep an inattentive child off his feet. But this was their playground and the dangers of the environment merely added to the excitement.

With Murray's help they built wood and kerosene-tin rafts, and on one frightening but memorable occasion Stan and Hal took to the river in full flood and Stan found himself swept out of control down the raging, foaming tide. After careening into an overhanging branch, Stan was tossed overboard and ensnared by the reeds and debris below the surface. Just as he was about to succumb to a state of panic, he felt the strong, sure hand of his older brother grasp him

Youth

by the collar and pull his head clear of the current. It was only Hal's quick reaction that allowed the boys to use their combined strength to drag Stan's legs free.

The headmaster of the local two-teacher school had the almost impossible task of contending with the antics of the assorted collection of scallywags masquerading as his pupils. The many football and cricket matches played against local teams from Doncaster, Templestowe, Eltham and Ringwood were far healthier pursuits than the lunchtime smoking of 'borrowed' Magpie cigarettes behind the school's toilet block. Stink-bombs were exploded in classroom ink wells. Pranks like this were harmless in comparison to one organised by mates Alan and Cecil Houghton.

Warrandyte was originally a gold mining settlement and the area was littered with abandoned shafts and rusting equipment. One hugely exciting discovery was a hidden cache of gelignite, fuse wire

The Yarra, 1923. Noel, Hal and Stan made rafts and explored the wilder sections of the river.

and detonators. Surely it would be impossible for two healthy twelve-year-olds to refuse the temptation to wag school and find something really good to blow up? A eucalypt with a hollow V at its base, well within audible distance of the school, seemed an ideal target and half a dozen sticks of 'gelly' did a magnificent job on the tree. The shower of splinters and rocks took quite a few minutes to settle. A good caning, written apologies and oodles of extra homework were small prices to pay for so much fun. From then on it was only the poor, unsuspecting Murray cod and Yarra River blackfish that had to contend with the odd 'plug' tossed into the stream.

The hunting, trekking, climbing, rafting and swimming enabled the children to develop an instinctive understanding of the outdoors, a profound sense of its beauty and a healthy respect for the dangers that lay in wait for the unsuspecting novice. These naturally developed instincts were to serve Stan well in his later life.

After only a few years at Warrandyte, the family moved back to Balaclava and Stan and Hal took up their studies at a state school in Surrey Hills, an inner eastern suburb.

In this era, tertiary education was reserved for the wealthy elite and while bursaries were available, there were few of them and it was normal for young men to enter the workforce in their early teens. Many sought apprenticeships where they could join a licensed tradesman. Others took any work they could find, and if they

Wattle Park, 1925. Stan ready for lessons at Surrey Hills State School.

were ambitious they studied part-time for some form of trade or professional career, usually at a college of technology. Hal was no different from the majority of his contemporaries and at age fourteen he found a position at Nye's, a local chemist shop. Ever keen to emulate his older brothers, Stan followed Hal into the pharmacy two years later. Full-time degrees in pharmacy did not exist in those days, so one sought an apprenticeship with the aim of doing several years of part-time study to gain a diploma.

The Bisset family members were strong supporters of the local St Margaret's Presbyterian Church near Surrey Hills and were among its most active parishioners. The five Bisset siblings found most of their social and recreational activities centred around the church. Murray ran a gymnasium out of the church hall, taking a group of local youths through sessions of weights, callisthenics, skipping and running. Stan's introduction to Murray's gym marked the humble beginning of a passion that was to consume him for the rest of his life. At the age of fifteen Stan became what could only be described as a fitness fanatic. After work in the chemist's shop and on every weekend he would spend countless hours training either in the gym or by himself: skipping, running or performing body-weight exercises.

By this stage, in the late 1920s, Noel had gone to work as a jackaroo on a property called 'Drivers' in the Riverina. Rural production had increased markedly after the First World War as many ex-servicemen took up soldier-settlement land-grants. By the mid-1920s, however, the harsh realities of life on the land began to take their toll and established pastoral properties like Drivers were constantly in need of new workers. Since Noel's letters home were full of enthusiasm for his new life he was soon followed by Hal. While Stan had always enjoyed good health, Hal had not been so lucky. No explanation was ever given for his lack of robustness — it was just accepted as being part of his make-up. But now, in his late teens and in this new and physically challenging environment,

Balaclava, 1927. Hal in his Sunday Best.

Hal virtually blossomed overnight from a pale, slim and somewhat fragile youth into a tough, robust young man.

Stan, still working in the chemist shop, was green with envy. The elder boys would arrive home tanned and fit on breaks from their work and Stan, always keen for adventure, longed to join them. When Noel moved to a new position on a cattle run in Western Australia and a spot became available at Drivers, Stan pleaded with his parents to let him go, but they insisted they needed at least one of their sons at home.

Doubly inspired not to fall behind his brothers in terms of fitness, Stan launched himself into his physical regimes with renewed vigour. He joined the YMCA and became a regular member of their basketball and gymnastics team. He also joined St Margaret's cricket team and it seemed every waking hour was consumed with some form of physical or sporting activity.

Stan also played tennis regularly throughout his teens, especially with his friends Colin and Maurice Long who had their own practice court. At the time, Colin was school captain of Melbourne Grammar and together with another friend, Alistair Righetti, they won the state schoolboys' doubles championship. Colin went on to have a long and wonderful career in tennis through the 1930s and in the late 1940s, after the war.

When he was sixteen Stan moved from the chemist shop to a new job as assistant accountant at the Royal Automobile Club of Victoria (RACV), again following in the footsteps of Hal who had joined the RACV before leaving to work as a jackaroo. Stan commenced an accountancy course through the Hemingway and Robertson Correspondence School. His new work role may have sounded somewhat dry and uninteresting but it proved to be anything but. Stan spent some of his day at work acting as a bodyguard for the club's accountant, or for one of the accountant's female assistants, as they made their daily visit to the bank with the club's cash takings. This role took on another level of responsibility when Stan was issued with a revolver. This necessitated his attending the local police station for training in the use of small arms.

As an adjunct to his new ad hoc role of bodyguard, Stan decided to take up boxing under the guidance of the former Australian lightweight champion, Sammy Grey. Stan's father had always been keen on skipping for fitness and would do up to 10,000 revolutions on the family's veranda every morning, a session that would take close to an hour. George had also taught Stan the skill and over a two-year period Stan gradually reached the point where he would do 20,000 revolutions in a non-stop, two-hour session. While Sammy Grey honed Stan's technical and tactical skills in the ring, his general fitness and conditioning training was overseen by former national sculling champion Jimmy Barton who, like the other coaches, was astonished at Stan's impressive stamina. Barton convinced Stan to take up sculling in addition to his boxing and general fitness routine.

While sport and fitness dominated his life outside the RACV, Stan was still able to find time for more cultural pursuits. The family was extremely musical. Olive was an accomplished pianist and gave lessons in her spare time. George was also more than competent and he could often be heard playing and singing hymns in his fine tenor voice. Family singalongs were a common form of entertainment and singing became a natural part of Stan's life. With his parents' encouragement, he began taking violin lessons with a family friend, Esther Rofe. Once described as 'the grand dame of Australia's composing community', Esther was a child virtuoso who had joined the Melbourne

San Remo, Western Port Bay, 1933. Stan was a gifted natural athlete.

Symphony Orchestra at age thirteen and performed on stage with Dame Nellie Melba. As a member of London's Royal College of Music, she was taught by Ralph Vaughan Williams, doyen of British composers.

Together with his siblings, Stan had always accompanied his parents to St Margaret's Church on the corner of Hotham Street and Denman Avenue and he was an enthusiastic member of their choir. Melbourne society strictly reserved Sundays for church and family and all formal sporting pursuits were actively discouraged. Far from rebelling against the norm, Stan loved the choir, which was gaining some notoriety. After one particular session Stan was approached by a gentleman who introduced himself as Mr Middleton. He complimented Stan on his fine baritone voice, explained that he was a teacher of note and offered Stan some free singing lessons. The Melbourne Conservatorium of Music was offering scholarships for young men with talent and Middleton believed that with some training, Stan would have the ability to audition for such a position.

Despite his initial scepticism, Stan enjoyed his music so much that he agreed to take Middleton up on his offer. Middleton was true to his word and with only a few months of formal training Stan not only gained an audition but won a scholarship for six months' tuition. The conservatorium, established as a private institution by George Marshall-Hall, was housed in the Victorian Artists' Society Building in Albert Street, East Melbourne, and was directed by Fritz Hart. Australia's famous diva Helen Porter Mitchell, better known to the world as Dame Nellie Melba, was closely associated with the conservatorium and taught there regularly until her death in 1931. Stan found it an extraordinary thrill to be part of such a wonderful institution and have the opportunity to rub shoulders with the stars of Australia's stage who regularly passed through its doors. The focus at the conservatorium was more on voice training than on any particular genre.

Balaclava, 1933. Stan (left) enjoyed a close and loving relationship with his family: Jonnie, Hal, George, Noel, Olive and Murray.

Music was undergoing an enormous change at this time, not only through the growth of professional musical productions and local amateur musical societies, but also because of the popularity of radio, which brought the latest music right into everyone's lounge-room. Hollywood musical movies were also tending to dictate local tastes and trends. Many homes had gramophones, most of dubious quality, so Stan was thrilled when his family purchased a new HMV Orthophonic Gramophone, which greatly improved the tone and volume control of the 78 RPM records. This meant he could play his favourite songs any time he chose — an easy and fun way to practise. All of this gave Stan the opportunity to learn selections from the classics right through to the latest hits. Many families, even those of modest means, possessed pianos, and family singalongs were hugely popular weekend activities.

Youth

The highlight of Stan's time at the Melbourne Conservatorium was when he was chosen to be a member of the chorus in J.C. Williamson's grand opera season production of Verdi's *Aida* at His Majesty's Theatre. It was a thrilling experience to be part of this dramatic story of an Egyptian Romeo and an Ethiopian Juliet, as Verdi had constructed the grandest of all operatic spectacles with bold melodies in staggering profusion and a score of unparalleled colour. When Aida died in Radames' arms for the last time, the show had run for an exhausting six months, and Stan had loved every minute of it.

CHAPTER TWO

It's Only the Game that Counts

Stan turned eighteen in 1930 and was leading a full and active life with a diverse circle of friends. Some members of his church group were members of a club called Power House and indulged in all kinds of interesting sports like athletics, rowing and lacrosse. One of the club members, Roy Luff, was a friend of Stan's and as one long weekend approached Roy proposed they undertake a leisurely ninety-five mile (150 kilometre) hike. This would entail a train to Camperdown and then a bus ride to the southern coastal town of Peterborough and then a trek back eastwards, finishing up at the popular holiday destination of Lorne. Agreed. They took a backpack each with some swags so they could sleep on the beach, as well as some light provisions. They arrived at Lorne unscathed but extremely footsore and camped by the Erskine River. After a refreshing dip and a hearty lunch, Roy had a pleasant surprise for Stan. They were going to 'take tea' with none other than Arthur Herbert Tennyson Baron Somers, Governor of Victoria, and his good Lady, who just happened to be holidaying at Lorne.

Balaclava, 1930. Roy Luff (left) and Stan about to depart on their Great Ocean Road trek.

When Stan realised that Roy wasn't joking, he was somewhat overawed. Stan needn't have been. Lord Somers, dressed in nothing but a short-sleeved shirt, shorts, broad brimmed hat and bare feet, greeted them with a casual handshake. They were then escorted to the rear lawn overlooking the ocean, seated at a table under a broad umbrella and served freshly squeezed lemonade. Lord Somers had clearly taken to the local way of life and an Australian summer was evidently far more appealing than a winter in his ancestral home at Evesham, County Worcester.

Stan was impressed by the Governor's charisma and personality. While his speech was aristocratic, it was delivered in a natural and self-deprecating manner. His pedigree and credentials were impeccable. His grandfather was a Victoria Cross winner and he himself had been decorated twice during the Great War. He had attended Oxford University and was an accomplished sportsman.

Lord Somers delighted in telling Stan the history of Power House. Interestingly, it had all begun with a game of rugby. One wintry afternoon in 1921, Prince Albert, Duke of York (later King George VI), found himself a fascinated spectator at a rugby match at the small town of Briton Ferry in South Wales, being played between fifteen 'industrial boys' from the local steelworks and a visiting team from the Royal College of St Peter, better known as the Westminster School. With Westminster boasting the highest acceptance rate into Oxford and Cambridge Universities of any British secondary school, the social difference between the two teams could not have been more marked. Despite this, the game was reportedly played with 'great keenness and good sportsmanship'.

The Duke was so impressed by the event that he conceived the idea of drawing together boys from different social backgrounds for extended periods of time with the aim of giving them a better understanding of each other. This led to the establishment of the Duke of York's camps at Littlestone-on-Sea, in south-east England.

In 1929 Lord Somers came to Australia as Governor of Victoria. He became good friends with a prominent Melbourne physician, Doctor Cecil Gordon McAdam. Together they decided to conduct a series of camps for young Melbourne men modelled on the Duke of York's camps in England, but they were also designed as a memorial to families who had lost fathers and sons in the Great War. Due to a national death toll of nearly 60,000 from a population of four million, there was hardly a family in Australia that had escaped a grievous loss. It was hoped that the camps would help to partially fill this void. Lord Somers was also Chief Scout of Victoria, later becoming World Chief Scout, and so the first camp was held at the scout camp at nearby Anglesea, south of Geelong.

Half the camp's participants were drawn from trade and industry, that is to say, early school leavers already engaged in the workforce, while the other half were boys who had attended private schools or Great Public Schools. Despite minor teething problems, the Lord Somers' Camps, as they were known, soon became an immense success, with the two groups of teenagers mixing amicably and participating in a whole range of activities. Pretensions deriving from differences in class or status were soon forgotten and many firm friendships were formed over the decades.

After the first camp in 1929, Lord Somers invited all the participants to a reunion at Government House. Doctor McAdam, known to everyone as simply 'Doc', and the Governor held an open discussion around the table.

When asked what he hoped to achieve from all this Doc said his aims were twofold. Firstly, to create an organisation that would bring together young men from all walks of life, irrespective of colour or creed, to develop a greater understanding and respect for each other. Secondly, to develop qualities of leadership and a desire to set an example to others in day-to-day living. He proposed to call it Power House.

It was agreed that the main camp would be an annual event held during the summer school holidays. Every boy who attended would automatically become a member of Power House. This was, in a sense, a continuation of the camp back in Melbourne — a social and sporting organisation to which the boys could continue to belong. It endeavoured to provide a greater than normal range of opportunities through which the boys could interact. Members represented Power House in every conceivable manner of organised sport and they were constantly attending social functions at fashionable venues and houses in St Kilda. There were, however, other attractions for Stan. Not having had the opportunity to finish fifth form at school, let alone attend university, Stan felt a slight gap in his social and scholarly experiences that membership of an institution like Power House might fill.

While, by its very nature, Power House was not a socially exclusive institution, acquiring membership was by no means automatic. One needed to be personally invited to participate in the summer camp before one could become a fully fledged member and Stan made this one of his goals.

As Roy Luff was already a member, and Stan had been received by Lord Somers at his Lorne holiday home, he felt his invitation could surely not be long in coming. It duly arrived, dated 5 December 1930, with a State Government House, Melbourne letterhead. 'Dear Mr Bisset,' it read. 'It will give me great pleasure if you could be my guest at a Camp to be held at Western Port Bay from the 18th to the 28th of January 1931 inclusive. In the event of you being able to accept this invitation, all necessary information will be supplied to you. Please reply to the Private Secretary, State Government House, Glenferrie Road, Malvern, by 14th December if possible,' and was signed, 'Yours Truly, Somers, Governor of Victoria'. It was not difficult for Stan to accept.

The January 1931 camp was at Balnarring East, on the eastern side of the Mornington Peninsula, at Western Port Bay. The small settlement was later renamed Somers. For the hundreds of young men who passed through Lord Somers' Camp and Power House, the Western Port campsite has always held a significant place in their lives. It had a stunning location. Tulum Creek, a clear tidal stream, ran onto a sandy beach directly opposite Phillip Island and the camp itself was built in a bend between the stream and the ocean beach. A group of philanthropically minded citizens had underwritten construction of the camp buildings. Five huts, each large enough for twenty boys, surrounded a central quadrangle. There was also a large mess hut that could accommodate the hundred or so boys. A bridge spanned the narrow stream where a path led to the camp's bush chapel. They felt truly blessed to have such a magnificent site.

It's Only the Game that Counts

In April, Stan was delighted to receive another invitation to attend the large Easter gathering. One day he started off with some intense physical training with his friends before cooling off with a quick dip in the stream. After a hearty lunch they lazed on the lawns, soaking up the strong afternoon sun. Meanwhile, another team of boys cleaning out the bush chapel for the Easter service was alarmed to discover a huge, newly formed bee-hive under the pulpit. A decision was made to smoke out the insects and so a tea-tree fire was hastily set ablaze adjacent to the hive. The odour of the burning melaleuca certainly had the desired effect, except that the bees headed directly across the stream and through the crowded camp. Stan and his mates were sprawled out in the sun in nothing but their swimming trunks and one of the more enterprising insects managed to find its way directly to Stan's nether regions, lancing its sting right into his most sensitive of appendages. Stan howled as he leapt to his feet, frantically grasping at the cause of his anguish. If he was expecting any aid or sympathy from his mates, it was slow in coming. They were incapable of doing anything other than writhe on the ground in fits of hysterical laughter.

The experiences of the Somers' Camps and the subsequent induction into Power House were hugely significant for Stan. Life is full of turning points and there are always decisions made along the way that don't seem immensely important but turn out to have a dramatic impact on one's life. Stan would soon be faced with just such an occasion, and it would revolve around a game of football.

It is difficult for anyone who has not lived in Melbourne to comprehend the passion the city holds for it own code of football — Australian Rules. No sports-mad youngster, especially in the 1930s when competition from other football codes or winter sports hardly existed, could possibly have escaped it. Like most youngsters, Stan had played football at school and had enjoyed it immensely. He was keen to play at a higher level but with work commitments, training, boxing, sculling and Power House activities, football had taken a back seat.

At the age of eighteen, Stan was invited to play Australian Rules with the Melbourne High School Old Boys team, which was about to be admitted to the Melbourne Amateur Football Association (MAFA). The club officials knew their first year in this competition would be a challenging one. Football club membership was not dependent on being a former pupil and Stan's recruitment was seen as adding great strength to their forward line. The MAFA, which changed its name to the Victorian Amateur Football Association in 1933, was one level below the senior Victorian Football League (VFL) and was the obvious stepping stone to this elite level. MAFA finals were always played as curtain-raisers to the VFL finals at the Melbourne Cricket Ground, where the best of the junior players could display their talents in front of the VFL managers.

Somers' Camp, 1934. Stan (left), Andy Barr, Max Carpenter and Jack Readhead give a friend a dunking in Tulum Creek.

It's Only the Game that Counts

Somers' Camp, 1935. Stan wins the shot-put competition.

Somers' Camp, 1935. Stan (centre, rear) with the club's senior boys and Pop Bremner (in the white hat).

Stan quickly befriended one of the club's other key recruits, Keith 'Bluey' Truscott. A dynamic and highly creative centre-man, Bluey became a legend within the club and was later recruited by Melbourne in the VFL. He played in their 1939 and 1940 premiership-winning sides and also represented Victoria. In the Second World War Bluey Truscott served with distinction in both the Royal Air Force in Britain and, on his return to Australia, in the Royal Australian Air Force. Feted as a national hero, he died in March 1943 when he went down with his plane during a target practice exercise in Exmouth. Another of Stan's team-mates was George Carter, who went on to play at the senior level for Collingwood and then Hawthorn.

There was no doubt that Stan matched it on the field with Bluey and George, and as his second season with the club drew to a close in 1931, approaches were made to all three players by senior VFL clubs. South Melbourne and St Kilda both asked Stan if he would attend the following year's preseason training. For Stan, this was the realisation of a childhood dream. As a youngster, he had adopted St Kilda as 'his' club and could even remember St Kilda patriotically changing its colours from Germany's red, yellow and black during the First World War.

Assessing his prospects as a senior footballer, Stan felt he possessed the necessary coordination, balance, ball-handling skills and kicking ability to play at the elite level. It was a self-confidence born of his childhood and teenage experiences. He just seemed to have that special knack of mastering any sport to which he turned his hand.

That same year, Stan was introduced to his future brother-in-law, Bill Wight, who had only recently arrived in Melbourne with his family. Bill had attended one of Sydney's Great Public Schools, Newington College, and had been a prominent member of the school's Rugby First XV. Keen to continue playing the game in Melbourne, he had joined the St Kilda Rugby Club.

There was the inevitable friendly rivalry between the boys over the merits or otherwise of the very different football codes. Like most Melbournians, Stan's love of Australian Rules was entrenched. The free flowing hand-balls, towering kicks and high marking made for a thrilling spectacle. Bill would have none of it. Rugby is a real man's game, and just to prove how tough it really was he suggested to Stan that he come along to their pre-season training and play a few trial matches. It seemed like a challenge Stan could hardly refuse. Maybe Bill had a point. Any footballer knows that there is a marked difference between how the body reacts under training conditions as opposed to match situations. Stan thought that the physicality of the rugby training as well as some actual match practice may well give him that extra hard edge needed to impress at the upcoming Australian Rules trials.

Although Stan had barely picked up a rugby ball before that first training session, he took an immediate liking to this most basic and, at times, highly confrontational sport. The anticipation of the physical competition was akin to the adrenalin rush Stan got as he sized up his opponent in the boxing ring. When it came to the first match the suggestion was that, despite Stan's size, he should start on the wing — a position that required pace. There was no problem with that — Stan could sprint with the best of them. He would be at the end of the attacking line, the last man likely to receive the ball but the one most likely to score a try. It would also give Stan an opportunity to observe the flow of the game and give him a better appreciation of the on-side rule that was one of the hardest concepts for a rugby newcomer to grasp.

As he walked off the paddock after that first game, Stan was hooked and he knew it. But could he really give up the opportunity of playing in the VFL for St Kilda or South Melbourne? Converting to rugby would be akin to a betrayal for some of the VFL's diehard supporters. After all, most Victorian youngsters would give just about anything they had for half the chance that Stan had been offered.

In his heart, Stan had already made the decision to play rugby, but he did have to step back and think through the consequences with a cool head. Firstly, there was the financial aspect to consider. Rugby Union was a strictly amateur code, and in 1931 Australia was still in the throes of the Great Depression. Unemployment was at astronomic levels. Stan was lucky enough to still be in work, but he could not supplement his income by playing Rugby Union.

Official payments to VFL players were endorsed as early as 1911, but the Coulter Law adopted by the VFL in 1930 severely restricted the size of these payments. Nevertheless, anything extra he could earn would be a wonderful bonus, and this consideration weighed heavily on Stan. He was only young, though, and nothing was forever. He could always change his mind if he received a genuinely tempting offer at a later date.

There were other aspects to consider as well. Rugby had a long tradition in Australia and offered more opportunities than Australian Rules to travel and play outside Melbourne, even outside Australia. Its traditions were firmly rooted in the English private school and university system and it was principally via the universities that rugby spread throughout and beyond the British colonies. Sydney University, for example, established its rugby club in 1863 and the Melbourne University Club was formed in 1909. Rugby unions had been established in the 1800s in England, Ireland, Wales, Scotland, South Africa, New Zealand and Canada. The game was even popular in the United States, again mainly thanks to the major universities like Columbia, Harvard, Yale, Princeton and Stanford, where rugby was the game of choice. The Australian national team, the Wallabies, had played their first international match against the USA in 1909 at Berkeley, only winning 12–8. The contrast with Australian Rules at this level was a stark one.

Stan could have mulled over the pros and cons of switching to rugby for an eternity, but when faced with a tough decision one often goes for the option that simply feels right at the time.

It's Only the Game that Counts

So rugby with St Kilda won out. The team had a great season and narrowly missed out on a place in the final. While rugby's heartland was in New South Wales and Queensland, the Victorian competition in the 1930s was particularly strong. Unlike today when AFL coverage dominates, a search through the Melbourne newspapers shows whole pages devoted to the city's rugby competition. There were guarded expectations that Victoria could well beat one of its northern rivals in the upcoming annual interstate matches.

During the early part of the season Stan switched to the back-row of the scrum, a position ideally suited to his physique. One of the most respected coaches in the state and a former All Black, a Mr Bellcliffe, made it quite clear to Stan that if his improvement continued through 1933, state representative honours would not be far off. In June the *Sun News Pictorial* reported on St Kilda's last match against University. 'S. Bisset was the most prominent forward on the field, competing well in the lineout, and was ferocious in the ruck and maul. It was his forays into the St Kilda backline, however, that most impressed, adding great thrust to the team's attack...He is clearly a player of the future.' This was no faint praise given that University boasted five state representatives and two internationals in its team.

In his first year with St Kilda Stan quickly became enmeshed in the rugby fraternity. The strength of this brotherhood would be difficult for non-rugby players to comprehend. The rugby code, strictly amateur at the time, had developed a male camaraderie that was unique. At the club level, the game had rarely sought to attract attention to itself. Players knew it was physically the most demanding and dangerous of sports. No quarter was asked or given on the field. Spilt blood and broken bones were often sported as badges of honour. But even after the bitterest of on-field battles, the minute the final whistle blew, all was forgiven and after-match bonding was as much a part of the ritual as the game itself. Friendships formed on the rugby field were akin to those forged in the heat of battle and not taken lightly.

33

Beyond football, Stan's other sporting activities and social life were mainly identified with Power House, so it came as no surprise that when their inaugural rugby club was formed in 1932 he was invited to join. He felt hard-pressed to decline, but the move would be a difficult one. Power House would be playing in the B Grade, or second division competition, whereas St Kilda was a formidable A Grade club. The move would hardly improve his chances of representative rugby.

Just as the origins of rugby hark back to the antics of William Webb Ellis at Rugby School, the origins of the Power House Rugby Club can be traced to similar shenanigans at the Lord Somers' Camp. 'Foot and Mouth Disease' was one of the more bizarre games that made up the activities programme. Played on an open field in shorts and bare feet, the aim was to get the ball through the opponent's goal. There were virtually no rules and it was an all-in melee where, among much laughter and buffoonery, there were inevitably many scratches, bruises, skinned knees and bloodied noses. So much so that after several seasons, Doc McAdam felt he had a responsibility to call a halt to the goings-on before someone was seriously injured.

With the outbreaks of Foot and Mouth Disease under temporary control, the unbounded spirits of the more active boys were clearly unquenched so Doc, forever positive, proposed the formation of a proper rugby club. By this time Doc had also become an important figure in Stan's life and his fireside chats — be they interesting stories from his own experiences in the Great War, current politics, or just his philosophical views on life in general — rarely failed to impress. As he was also a great believer in British institutions and sport, the very British game of rugby clearly represented these ideals perfectly.

The first Power House team, formed in 1932, was not entered into a competition and only played scratch games against Scotch College, the Naval College and Geelong. The very first of these games was played on a field near the Melbourne Zoo on the north side of Royal Park, adjacent to the railway line. There were no dressing sheds and the boys simply had to hang their clothes on the fence — no changing of underpants allowed while the train was in the station. Interest in the game grew so rapidly that in May of 1933 it was decided to enter the team in the Victorian Rugby Union competition. The club's colours were obviously those of Power House, the green, black and white of Lord Somers' himself. After much debate, the traditional horizontal hoop pattern was chosen for the guernseys, and as a further tribute to the good Lord Somers, a baron's coronet was added to the left breast.

Doc became president of the new club and the role of vice-president went to a great patron, Mr George Nicholas. Wing Commander Francis Bladen, affectionately known to all the boys as 'Dad', became secretary. As a former pupil of Melbourne Boys High School he was well acquainted with Stan's achievements in the Old Boys Australian Rules side and had followed his first year in rugby with great interest.

A graduate of the Royal Military College Duntroon, Bladen had been seconded to the Royal Australian Air Force. He went on to have a distinguished career in the RAAF during the Second World War and subsequently retired as an air vice-marshal. Despite his firmness when it was required, Stan found nothing harsh about the man. Abstemious when it came to alcohol, he loved his pipe and if ever one of the boys was called over for a chat one knew it would be almost impossible to resist any request. So it turned out with Stan.

It was a done deal then. Power House had bagged a star recruit for their 1933 season. Stan had been a willing participant in the Foot and Mouth Disease games at Somers' Camp so he was well versed in the club's traditions. But more seriously, his understanding of the intricacies of rugby had developed quickly during the season with St Kilda.

Stan's strict personal discipline with regard to his fitness and lifestyle, together with an absolute commitment to the game, was something of a culture shock for many in the club—something attested to by notes in the committee books. For some of the younger team members, rugby had simply been seen as little more than a way of letting off steam and an excuse to socialise in the pub after matches. The then teetotalling Stan provided a very different role model.

Twenty-one-year-old Stan was nearing full physical maturity. He weighed in at thirteen and a half stone (about 85 kilograms) and stood at just over six foot two (187 centimetres). Stan was relatively tall for that era, but it was more the combination of his size, strength, speed and mobility that made him such a formidable competitor. He was ideally suited to the back row of the forwards. Their role, which is to win possession for their side by contesting for the ball in rucks and mauls, was Stan's speciality, and his speed to the breakdown was exceptional. If a team-mate had the ball, Stan would ensure he retained possession. If the opposition had the ball, Stan's aggressive rucking, if the opposition player was on the ground, or his mauling, or wresting of the ball from a player still standing, often resulted in a turnover of possession. It was Stan's skill in attack, however, that had improved markedly through his season with St Kilda. Stan learned how to break away quickly from the set pieces or the rucks and mauls and follow the ball as it was passed along the attacking backline. Gifted players somehow have a knack of being in the right place at the right time, ready to receive a pass just as they hit the advantage-line at full pace. This free-ranging role in attack had the effect of adding an extra man to the team's backline.

The 1933 football season drew to a close with Power House finishing in the final four—a more than creditable result in their first full year in the competition.

In addition to rugby, Stan was involved in other Power House sports including athletics, rowing and wrestling. It was also at this time that Power House decided to hold one of its first dances. Stan was a keen dancer and he and his friends regularly frequented Carlyon's Ballroom, Wattle Park Palais or the Palais de Danse at St Kilda, Leggett's Ballroom at Prahran, the Palais Royale at the Royal Exhibition Building or the Green Mill, where the Arts Centre is now located.

Popular as these venues were, they were hardly suitable for young, single women of good breeding. This was the reason the Power House dances became so popular. The club was incredibly fortunate to have its own substantial clubhouse, built on land leased to the Lord Somers' Camp by the Albert Park Trustees. The cost of construction had been met by the vice-president of the rugby club, George Nicholas, a prominent citizen with a fascinating background. When German imports of acetylsalicylic acid, better known by its trademark name 'aspirin', were cut off at the commencement of the First World War, George set to work in a primitive plant using kerosene tins and kitchen utensils borrowed from his wife. After much trial and error he made the first Australian-produced aspirin. With a new license he was able to corner the entire domestic market. Realising that the name 'aspirin' could be reclaimed by the German pharmaceutical company Bayer after the war, George sought his own trade mark. Aspro, along with Vegemite, became one of the best-known brands in Australia's commercial history. This great success enabled George and his brother Alfred to endow the public with lavish gifts, often made anonymously, and Power House was on their list of beneficiaries.

Being right on the lake, the new clubhouse provided a wonderful inner city meeting place for all the members and their young male and female guests. And given the club's impeccable credentials, young women simply flocked to its dances. The club Auxiliary was always in attendance, providing supper but quite clearly unofficially chaperoning the unattached young ladies. This was an accepted convention for that era.

Stan and the young male members of Power House were delighted with these arrangements. The boys were quietly coached in good manners and respectful behaviour, essential if one expected to receive an invitation to one of the finer private homes on St Kilda or Toorak Roads. Doc McAdam frequently entertained a wide spectrum of Melbourne's society at his grand St Kilda home, Stormont. Cocktails, dinner parties and musical evenings were frequent occurrences, and Stan was high on the list of favoured invitees. Always respectful, unassuming and thoughtful, he accepted his sporting prowess and natural good looks without affectation. He was extremely hard working and disciplined — it would be another four years before he drank his first glass of beer. His fine baritone voice was a welcome addition to social evenings at a time when singing around the piano was one of the most popular forms of home entertainment.

Not only were the dances hugely popular social events, they were profitable fund-raisers. With an entrance fee of two shillings and sixpence per couple, the first event raised a whole £8. This may not seem a great deal but many of the younger men, especially those unable to find work, found it difficult to pay the annual subscriptions. Film nights also became popular social fund-raising events.

In 1934 there were enough players to field two teams in the Victorian competition. It may have come as something of a shock to the rugby community when the Power House A Grade team won the premiership in only their second full year in the competition; however, the Rugby Club committee had predicted as much in their March Annual General Meeting.

If 1934 was a year to remember, 1935 was something else again. Power House's commitment and approach to the game had moved to a level that no other club was likely to match. Their early season performances were so dominant that they burst into the media spotlight. Melbourne newspapers' main focus was obviously on Australian Rules, but they still gave great coverage to rugby and could recognise a good story when they found one. Power House claimed the second-division premiership with an amazing season that boasted a sixteen-win, no-loss record, amassing 630 points and conceding only 23. Much of this success was rightly attributed to Stan and his inspirational influence. 'They have, in Stan Bisset, a forward of great promise,' wrote the *Age* at the end of the season. 'He has a splendid physique, is fast, and plays with great dash. He will be a strong contender for a place in the Victorian pack in the years ahead.'

During 1935 HMAS *Australia*, a Country class heavy cruiser, was sent from her home waters to the Mediterranean for a year. Since her crew had formed the backbone of the first division Naval College side, their club was relegated to the second division. Power House's total dominance of the 1935 season made them obvious candidates for promotion and Stan once again found himself a first division footballer.

Stan's contribution to the side and his natural leadership abilities were recognised when he was made captain for the 1936 season. Stan made meticulous preparations during the off-season. Every member of the team, including an extended reserves list, was given a personal training regime to follow in addition to regular one-on-one or squad sessions to check on progress. The whole team was called together in February and arduous training sessions were prepared for the forwards and backs to coordinate teamwork. As rugby was a strictly amateur sport, practice had traditionally been only once a week, but Stan set about changing all this. Tuesdays and Thursdays were set aside for training but the real coup was a new training venue — the Young Women's Christian Association field, equipped with electric lights. Now, training could take place for an intense two full hours, covering all aspects of ball-work with essential drills repeated and repeated until they worked faultlessly.

Stan's brother Hal was a welcome new addition to the team that year. Fresh and extraordinarily hardened by his heavy work in the bush, he added great strength to the forward pack. Many members of the side also represented Power House in athletics. Stan had been Power House's standout athlete in a variety of track and field events in 1934 and 1935 and represented the state in the javelin, but on the sprint-track major honours had gone to two young sprinters, Andy 'Nicky' Barr and Reg Talbot. Reg, who was captain of the backline, played at five-eight while Stan played Andy Barr on the wing.

The club fielded four teams in 1936, one in the first division A Grade competition, one in B Grade and two in C Grade. Stan's A Grade side began with comfortable wins against Harlequins and Geelong, but it was the match against Footscray that presented the first real challenge in the top grade. The match was keenly

Power House Rugby Team 1936

Eric Bull - Reg Talbot - Geoff Cooksley - Dick Hair - Wal Snelling - Orm Watt - Max Carpenter
Frank Redhead - Andy Barr - Bert Browning - Stan Bisset - Morry Blundell - Harold Bisset
Harold Blundell - Lisle Barnden - Bruce McLeish - Fred Kerr - Jack Redhead

anticipated in the press and it was generally accepted that the newcomers would be no match for a Footscray side that was regarded as the best in Victoria. Despite the predictions, Stan and his team defended their line with unexpected ferocity, holding the much touted favourites to a scoreless first half. Footscray's last-minute try gave them a narrow win but Power House had done more than enough to prove it was a team of great talent.

Stan was elated when he received a telegram from the Victorian Rugby Union to say he had been selected to play in a trial match that would determine the Victorian state team. Victoria was due to play in the annual interstate series against NSW and Queensland in Sydney. The 'Victoria' team was primarily made up of the already established state representatives, while Stan would be playing in the 'Rest of Victoria' team comprised of the up and coming players. The game was played on 27 June 'on a soft and muddy arena at Western Oval Footscray,' reported the *Melbourne Herald*. 'The selected Victorian team to compete in the triangular tourney in Sydney next weekend was soundly defeated by the Rest of Victoria, 27 points to 21, much to the surprise of the selectors,' and much to their embarrassment also, one presumes. The only photograph displayed in the newspaper was of Stan. 'For the Rest,' the article continued, 'S. Bisset, the young Power House athlete, was doing a tremendous amount of work and causing havoc among the Victoria forwards.' No faint praise indeed given that the Victoria side included three internationals — Denis Cowper, Owen Bridle and 'Weary' Dunlop — in addition to their regular state players. Stan was disappointed to learn he did not win a spot in the final selection but he knew his time would come.

The highlight of Power House's club season was the defeat of the previous year's premiers, Melbourne, in the semi-final. This gave Power House a spot in the final against Footscray, but due to several key players being out with injury the result was a disappointing 27–0 defeat. There was a personal upside for Stan, however, from the encounter with Footscray. At the after-match celebrations he made a particular point of seeking out one of the prominent Footscray players, Gordon 'Max' Carpenter, who until then he had only known by name. It was a fortuitous move because Max, a sensational all-round athlete, subsequently decided to join Power House and went on to become one of Stan's closest rugby companions. With Stan, Max went on to have his own outstanding career in rugby.

Stan was again captain of the A Grade side in 1937 when the club once more fielded four teams. The club committee noted that the players 'were the fittest to have ever represented the club'. Tuesday and Thursday night training sessions commenced at 7.30 p.m. and finished at 10 p.m. These hours were unheard of for an amateur club. There was a major focus on individual skill training and the club created a little piece of history when it acquired the state's first scrum-machine. It caused such a sensation that the Victorian team coach pleaded to be able to use it for the state side's training sessions later that year.

Although the A Grade team did not reach its potential in 1937, finishing fifth on the ladder, the year marked a highpoint in Stan's rugby career. In May he was selected to represent Victoria for the clash against South Australia at Adelaide's Norwood Oval. With Stan playing in the second row, Power House was also represented by four other players while Pop Bremner, one of Power House's stalwarts, was the team manager. As was the case with Victoria, South Australian rugby in the 1930s was exceptionally strong. While Victoria had won all four previous interstate encounters, they had been close run affairs. Their expectations this year were no different against a team led by Fred Ward who also represented South Australia in Sheffield Shield Cricket. Only Reg Watson's last-minute tackles salvaged a two-tries-to-one win. 'Narrow Win to Victoria,' ran the *Age*'s headline, with the sub-title 'Bisset best Victorian' then recording that, 'He led the forward rushes and was responsible for eight of the team's eleven points, equalling a record in scoring in every possible way. He scored a try, converted it, and kicked a penalty goal.' The tour became a memorable occasion for another reason — it was the first time in his life that Stan had ever tasted beer.

Unquestionably the highlight of the domestic rugby year, indeed that of the decade, was to be the visit of South Africa's national side, the famous Springboks. As a lead-up to the two Tests against the Wallabies, the Boks were to play various Australian state sides as their ship took them on to the nation's rugby capital of Sydney, where both Tests were to be played. When the Victorian team was announced, it wasn't only Stan who had cause to celebrate. There were six other Power House players selected to engage the visitors.

Stan was clearly elated with his selection. When Stan moved to Power House in 1933 there had been no guarantee, indeed no expectation whatsoever, that Power House would gain promotion to A Grade. Since there was little probability that the state selectors would choose a second division player, Stan had potentially forfeited a representative career for the sake of supporting Power House. As it turned out, he could not have written the script better. Most footballers peak in their mid to late twenties. At the age of twenty-five, Stan's opportunity to play for Victoria could not have been better timed.

However, as proud as Stan was to represent his state, he secretly aspired to greater things. He saw the Victorian colours of blue and silver as a stepping-stone to the myrtle green jersey and gold ringed socks of the Wallabies.[1]

Over the previous sixty years, Victoria had struggled to gain recognition of its players at a national level. The Australian Rugby Union selection panel was dominated by New South Welshmen.

---

[1] When the South Africans toured in 1937, Australia changed its colours to a white jersey with green and gold hoops, so as not to clash with the traditional green of South Africa. Australia then reverted to their myrtle green jerseys. The present-day all-gold jersey was first introduced for the Wallabies' tour of South Africa in 1961.

Queenslanders often had cause to vent their spleen at what they regarded as discrimination. In fact, only one Victorian-born player had ever represented his country in rugby and that honour had gone to Benalla's Edward 'Weary' Dunlop in 1932. Other players had been chosen for the national side while playing for Victorian clubs but they had all been born north of the border or in Evan 'Ted' Jessep's case in 1934, across the Tasman.

Despite the odds of recognition being against them there was a general feeling that Victorian rugby had made such great advances in recent years that claims for national selection for its players could not go unheeded. This was due in no small way to the impact made on the game by the man with whom Stan would be packing down in the Victorian scrum — the lock, Weary Dunlop. In fact, Weary was not the only member of the 1937 Victorian team who would go on to become an Australian household name, more for his achievements off the rugby field than on it.

Stan had played against Weary during the previous two seasons and they had mixed together at after-match functions. Stan says that no one who met the man could fail to be captivated by his personality and character and he recalled many of their memorable times together. However, none of Weary's exploits on the field matched the courage and ingenuity he displayed as a prisoner of the Japanese in the Second World War, particularly on the Thai-Burma railway. Totally unbowed, he defied Japanese authority almost at will. Such extraordinary bravery made him, as one man attested, 'a lighthouse of sanity in a universe of madness and suffering'. Thanks to Weary Dunlop and a number of other Australian doctors, Australian survival rates were higher than those of all other Allied prisoners-of-war.

By the time Stan joined him as a Victorian team-mate, Weary had already become a legend in the close-knit rugby fraternity. Weary, having played all his early club football for Melbourne University, had by this stage joined the Old Boys Club as captain. The Old Boys were renowned for their great camaraderie, their love of the game, and for their hard drinking, mainly in the old London Hotel on Beach Road, Port Melbourne, where they had established their base. They were no pushovers on the field, however, and were having one of their best seasons on record. One rowdy evening at the London pub the discussion turned to the choice of a motto and emblem for the club. Weary sketched a rampant unicorn with the words, *Nulla Vestigia Retrorsum*—Never a Step Backwards—on the tablecloth. From that week onwards the unicorn adorned the team's blue and white ringed jerseys. When the club eventually amalgamated with the Melbourne Club in 1939, Melbourne adopted the unicorn.

Stan vividly recalled a club match against Weary's team during the 1936 season. Early in the season Old Boys had beaten Power House by several points, but in the week following the match a member of the Power House committee had written to the Victorian Rugby Union appealing against one of the Old Boys' tries. The appeal was upheld and the result of the game was reversed. Stan had known nothing of the appeal, which seemed to run counter to the club's ideal as summed up in their team song: 'No matter if we lose the match, or from defeat a victory snatch, it's only the game, the game that counts, and only the game that counts.'

When the return match against the Old Boys took place, Stan knew that perceived injustices would be high on the list of things that might spark what became known as one of Weary's 'Elephant Acts'.

In the return match Power House won the toss and Stan made the Old Boys play the first half into a bitingly cold and blustery southerly. Power House managed a scrambling try in what was obviously going to be a low-scoring game and went to the break with a three point lead. As the teams changed ends for the second half the extraordinarily fickle Melbourne weather performed one of its famous tricks and the wind dropped to a virtual zephyr. Any advantage the Old Boys had hoped to gain as muscles tired late in the second half had vanished with the wind. With only minutes remaining Stan felt Power House had well and truly gained their adversaries' measure. Suddenly Weary's blood curdling battlecry split the air and there was an explosion of energy from the Old Boys team. The Power House forwards were hurtled out of the way as Weary emerged from a maul at full gallop, ball in hand and with the look of a raging bull. Weary could remember the incident decades later and was quoted by his biographer, Sue Ebury: 'I went charging through and gave someone such a tremendous hand-off that I broke my finger. I remember being tackled just short of the line but someone else managed to gather the ball and we scored wide out.' The result: three all.

The whole experience is also etched in Stan's memory, as are the lessons to be drawn from it. The original appeal against the Old Boys was, in essence, contrary to Power House's own principles. How often do things turn against you when you fail to live by your own ideals? Then there was the evidence of the power a team could generate if it really believed in its leader and heeded his call to arms. Finally, there was the impact one man could make on a game, or any event for that matter, if and when he chose to impose his will on the situation.

All of this was more impactful given the essentially quiet and unassuming nature of Weary the man. When the Victorian team gathered for training there were quieter moments when he and Stan could talk. Weary confided to Stan that he felt self-conscious when he had first arrived at Melbourne University's Ormond College as the son of a modest country family and the product of a state school education. Suddenly he had found himself an outsider, surrounded by boys from privileged backgrounds. In fact, for Weary, his success on the rugby field and in professional life, the reports in the media, the meetings with dignitaries and his growing maturity, never quite compensated for this early insecurity and lack of full acceptance.

Stan could easily identify with the situation into which Weary had been thrust. After all, the boys from Power House had come from vastly different backgrounds. On reflection, though, Stan also saw some major differences between their two experiences. Many of

It's Only the Game that Counts

the university students Stan had met seemed to delight in displaying their perceived elitist positions, sometimes belittling anyone of lesser background. By contrast, the privileged private school boys from Power House had set out to develop a rapport with the other members of the club regardless of social status. Additionally, Stan felt he had a more outgoing personality than Weary, one that had been encouraged by his participation in voice training and singing. Stan appeared to be much more comfortable in public situations and would think nothing of breaking into song, for example, at any appropriate moment. He also seemed to be the one asked to speak at public occasions, a role he had to fulfil frequently as captain of the rugby club.

The approach of the two men to sport was also different. Whereas Stan threw himself into every activity that was on offer, Weary had to be coaxed into participation. Weary just happened to be gifted with a superbly lean and athletic body, and he was *big*. He weighed over 15 stone (95 kilos) and stood at six foot five (198 centimetres), yet he was also nimble and well coordinated. However, he simply wasn't keen to throw his weight around. Essentially, he lacked the natural killer instinct that often goes with international sporting success. For example, he had always been handy with his fists but he had to be persuaded to represent university at boxing, a sport that was extremely popular in Australia in the 1930s. Weary was good enough to go on and become the inter-collegiate boxing champion but he only ever did just enough to win.

For the Victorian match against the Springboks, Stan was chosen to partner the team captain, Cliff 'Haggis' Lang, a coarse and dour Scotsman, in the second row. Weary would play in the Number Eight position.[2] Despite their different backgrounds and

---

[2] In those days, other than the lock, team numbering was different. The fullback wore number 1, the wingers 2 and 5, the centres 3 and 4, the five-eight 6, and the half-back 7, while in the forwards, the lock (now called 'number-eight') wore 8, the breakaways and second rowers (now also called locks) wore 9, 10, 11 and 12, and the front rowers 13, 14 and 15. Today, the forwards are numbered from 1 to 8, and the backs are numbered from 9 to 15.

personalities, the three tall, powerful forwards soon became friends and developed a great understanding on the field. Being thirteen years older, Haggis Lang took Stan under his wing. Haggis was tough but versatile, could play any position in the forwards and his experience was of great assistance to Stan during his first taste of elite rugby.

It was no surprise that the South Africans easily defeated Western Australia 37–8 and then South Australia 55–3 in the opening games of the tour. When the Springboks disembarked from the *Ulysses* at Melbourne's Station Pier on 9 June 1937, the reporters were waiting for them. Percy Day, their manager, admitted that the match against the local side would be the first serious challenge for the visitors and a real measure of the quality of both teams. Several of the players left a great impression on Stan. Amongst them were the big utility forwards, Stephanus 'Fannie' Louw and Matthys Michael 'Boy' Louw, two of ten footballing brothers. If Boy had a sense of humour, he masked it well. Much to Boy's rage, Stan called him 'Adolf' on the field, due to his stern expression and Hitler-like lock of hair that he kept tossing back from his forehead. It was a brave call on Stan's part, as goading these unsmiling assassins on the football field was not a healthy pastime.

Over 18,000 supporters packed Carlton Oval for the match. Stan had never played in front of so many people, but when he and his team-mates took to the field it wasn't the size of the crowd that was overawing, it was the prodigious size of their opponents. As the teams lined up in centre field to shake hands it became obvious just how enormous the famous Springbok pack actually was.

It was certainly not the case that the Victorians were undersized. Quite the reverse. When the Victorians had played NSW at North Sydney Oval, the *Sydney Morning Herald* reported that there was an audible gasp of awe from the crowd when the Victorians took to the field. They were described as akin to an All Black pack. 'Dunlop, Perrin, Lang and Arnold are magnificent specimens,' enthused the

Carlton Oval, June 1937. Stan supports the ball-carrier in the Victoria versus South Africa match.

Herald. 'New South Wales seemed flustered by their All Black tactics.' Well spotted by the reporter. The Victorian hooker was the former New Zealand international, Evan 'Ted' Jessep, who was then playing in Melbourne and he had drilled the Victorians in All Black tactics for seven weeks prior to the encounter. The Victorians' second rower, Tom Perrin, was sixteen and a half stone (105 kilos) and six foot two (187 centimetres). Haggis Lang was sixteen stone (101 kilos) and over six foot (183 centimetres), and Weary was by far the tallest man on the field. 'They are big and fast and can ruck like the devil,' concluded the *Herald*'s match report.

It was probably the demeanour of the Afrikaaners rather than their actual size that impressed and intimidated their opponents. The player profiles revealed that they were no taller than the Victorians, they just seemed to be as broad as they were tall and their mobility was truly impressive. In the winter of 1937, Stan was approaching the prime of his life. With his imposing stature, he was accustomed to dwarfing most of the men he passed on the street. But now, as he faced Mauritz van den Berg, a 'Great Block from the Veld', as Stan described him, it was the first time he had ever felt physically intimidated by another man's presence. The unflappable Haggis Lang nudged Stan and gave him a quick wink. 'This should be fun now, eh laddy?' he muttered. 'Some fun,' thought Stan, but Haggis was opposing the South African captain, Philip Nel, the biggest of them all.

Pre-match expectations of Victoria extending the South Africans were tested in the game's early minutes. The Boks scored from the kickoff and went on to dominate the half, particularly during the set-pieces.

The South Africans only spoke Afrikaans on the field. Stan took the ball into a ruck early in the game, and as he was tackled and fell forward he placed the ball on the ground next to his midriff and rolled over with his back to the South Africans, as he was entitled to do, to protect possession for his team. As he got to his feet, Mauritz van den Berg growled, 'Do that again and I'll kick your bloody head in'. It was the only English Stan heard from him all match. The first tackle Stan attempted on van den Berg was from almost head-on and proved a near fatal experience. The old adage of 'take them low around the bootstraps' was never more applicable. The South Africans carried about them an aura of personal hostility that was foreign to the Australian players and ran counter to their own rugby culture. It created an atmosphere that could best be described as intimidating.

As the teams made their way to the sidelines at the half-time whistle, with the scoreboard reading 30–3 in favour of the tourists, Stan's wily old second-row partner grabbed him by the shoulder. 'A quiet word, Stan. Weary's the only bloke on this team who can match the buggers up front,' Haggis whispered, 'but I don't think he's going about it quite the right way.' Haggis was absolutely correct, as Weary had been strangely subdued. 'Right, laddy, here's what we're going to do about it …'

The South Africans put the ball into touch from the opening kick of the second half and as the forwards formed up for the lineout, Stan and Haggis took up their positions at numbers one and three, sharing the responsibility of protecting Weary, who was jumping at number two. As the hooker tossed the ball in and Weary and van den Berg jumped to compete for possession, Stan leapt up and slammed himself into Weary's back while Haggis drove into his thighs at almost the same instant. Weary crashed to the ground, stunned by the impact, but then leapt to his feet in a towering rage. Weary naturally assumed the other South African jumpers were the culprits and unprintable words in English and Afrikaans were exchanged. Haggis pulled Weary away by the jersey and swung him round, then pushed him towards the breakdown. Weary bounded off fairly trembling with rage and indignation. No doubt about it, Weary was in Elephant Act mode so it was just a case of hang on to your hats. Weary hurled his shoulder into the ruck and a Springbok flanker was jettisoned out of the melee like a rag doll. Stan and Haggis followed closely behind as they grabbed each others' jerseys and drove low into the exchange. For the rest of the half the three rangy forwards created havoc for the Springboks at the breakdown, Stan and Haggis rucking and mauling with their typical savagery and Weary charging into the breakdowns and cleanouts with his new-found aggression.

The new tempo set by the Victorian forwards ensured the second half was a far more interesting and close-run affair than the first. At the final whistle, the Victorians had held the Boks to a creditable 41–13 result, having scored 10 points to South Africa's 11 in the second forty minutes. The huge crowd that included the Governor-General, Baron Gowrie, relished the challenge the state side had presented to the visitors. It was clear from post-match reports that Stan's performance had not gone unnoticed. The *Age* described the South African forwards as weighing 'ten to a ton'. The Victorians, however, were reported to have, 'played an aggressive game against the imposing Springboks, especially those doughy forwards E. "Weary" Dunlop, Lang, Baker and Bisset'.

Everyone fully expected Weary, at least, to gain a spot in the Australian side to play in the first Test at the Sydney Cricket Ground on 26 June. However, on 19 June the South Africans played NSW on a boggy SCG pitch and the New South Welshmen, led by the imposing Randwick captain and centre-three-quarter Cyril Towers, stunned the rugby world with a 17 points to 6, five-tries-to-nil, thumping of the visitors. (In this era, tries were only worth three points.) This victory dashed Weary's chances and those of any other Victorians who might have held slight hope of a call-up to the national side. The selectors clearly did not want to break up what they saw as a winning pack of primarily NSW forwards. The gamble almost paid off. The following Saturday the Springboks scrambled home in the first Test by 9 points to 5 in front of 18,296 spectators at the SCG.

That very same evening in Melbourne, the selectors clearly marked Stan as a player of the future when he and Power House team-mate Mo Blundell received telegrams informing them that they were selected to play for an 'Australian XV' against South Africa at the Exhibition Ground in Brisbane in just one week's time, Saturday 3 July. It was not an official Test match and players would not be capped.[3]

The game in Brisbane was effectively a trial match for the second Test, with the Australian XV made up of a combination of established Test players and newer, as yet uncapped players. Arrangements for the trip to Brisbane were vague and Stan and Mo had to organise their own travel. Acting on another cryptic telegram to the effect that all expenses would be reimbursed on arrival, they found themselves two second class seats, and felt very much like second class citizens, as they departed Spencer Street Station on the Monday evening train.

---

[3] The Australian Rugby Union retrospectively awarded Stan a cap in 2002.

They passed the long and agonisingly tedious trip by reading books and playing vingt-et-un. After the change of trains in Albury they came upon a state of chaos. The NSW train was overcrowded due to an earlier cancellation so they decided to splurge on sleepers for the Sydney to Brisbane sector. After all, the whole exercise would be a complete waste of time if they arrived in a state of total exhaustion. As it was, they had no opportunity to meet with the other members of the team before the game, which hardly augured well for any sense of teamwork. On the field, the established players, already assured of selection for the second Test in Sydney, played with a distinct lack of passion. However, Stan and the other new boys naturally gave it their all. Stan played in his favourite position of breakaway (flanker) and marked Ebbo Bastard. Ebbo was the same age as Stan and was rated by the renowned South African rugby critic Arthur Cyril Parker as 'the best and most consistently good all-round forward in the side'. The day after his encounter with Ebbo, Stan was judged by the Brisbane *Courier Mail* to be 'the equal of any on the field'. Despite the efforts of the younger team members, the Australian XV lost 36–3 in front of 25,000 enthusiastic spectators.

At the after-match reception Stan was approached by the Australian selector, Sydney King. King was only a slight fellow, weighing just on seventy kilos, but there was no doubting his courage. A former centre-three-quarter with Sydney's Western Suburbs, he had toured Britain and France in 1927–28 with the Waratahs and had been capped fourteen times for Australia, during which time he formed a legendary partnership with Cyril Towers. King was widely respected for both his big heart and his knowledge of the game. 'You played extremely well,' he told Stan. 'I was most impressed. My one suggestion to you is that you put on another half a stone or more. I'd just like to see you gain a little more body weight. If we were confident you could cover positions in the second row as well as the back row, you will definitely come into our considerations for next year.' Stan got the gist of the message:

he would be overlooked for the second Test, but he shouldn't give up hope. A tour of Great Britain beckoned.

The Wallabies once again demonstrated that Australia was a genuine rugby power when they extended the Springboks the following Saturday at the SCG, losing 17 to 26 in front of 30,000 fans. The South Africans went on to defeat New Zealand by two Tests to one — the only Springbok side to win a series in New Zealand and for many years considered the best side to have visited the country. This puts the win by NSW and the two narrow losses by Australia into their true perspective.

Stan arrived back in Melbourne with Syd King's words still ringing in his ears. He rarely needed inspiration for his training, but once the regular club football season concluded in September his off-season regime would have a very specific target. He joined Aaron Beattie's gym in the city and also held a series of meetings with Jimmy Barton on how he could most effectively achieve his goals.

An exceptionally talented trainer, Jimmy was a national sculling champion having won the 1924 title on Port River, North Adelaide, covering the two and a half mile (4 kilometre) course in just over eighteen minutes. He had experimented with his own exercise and diet regime and had come to an insightful understanding of how the body functioned. He made a point of developing different regimes for different sports. For example, boxers needed maximum strength and endurance but at a minimum body weight. It was the same with rowers. Long-distance runners, sprinters, swimmers and rugby players all had different requirements.

Stan wanted to put on weight and build muscle while retaining his speed and mobility. During previous off-season regimes he had focused on doing relatively light weights at high repetitions. For the summer of 1937–38, Jimmy completely reversed this program. He focused on a broad range of weight exercises for the upper and lower body, always in three lots of ten repetitions, always at maximum load, and always under strict supervision to avoid injury. By the last repetition of any set of exercises, Stan's muscles were fairly quivering with the stress, and the supervisor often had to assist with the last one or two lifts. And yet every few days, Jim and Aaron would add another half-a-pound or so to the weights, so as the weeks slowly turned into months the pounds slowly turned into stones, both on the weight bar and on Stan's body. In an era when little or no science had gone into sports nutrition, Jimmy had simply followed his intuition and the messages his own body gave him while practising his sport of sculling. The wisdom of the day was that athletes would benefit from a high protein, high sugar diet. It was quite common for footballers to gorge on steak and eggs only hours before a match. Jimmy was a great believer in a more balanced diet and had made the connection between carbohydrate intake and physical endurance. He made Stan maintain a diary in which he recorded not only his weight training regime but also his daily dietary intake. Variations were made on a weekly basis. By April 1938, Stan weighed over fourteen and a quarter stone (92 kilos) and it was all muscle and bone.

The 1938 club competition opened with a run of victories for Power House. 'Brilliant Rugby', 'Speed Rugby on Saturday' and 'Power House Burst Shocks Footscray' ran a string of Monday evening *Sun News-Pictorial* headlines. The team was still undefeated when, in the second week of May, the competition was suspended to allow for the annual state trial match, the Possibles versus the Probables, at Middle Park. Stan's form was such that he was an automatic selection in the state side.

The following week the team left by train for Sydney for the triangular series against NSW and Queensland. The team was based at the Oceanic Hotel in Coogee but on the Friday evening prior to the first match against NSW, the team decided to dine at Aarons' Exchange Hotel in the city. It was akin to the Christians deciding to dine with the Romans on the eve of the Circus. The

Exchange Hotel was holy ground for the NSW players and dining there could only be viewed as a provocative act by the southerners. As they entered the saloon, one of their forwards was accidentally-on-purpose shoulder-charged by another patron as they passed one another in the doorway. It was none other than 'Wild Bill' himself. Bill Cerutti was acknowledged as the toughest front-rower in the game. The son of an Italian immigrant, he had a thick bull neck, a great stocky frame and a deep, throaty laugh. He relished body contact and dished it out with regularity. He received his own share of hard knocks but always observed the prop's code of never complaining or squealing on an opponent.

At the Exchange Hotel, Cerutti shook hands with several of the Victorians and had a jibe for each of them. 'Looking forward to Saturday are you, Bisset?' he said as he paused in front of Stan. 'Well all I've got to say to you is just lay off the grog, the women and the fags.' This was very handy advice for a teetotalling Presbyterian. With that, Wild Bill took a deep drag on the Havana cigar he was smoking and blew in Stan's face. Well, the Victorians *had* chosen to eat in this particular establishment.

As the visitors jogged onto North Sydney Oval on Saturday 11 June they were shocked at the state of the pitch. Like many Australian football grounds, North Sydney Oval was a cricket ground in summer. The entire central square area, extending to both twenty-five-yard lines, was covered in black Bulli soil, renowned for its thick binding qualities. When rolled, it formed the type of rock-solid bouncy wickets that fast bowlers dream about. After it rained, though, and was cut about by boots and then re-baked into a solid mass by the winter sun, it was akin to playing on jagged concrete.

Stan played opposite the NSW captain, Russell Kelly, three years Stan's senior and a genuine athlete, having been a schoolboy sprint champion. He had debuted for NSW in 1933 and toured New Zealand with 'Dooney' Hayes' Australian team in 1936. Stan remembers his dashing speed off the mark and great ball-handling skills. NSW scored late in the game to snatch a 14 to 12 win. Scarcely a man left the field without injuries of some description. 'Dressing Rooms Resemble Casualty Ward,' ran the headline of *The Referee*'s match report. Stan had skinned both knees, had badly bruised hips and thighs, and sported an ugly graze down one side of his face. In possession of the ball early in the first half, he had broken through the opposition backline when someone ankle-tapped him from behind. Off balance, he had almost fallen into the path of sixteen stone (101 kilos) John 'Steak' Malone who, clasping him with both arms, fairly fell on him and drove him into the turf, or more correctly, what should have been the turf. The tackle could count as being legitimate, but the elbow in the back of the head that ground Stan's face into the baked soil definitely wasn't. It was Steak Malone's way of saying, 'Welcome to Sydney'.

Stan developed an infection in one of his knees, which he was sure had come from the yellow limestone chalk that marked the sidelines, and when he woke on Sunday morning he could hardly bend it. The return match was on the Monday and so he spent much of Sunday having a series of long hot baths to increase the blood flow and ease the swelling. There was plenty of time to survey the Sunday papers. The *Sydney Sunday Times* reported that, 'the Victorians played like a Springbok pack. Bridle and Bisset secured possession and their big forwards, Redhead, Lang, Pearson and Wilson drove in over the top in impressive style ... a tactic that continually flustered NSW. A win by NSW on Monday can not be assured.'

It was a prophetic conclusion. When the Victorians took to the field at Manly Oval at 3.15 p.m. on the Monday there were so many limbs covered in bandages and strapping that it looked as if the players had risen from their hospital beds to attend the match. The Sons of Lazarus gave the New South Welshmen a five-tries-to-two, 23 points to 14, thumping. When the final whistle blew, the Victorians hardly had the energy to celebrate; they just fell into a huddle holding one-another upright, allowing the moment of victory to sink in. As Stan turned around, the NSW team was walking over to shake hands. The first to greet him was Steak Malone, sporting a huge grin and an apparently sincere, 'Well done, mate'. When Stan walked through the tunnel of NSW players as they clapped the visitors off the field, the last man to shake his hand was the NSW captain, Frank 'Fob' O'Brien. O'Brien was inconsolable and near to tears. He had played his representative career to date in the centres, outside the majestic Cyril Towers, the regular NSW captain who was unavailable through injury. The team was effectively trialling new players in the role and in this, Fob's first go at the job, he felt he'd let his state down. The match report in the *Sydney Morning Herald* compared the Victorians to another world rugby power. 'They have the physique of the All Blacks and play in their style. The influence of Evan Jessep is still evident.' The *Sydney Mail* recorded that 'rugby has now entered a new era. NSW can no longer claim supremacy in this sport. Difficult as this is to accept by the NSW public, it augurs well for the future of the game.'

The two states had first played one another in 1889. In the eighteen matches up to the previous Monday, Victoria had only won on four occasions. The 1933 side with Weary Dunlop had won under eerily similar circumstances, losing their first match on the Saturday at North Sydney Oval but winning 14–8 at Manly on the Monday. Victoria had also won again in 1935. The difference in 1938, however, was the emphatic nature of the victory. According to the *Age*, 'it has risen Victorian Rugby to the highest traditions of the game'. Sadly, it was the last victory Victoria ever recorded over NSW.

The team returned to a hero's welcome in Melbourne. Stan's fine form continued for the remainder of the domestic competition and the minutes of Power House's Annual General Meeting summing up the 1938 season hardly convey the elation the club experienced by winning its first A Grade premiership. The secretary Reg Talbot wrote, 'A Grade played twenty matches of which seventeen were won, two were lost and one was drawn, and won the premiership by comfortably defeating Footscray in the final'. The Footscray side, which had won the premiership for the past two seasons, was beaten 18 points to 8 by Stan and his men and the first grade flag was triumphantly brought to the Lakeside clubhouse for the first time. The reserve grade was a narrow runner-up, losing to Harlequins in the final. One could not have found a bookmaker willing to take any odds on the possibility of Power House winning the C Grade premiership. The reason? The two Power House C Grade teams played off against one another in the final. As a fitting finale to the season, Stan captained Power House on its first interstate tour. Several prominent players from other clubs joined the team and the Victorian Rugby Union accorded them representative status, allowing them to wear the Victorian jumper. They were defeated 19–18 at Norwood, but the game was played in such good spirit that scant regard was paid to the scoreboard.

CHAPTER THREE

Green and Gold

The 1939 Australian rugby season opened with a buzz of excitement. Confirmation had just been received that the rumoured tour to Great Britain, scheduled to depart in July, was definitely on. The team would be called 'The Second Wallabies'. Had it not been for the foresight of Doctor Herbert 'Paddy' Moran, they might well have been called 'The Second Rabbits'. Moran had been the captain of Australia's first full tour of Great Britain in 1908 and was aghast to learn that in the weeks prior to the team's arrival at Plymouth the British press had given the Australians the moniker of 'The Rabbits'. In his first press interview, Paddy made it clear he had no intention of allowing that name to stick.

Thousands of rugby fans wrote to the newspapers with suggestions: Kangaroos, Wallabies, Wallaroos, Kookaburras. In fact the players wore the NSW emblem of the Waratah flower on their pale blue jerseys with the word 'Australia' embroidered underneath, so there was a strong argument to say the Waratah should be retained for the national team. Paddy called a team conference. The Waratah and pale blue jerseys were associated with NSW and hardly representative of the whole nation. Given that the epithet 'Kangaroos' had already been snaffled by the breakaway Rugby League for their national team, 'The Wallabies' won out on the day.

And why was this 1939 team to be called the 'Second' Wallabies when, since 1908, there had been major Wallaby tours to the USA, South Africa and New Zealand? The only possible answer was that this tour was to be on such a grand scale and so prestigious that, by comparison, all other tours paled into insignificance. The press called the tourists 'The Lucky 29'. How ironic that label would turn out to be.

On the domestic Victorian scene, the 1939 season was shaping up to be one the biggest in Power House's history with the club fielding five teams. The club needed to draw on all its obvious depth because from early June, six of their key players were away for extended periods on representative duties. State trials and interstate tours had become a regular part of the annual calendar but this year they had taken on monumental significance.

The Lucky 29 were really going to earn their jerseys. The Australian Rugby Union ensured the selection process was as thorough and as inclusive as possible. They did not want a repeat of 1927–28 situation when the NSW Waratahs toured Britain, Ireland and France, and with a token Queenslander Tommy Lawton in the team, assumed the mantle of the nation's representatives. The Australian Rugby Union retrospectively accorded Test status to the international games they played, but it was hardly the way to go about building the code on a national basis.

In 1939, Victoria and Queensland went through a rigorous Possibles versus Probables and State versus The Rest series of trials. NSW country, where rugby had a strong following, was divided into six regions that would all compete against one another before selection of the NSW Country team. It would then play against a City side and the NSW side would be selected after this round of matches. Additionally there was a Union team that included players from other regions such as Western Australia and South Australia — a process deemed more efficient than sending full teams from these weaker regions.

All of this would culminate in a series of interstate matches in Sydney in early June. The nation's best players would then face off against one another in two matches at the SCG on 17 June. That evening, the five selectors would sit down and choose the players who would take up berths on the SS *Mooltan*, which would be waiting for them a month later at Circular Quay.

Given what was at stake, the interstate series was fought with more than typical intensity. Queensland had emerged from something of a slumber in the 1920s to again be a major power in Australian rugby. In the first match of the series they shocked NSW by beating them 20 to 17 in Brisbane and then rubbed salt into the wound by winning 21–14 at North Sydney Oval. This did not augur well for the Victorians. The national team was sure to be dominated by NSW players and now, with two wins already under their belts, it would be the Queenslanders knocking on the selectors' door for any contentious positions. It was absolutely imperative that Victoria put up a good showing against Queensland when they met at the Sydney Sports Ground on Wednesday 7 June. Although Victoria lost 11–6, the match was much closer than most pundits expected. The most widely read and well respected national sports newspaper of the day was *The Referee*. Its banner headline the following day read, 'Victoria's fine showing against Queensland' and according to the journalist C.V. Davis, 'Bisset and Lang were in tip top form'. The headline on the *Daily Telegraph*'s main sports page read 'Bisset's Strong Claim For Tour'. Unfortunately the Victorians did themselves no favours by losing comprehensively to NSW, 27 to 6, at North Sydney Oval on the following Saturday, but they put in a much more solid performance in the second match, losing narrowly by 18 points to 22.

Sydney, 8 June 1939. The **Daily Telegraph**'s *Syd King was a former international rugby player and selector. At the time this article was written he was one of Sydney's most respected journalists. Along with other sports writers, King believed that Stan's form in the trial matches was so outstanding that his selection for the 1939 Wallaby tour was almost assured. (Note: Bisset is spelt incorrectly).*

News that the Victorians had gained four places in the final Australia XV versus The Rest trial on 17 June was greeted with wild jubilation at their base, the Coogee Oceanic Hotel. To be fair, given the level of competition they faced, it was all they could have hoped for. For the Australian XV, Stan was picked to play with Haggis Lang in the second row. This was something of a surprise as he had played most of his football in the back row at breakaway. In his previous two matches, however, he had switched to the second row and his scintillating form had obviously caught the eye of the selectors.

The following Saturday, 20,000 fans packed the SCG to watch the kick-off of the 1.15 p.m. trial match between a NSW XV and a Combined XV. The Australia XV versus The Rest match commenced at 3.15 p.m. The selectors had made it quite clear that selection for the later game by no means guaranteed a spot in the final squad. Any of the sixty players, plus reserves, could be considered for selection. The Victorian team manager, Pop Bremner, while having no official role in proceedings, was still allowed access to the field and he watched the game nervously, sitting beside the St John Ambulance men who always attended big matches at the SCG. Pop never missed an opportunity to run onto the field with the ambulance men, ostensibly to render first aid but in fact to whisper furtive instructions and advice to the four Victorians. His advice to Stan was for him to try and check the Queenslander Bill McLean, who was breaking early and illegally from the lineout, harassing the Australia XV's half-back and severely disrupting clean ball to the backs. At the half-time break, Pop gave Stan more specific instructions: to watch McLean like a hawk, to break at exactly the same moment as he did and to physically impede his advance. If the referee was incapable of enforcing the rules, it was up to Stan to take things into his own hands. At the first lineout in the second half, McLean again broke early and from only two metres away Stan hurled himself at the Queenslander. He only meant to knock

McLean off his stride, but there was a violent clash of heads and both players fell stunned to the ground. The match was stopped while McLean was led to the sideline to have a gash on his right eyebrow taped and strapped. Most of the crowd thought the clash was just an accident — the clash of heads was — but those with a knowledge of the game, and McLean himself, got the message that Stan had delivered: stay on-side until the ball was clear of the forwards. Stan was fortunate to have the NSW lock Aub Hodgson beside him in the back row, and they began to dominate their opponents. There was little separating the overall performance of the teams, but the The Rest backline was slightly better on the day and they won 29 to 14.

All the players mingled in the dressing rooms and then gathered in their various state huddles, each dissecting the day's play and the merits or otherwise of their performances. Stan thought he had played well but the head clash had left him slightly concussed. Pop assured him that he was one of the best forwards on the field. It was too late to worry anyway, because his destiny had now passed into the hands of others.

Immediately after the match, the five selectors retired to Rugby Union headquarters in the city. By 9 p.m. they had made their decision. Three copies of 'The Lucky 29' were typed up, sealed in three different envelopes and given to the state representatives. First thing the following morning, all the interstate players boarded their trains for home at Central Station. The big announcement would be made simultaneously in all three eastern state capitals at 7 p.m. on Monday 19 June.

The Melbourne rugby clubs had partitioned offices in a large building at Middle Park that had served as the Victorian Rugby Union headquarters since 1934. All the players and hundreds of their families, friends and supporters gathered outside the main door for the announcement as the meeting room was too small for such numbers. A hush of nervous expectation descended on the crowd as Mr W. J. Christie appeared, envelope in hand, and mounted a small podium. Christie had played his rugby with the Royal Military College Duntroon, and sensing the drama of the moment began his announcement in his best officer's voice. After an excessively long speech explaining the selection process—'Get on with it, Bill, for God's sake,' yelled someone in the crowd—he began to read out the names, starting with the fullbacks and working his way through the list. There was a huge cheer when Max's name was called out. 'Wingers: Carpenter, Victoria.' But there were no more Victorians in the backs. No Denis Cowper, no Ru Dorr, no John Hammon. Their heads slumped and they were consoled by friends.

'And now to the forwards,' said Christie. 'Back-rowers: from NSW, Hodgson, Oxenham, Windon. From Queensland, Oxlade, McDonald, McLean.' Stan's head dropped and he felt unsteady on his feet. A horrible gut-wrenching feeling of bitter disappointment welled in his throat. He had done his sums. The selectors would pick six back-rowers. That was it. It was all over.

He turned to walk away, wanting to be by himself, knowing he'd be asked how he felt and knowing he would be incapable of speaking. Christie went on. 'Second-rowers: From Queensland, Monti. From NSW Turnbull.' Christie then paused for dramatic effect. 'And from Victoria … Bisset.' It was unbelievable. He had been selected as a second-rower after all. Syd King had predicted it two years ago. Stan looked up, stunned and speechless. Two men were looking at him and laughing uncontrollably. They were Aaron Beattie and Jimmy Barton.

One of the first to congratulate Stan was Haggis Lang, who must have been devastated to have missed out, but made no sign of it as he shook Stan's hand and wished him all the best. It took minutes for it all to sink in. The unprecedented had happened. In fact three players from the one Victorian rugby club, Power House, were to wear the emerald green and gold of Australia. George Pearson, a theology student, a big dashing prop with the University club, was also in the side. In an interview with the *Age*, George said he owed it all to Pop Bremner. He explained that Pop had pulled him aside at half time in the trial match and said he was going well but his work-rate in defence was not up to his best. 'In the second half, I crash-tackled everything in sight. I think I even got the ref once.'

Apart from his own selection, none could have been more thrilling nor more satisfying for Stan than that of Andy 'Nicky' Barr. Andy was three years younger than Stan and only a fifteen-year-old when they first met at the 1931 Lord Somers' Camp. They had taken an instant liking to one another, not the least because of their mutual love of sport. Andy could sprint 100 yards in football boots in just over ten seconds. He played first grade for Hawthorn in the VFL at age nineteen before a fateful game of Rugby Union in 1935 where Stan had asked him to fill in for an injured player. Like Stan, he had fallen for the game; like Stan, he had also started on the wing and then moved to breakaway. Later, he switched to hooker, in which position he was selected for the Wallabies, along with Alby Stone from NSW. Andy went on to become one of the RAAF's most decorated fighter pilots. His exploits earned him membership of several exclusive aircrew 'clubs'. First was the Caterpillar Club, where one qualified by having to bail out of a disabled aircraft. He qualified three times for The Late Arrivals Club, that is, he was shot down behind enemy lines, was captured, escaped, and made it back to his unit to resume flying operations on three separate occasions. He acknowledged his Homeric deeds on the football field and in the war-torn skies of Europe with an air of total modesty.

Reflecting on how he felt on hearing the news of his selection, Stan found it hard to express his emotions. Australia's almost wholly white, Anglo-Saxon population of seven million, situated in a vast country at the southern tip of a culturally alien Asian continent, felt a genuine isolation from their spiritual home of Great Britain. The luxury of foreign travel was reserved for an elite few. Sea voyages to the UK took six weeks and the return fare for a second class cabin was £130. The idea of flying overseas was an even more remote possibility. The first regular aerial passenger service had only commenced in 1934 with Qantas Empire Airways flying as far as Singapore and Britain's Imperial Airways continuing on to London. The voyage took twelve and a half days and the large four-engine flying boats could only carry fifteen passengers. The fare of £275 was astronomical, given that the average weekly wage at the time was only £3/9/-.

Stan could well remember the envy he felt on the odd occasions he had reason to visit Station Pier at Port Melbourne to farewell privileged friends as they departed on an overseas voyage. The sight of jostling crowds clutching at masses of different coloured streamers linking family and friends on board with those on the wharf made for an unforgettable sight.

He was at the pier when the Wallabies had sailed for their South African tour in June 1933. He was there again that same year when Douglas Jardine and his English cricket team had set sail for home at the conclusion of the Bodyline series. Stan had attended the second cricket Test in Melbourne in January. The crowd was in shock when Bradman was out for a duck in the first innings, clean bowled by Bowes. Voce and Larwood terrified the other Australians with their vicious speed bowling directed at the batsman's body. Then Bill O'Reilly had ripped through the English batsmen with his fast leg-spinners, and Bradman's classy century in the second innings sealed the match for Australia. The victory did little to cool the animosity that the Australian fans held for the Englishmen and Stan still remembers the lone figure of Jardine, standing at the ship's rail, well away from the rest of his team, as if they too wanted no association with the man who the cricketing world now loved to hate. Jardine fanned himself with a newspaper in the scorching, late summer heat. 'You leave our bloody flies alone, Jardine,' yelled a wag standing beside Stan as the *Mooltan* pulled slowly away from the dock.

Could Stan have possibly imagined that in six years time, he himself would stand on the very spot where Jardine had stood, on the very same deck, on the very same ship, also en route to England?

The itinerary of the 1939 Wallaby tour read like a trip to Rugby Heaven. It was to be one of the longest, most involved and most interesting trips ever undertaken by an Australian sporting team. It was to last ten months and encompass twenty-eight matches. Commencing in Devon in mid-September, and playing one mid-week match and another on a Saturday, they would travel through Wales and the Midlands to Scotland. By November they would be back in London and then play Oxford and Cambridge Universities. The first Test would be against Scotland on 25 November, the

PROGRAMME

*

Chairman - - - Mr. W. W. HILL

TOASTS

"THE KING"

"THE 1939-1940 AUSTRALIAN TEAM"

Proposed by:

Mr. W. W. HILL,
President, N.S.W. Rugby Union.

Right Hon. W. M. HUGHES, K.C., Attorney-General.
Representing the Prime Minister.

Lt.-Col. Hon. M. F. BRUXNER, M.L.A., Deputy Premier,
Representing the Premier.

Mr. J. M. TULLY, M.L.A.,
Representing the Leader of the Opposition.

Response:

Dr. W. F. MATTHEWS, Manager.

Mr. V. W. WILSON, Captain.

Mr. E. de C. GIBBONS, Vice-Captain.

* * *

DIVERTISSEMENT

Mr. LESLIE HERFORD   Mr. PAT. FLANAGAN
Mr. FRANK RYAN   Mr. ALFRED WILMORE

MATCH RECORD

DATE		MATCH	RESULT	For	Against
Sept.	16	Devon and Cornwall at			
,,	20	Cumberland and Yorkshire at Workington			
,,	23	Somerset and Gloucestershire at Gloucester			
,,	27	Abertillery and Cross Keys at Abertillery			
,,	30	Cardiff at Cardiff			
Oct.	4	Midland Counties at Birmingham			
,,	7	Combined Services at Aldershot			
,,	11	North of Scotland at Aberdeen			
,,	14	South of Scotland at Galashiels			
,,	18	Glasgow and Edinburgh at Glasgow			
,,	21	Northumberland and Durham at Sunderland			
,,	26	Newport at Newport			
,,	28	Neath and Aberavon at Neath			
,,	31	Llanelly at Llanelly			
Nov.	4	London Counties at Twickenham			
,,	9	Oxford University at Oxford			
,,	11	Hampshire and Sussex at Bournemouth			
,,	15	Cambridge University at Cambridge			
,,	18	Leicestershire and East Midlands at Leister			
,,	25	SCOTLAND at Murrayfield			
,,	29	Lancashire and Cheshire at Blundellsands			
Dec.	2	Ulster at Belfast			
,,	9	IRELAND at Dublin			
,,	14	Pontypool, Talwain and Blaenavon at Pontypool			
,,	16	Swansea at Swansea			
,,	23	WALES at Cardiff			
,,	26	London Counties at Twickenham			
Jan.	6	ENGLAND at Twickenham			

Wentworth Hotel, Sydney, 19 July 1939. This was the program for the dinner hosted by the Australian Rugby Union to farewell the Wallabies. The tour was to be on a grand scale, lasting ten months. After playing in the British Isles, the team was to play Tests against France, Germany, the USA, Canada and New Zealand.

second against Ireland on 9 December, the third against Wales on 23 December and they would conclude the British leg with the clash against England at Twickenham on 6 January 1940. Two Tests were planned for France and one in Germany. Rugby Union had reached Germany through affluent British students who had attended private grammar schools during the time of the German Confederation. British students had also studied in the major universities towns while others had completed their military service in Hanover. The German Rugby Federation was established in 1900 and the country won the silver medal in Rugby Union at that year's Olympics in Paris. Their national side was extremely well respected and had beaten France twice in the 1930s.

After returning to London, the Australians would then sail for the USA and play two Tests against America and one against Canada. They would then cross the Pacific and conclude their tour with two Tests against New Zealand. While the players were all strictly amateurs, the team would fill stadiums like Twickenham to capacity. With anticipated crowds of up to 30,000 paying an average entrance fee of two shillings and sixpence, the tour would make a colossal profit. The contract each player had signed guaranteed first class sea and rail travel and stated that all meals and 'reasonable expenses' could be billed to the Union. Irrespective of one's background or experiences in life to date, this was truly the opportunity of a lifetime.

All of Stan's many friends and all his family flocked to the pier to see him off. They inspected the two-bedded cabin he expected to share with Andy Barr and admired the recently installed ceiling fans that would hopefully bring some relief during the long crossing of the tropics. Prior to sailing, Stan held more than thirty streamers in one hand and waved at everyone he could recognise with the other. Three more blasts in quick succession signalled the time for departure. Tears literally streamed down people's cheeks as the crowd burst spontaneously into the haunting melody

Green and Gold

*Sydney, 21 July 1939. the **Mooltan** departed Sydney with seventeen NSW and eight Queensland players who made up the Wallaby touring party to Great Britain. The four Victorian members boarded the ship in Melbourne on 25 July.*

Melbourne, 25 July 1939. The four Victorian members of the Wallaby Team: (left to right): George Pearson from the University Club, and the three Power House team-mates, Andy Barr, Max Carpenter and Stan.

71

*Melbourne, 25 July 1939. It was unprecedented in Australian Rugby history that three members of the one Victorian rugby club, Power House, should be selected for the national team. Wearing their Australian Team blazers on board the **Mooltan** (from left to right): Stan, Andy Barr and Max Carpenter.*

Melbourne, July 1939. Andy Barr and Stan proudly wear their new Wallaby kit while holding the travelling rugs issued to each player.

of the Maori Farewell: 'Now is the hour, when we must say goodbye. Soon you'll be sailing, far across the sea. While you're away, oh then remember me. When you return, you'll find me waiting here.'

The *Mooltan* departed Sydney on 21 July 1939 with the seventeen New South Wales and eight Queensland members of the squad on board. It was 25 July when the four Victorians boarded ship in Melbourne. A week before departure, Power House had organised a lavish celebratory dinner for its three heroes at the Victoria Palace Hotel. Many toasts were proposed and many speeches delivered. Doc McAdam was brought to tears as he recalled how he felt like a killjoy when compelled to call a halt to the Foot and Mouth Disease games at Somers' Camp seven years previously. How could he, or any of the other founding members of the club, imagine that their fledging venture would produce three national representatives in the one year? It was truly an unprecedented honour for them all. The following day the *Sporting Globe*'s headline ran, 'Wallaby representatives bring great honour to Melbourne'. The article concluded by saying that, 'At last, Victorian rugby has gained its rightful place in the lexicon of Australian sport'.

The week prior to departure had passed in a whirl of private and public farewell dinners, and the emotional send-off had left lumps in the four Victorians' throats. Their heads were still giddy from the back slapping and elevation to celebrity status in their beloved city of Melbourne. They had not even had time to visit their cabins before they were summoned to their first on-board team meeting as the *Mooltan* slipped quietly through the narrow Port Phillip Heads with the outgoing tide.

As they entered the large meeting room adjacent to the dining salon the chilly reception awaiting them came as a total and bewildering shock. The four Victorians were treated with total disdain and contempt by the largely New South Wales squad. Unbeknown to Stan and his Victorian contemporaries, the rest of Australian Rugby Union was furious that these upstarts from Melbourne had the gall to actually steal Wallaby caps from the men of New South Wales and Queensland to whom they rightfully belonged.

Cocooned as they were by their supportive family and friends and a doting Melbourne press, the Victorians had been totally oblivious to the controversy and barely concealed acrimony that had swirled around Sydney rugby circles in the weeks following the team's selection. With the benefit of hindsight, Stan feels the 'state versus state' issue was not at the heart of the matter. One of the biggest shocks for rugby supporters had been the omission of Cyril Towers from the team. It was true that at the age of thirty-three, this Prince of centres was nearing the end of his illustrious career, but given his experience, his goal-kicking abilities and his recent form, many judges were at a loss to explain his exclusion.

Towers, who was present at the Sydney Rugby Union headquarters when the team was announced, was so upset he refused to be interviewed by the press. The manager selected to lead the tour, Doctor Wally Matthews, had managed the Australian team on its tour of South Africa in 1933. While Towers was in that squad, he was a notable omission from the Tests. Matthews was alleged to have said that Towers' forthrightness was so disruptive 'it would destroy team morale'. It looked as if there was only room for one of the two men on the 1939 tour and it was Matthews who received the selectors' nod.

Was it the case that the selectors were incompetent, or had they been acting with genuine vision and with the best short and long term interests of the game at heart? Towers kept his views on the matter to himself for a while, but then in an interview with the Sydney *Daily Telegraph* he let fly with both barrels, giving the Rugby Union administration a great serve. 'The Union's administrators were muddling and stupid,' he claimed. 'They've killed my enthusiasm for football. Until they put men at the head of affairs who understand football, the game won't have a chance.' Maybe he was right. Yet in the very next sentence, Towers appeared to contradict himself. 'Young and promising players are not in the race unless they are in big with the executive.' If that was the case, how could he explain the selection of Des Carrick, a hard-running nineteen-year-old centre who had only recently left school? Carrick had effectively been selected to take Towers' place. Another NSW back, the five-eight, Paul Collins, admitted his selection had come as a genuine shock.

The Victorians could claim that they too were poorly treated by the selectors with the omission of their 'own' Denis Cowper. Educated in Sydney and having played for Norths before moving to Victoria, Cowper had represented Victoria and played for Australia in Tests against New Zealand in 1931 and 1933. He toured South Africa in 1933, and when the captain Alec Ross was sidelined with appendicitis he took over the captaincy. Cowper had no beef with the selectors, nor with the Union administration. Presumably, like Towers, had been omitted to make way for new blood.

Another prominent omission was that of Wild Bill Cerutti, who many considered to be one of the toughest and most competent forwards still going around in NSW. Cerutti had made his international debut as a nineteen-year-old and his play during the Wallabies' tour of South Africa in 1933, when Australia won two of the Tests, was so dominant that South African rugby critics named him in their 'best ever' world XV for decades to come. Cerutti was known for his love of a scrap. In one famous incident on the South African tour, both teams had been called together for an official dinner in an attempt to douse the fiery on-field exchanges that were in danger of ruining the series as a spectacle. The managers of both

Sydney Cricket Ground, 1938. Two of the most influential Australian rugby players of the 1930s were Cyril Towers (ball in hand) and Aub Hodgson (moving in to make the tackle). Towers was a shock omission from the 1939 Wallaby team.

sides made speeches saying that if the players did not respect the rules and play in the spirit clearly enshrined in the fine traditions of the game, they would never again appear in their national colours. Cerutti was sitting next to the famous South African brothers, Boy and Fannie Louw. Fannie turned to Cerutti and said, 'Well, it'll be all-on tomorrow', to which Cerutti quipped, 'Why wait until tomorrow?' and a wild brawl erupted on the spot.

All in all, it had been an ugly few weeks in Sydney that had left a bitter taste in everyone's mouth. Even the NSW newspapers agreed that the four Victorians had earned their places fairly and squarely, so there was no logical reason why their selection should have been resented by anyone. The only explanation for the hostile reception the Victorians received was that they were unknown to the rest of the touring party and that this was an era when parochial attitudes and state rivalries were much more marked than today. As is often the case with 'new boys' joining a team, the Victorians were apparently going to be forced to earn the respect of the established players. Still, it was hardly the start to the great adventure that they had been anticipating. One thing Cyril Towers did say in his interview with the *Daily Telegraph* with which Stan could certainly agree was, 'It's more than brilliant football and ability on the field that gets you into the team'. How true, indeed.

Such had been the focus on their own world of sport, and living as they had done, some 12,000 miles from their destination, virtually no one in the Wallaby squad had given much thought to world political events. As the ship sailed across the Indian Ocean, however, the political situation on the Continent was beginning to deteriorate rapidly. In fact it had been deteriorating since September 1938, when Britain had ceded the Sudetenland, in Czechoslovakia, to Germany as part of the infamous Munich Agreement. The world had viewed this event with mixed feelings. Many observers, particularly in Britain and on the Continent, felt that Chamberlain and Hitler had reached a reasonable compromise that would

*At sea on the **Mooltan**, August 1939. The on-board pool was popular with the team as they passed through the tropics.*

ensure 'Peace in our time'. However, some other observers, like Doc McAdam who followed such events with great interest, saw it as a step towards continuing German expansionism. The international community should be confronting Hitler rather than compromising with him.

Europe seemed to be rushing headlong into war, but these events were far from Stan's mind during the voyage. This Indian Ocean leg of the voyage might have been uneventful weather-wise, but storms of activity were brewing on board. In addition to the normal entertainment, which included a dance band, an English theatrical company was en route home and the rugby players were simply thronged by a bevy of flashy showgirls and shapely dancers. Stories of a moving feast of love affairs abounded, be they true or simply told to impress, Stan never really knew. But having come from a respectable church-going family in what was a conservative city, Stan's first overseas trip was becoming something of an eye-opener.

As they passed into the tropics, temperatures in the cabins reached an almost unbearable 100 degrees Fahrenheit during the day and sleeping at night became an uncomfortable, sweat-soaked experience. The evening they were to cross the equator, a fully dressed Neptune appeared with his obligatory trident to lead everyone into the salon for a grand celebratory feast to be followed by a huge Crossing of the Line party. Stan lined up with all the other uninitiated 'Pollywogs'—that is, those crossing the equator for the first time—and prepared for his 'baptism' by water. As the night wore on, the party got out of hand, with people being tied up and having eggs cracked over them while others had shaving cream lathered all over their heads.

Stan and Andy Barr, in particular, had become the butt of a series of jokes based on the contrast of their build and complexion. Andy was slim and fair with sandy coloured hair while Stan was broader and stronger and had a darker complexion. They were nicknamed 'Pale and Darkie' or 'Black & White' whiskey. On the evening of the Crossing, as everyone filed into the dining hall Steak Malone yelled out to Stan from across the crowded diners, 'Hey Blackie, I hear you're going to be leading us in some gymnastics in the morning. Bet you can't do this though,' and he leapt into a handstand position with the intention of doing a handspring. At the crucial moment, his hands slipped and his fifteen stone body came crashing down on its backside in full view of scores of bemused black-tie diners. Stan simply smiled, executed a perfect forward somersault and without breaking step, flopped into his seat beside an aghast Doctor Matthews. Throughout dinner there were some quiet mutterings about how Stan and the Power House boys would fare on tour. 'Sure, these lads are fit, but look at them. I don't know how those boys are going to scrummage against the biggest pack in the world.'

The team management had seen the friction developing and, to their credit, took measures to alleviate it. Wally Matthews had

*At sea on the **Mooltan**, August 1939.*
Stan playing cricket in the nets on deck.

played as half-back for NSW against Queensland and Great Britain, had managed the First AIF side and the 1933 Wallaby tour of South Africa. He was a well-respected medical practitioner and the Mayor of Orange. Secretary to the manager was Mr Jeff Noseda, who had fifteen years experience in rugby administration. The captain, Vay Wilson, was a big, studiously contemplative Queenslander who had played for Australia in 1937 under Cyril Towers, from whom he had taken over the Australian captaincy for the subsequent Tests against New Zealand. Wilson later admitted to Stan that he had little time for Towers, who 'rarely found time to discuss tactics with his players'. Wilson was above such pettiness and was keen to find a way to bind the current team together. The first suggestion was that Stan and Andy change cabins and be allocated new roommates. Stan was delighted to share with Queenslander Boyd Oxlade who had been a team-mate in the Australian side in the final selection trial. Boyd had played for Australia in the three home Tests against New Zealand in 1938 when, according to the Australian coach Johnny Wallace, rugby reached a standard rated the highest ever seen in Australia.

Stan also became close friends with Andy Barr's cabin-mate, Ron Rankin. A talented, hard-running fullback from the Drummoyne club who could kick goals from just about anywhere on the field, Ron had already played seven Tests. He was a master at Sydney Grammar School and like Andy Barr, he subsequently joined the RAAF and won the Distinguished Flying Cross with Bar. He also received the Belgian Croix de Guerre.

The second and perhaps more effective move was Wilson's suggestion that Stan take responsibility for some of the team's physical training, a role traditionally filled by the captain. It was Jeff Noseda who approached Stan. 'I hear you're quite keen on the gym work and I believe you've trained with Aaron Beattie in Melbourne. Why don't you take over some of the PT in the mornings after breakfast?'

The presence on board of the strapping rugby players had caused more than a stir of interest, possibly much more, and the sight of them on deck, stripped down and ready for action, soon attracted a crowd of curious onlookers as Stan put the squad through its paces. For a good hour, he bombarded the men with push-ups, callisthenics, squat jumps, gymnastics and half an hour's skipping. It made Vay Wilson's sessions seem like a warm-up and the deck was soon awash with sweat. The only men used to this kind of physical

*At sea on the **Mooltan**, August 1939. The Australian skipper Vay Wilson (back to camera, No. 11 jersey) puts the players through their paces. When Stan assumed responsibility for this type of training he greatly increased its intensity and effectiveness.*

punishment were the Power House boys and there were groans of protest from the others as the session ground interminably onwards. As the squad neared a state of collapse at one session, Stan said, 'OK boys. Not a bad loosener. We'll get serious tomorrow.'

While they paraded on the deck the following morning, the team found Stan standing beside a series of iron bars laid out along the wooden decking. 'Without a proper gym,' he announced, 'scratch-pulling is the best we have to do some strength training.' While the team looked on, bemused, Stan made a show of scanning the team for a suitable partner for a demonstration. He settled on Aub Hodgson and asked for his assistance. Aub shifted his ponderous bulk and came out to the front of the team.

Scratch-pulling was a strength training exercise commonly used by rowers. Two men would sit on the ground facing one other with legs outstretched, their feet braced together, both gripping the same bar and heaving away from each other as if pulling an oar. The winner was the man who managed to pull his opponent up off the ground. 'Take the strain,' said Stan, and the two men steadied themselves. 'Ready?' Hodgson only grunted. 'Right. Pull!' The assembled Wallabies and the growing crowd erupted with cheers as the two men heaved against one another. Hodgson, a grazier weighing over 100 kilos, was a genuinely formidable opponent. Both men's legs and chest muscles quivered under the strain, but slowly, almost imperceptibly, Hodgson's backside began to slide forward across the deck. Hodgson knew what was happening and threw all his effort into one last desperate pull, but Stan was too

*At sea on the **Mooltan**, August 1939. Vay Wilson (standing) holds the head of Aub Hodgson as a neck-strengthening exercise. Aub was considered the biggest and toughest of the Australian forwards. The Victorian players had initially felt like outsiders, but the attitude of the squad turned in their favour when Stan out-muscled Aub in scratch-pulling, another body-strength exercise.*

strong, and with a final heave of his own he dragged his opponent clear of the deck and onto his feet.

Hodgson was one of the toughest, most flamboyant and most gregarious forwards Australia has produced and separating fact from fiction regarding his antics was never easy. What is true is that by 1939 he had represented NSW twenty-four times, played eleven Tests including those on the Wallabies' famous 1933 South African tour under Alec Ross. South African rugby writers invariably included him with Cerutti in their World XV, such were his performances on the 1933 tour. That he relished fierce physical encounters was undisputed, and to his credit Hodgson took his loss in the scratch-pull competition well. 'Good one, Blackie,' he said as he helped Stan to his feet. It was the first time he'd used Stan's nickname. Hodgson's defeat in such a blatantly fair and public test of strength completely changed the dynamics within the squad. The Victorians were no longer the new boys and they enjoyed universal acceptance within the team.

The *Mooltan* made its first port of call at Colombo. Significantly, it was Aub Hodgson who invited Stan and Andy to make up a group of ten who were going to hire two cars and drivers and go for a sight-seeing and shopping tour. After admiring the views from Mount Lavinia and being fleeced by a crafty Sinhalese shopkeeper in a drapery store not dissimilar to the one he had known in Prahran, Stan returned to the ship marvelling at his first experiences in a foreign land.

The ship struck wild weather on the Arabian Sea, then passed through the Suez Canal and took on supplies at Port Said. In the lounge, they read through the week-old selection of British newspapers. 'War Clouds Gathering in Europe,' read one headline. 'Good Lord. I hope we don't get wet on the way,' was one throw-away remark, but it merely masked a growing sense of foreboding that no one, until now, had wanted to acknowledge. Surely they could not be sailing into a military maelstrom on the eve of their approach to Europe?

As the *Mooltan* drew near to Marseilles, the Wallabies emerged from their cabins in the late afternoon, keen to be among the first to sample the local hospitality, but that evening they were greeted with a startling sight. The entire city, reputed to be one of the most vibrant and lively towns on the Mediterranean, was plunged into a blackout, apparently due to fears of German air raids. During the preceding three years the city had been witness to streams of immigrants fleeing the Spanish Civil War and the inhabitants had heard accounts of the unprovoked air strikes by the German Condor Legion. The citizens had no intention of being caught unprepared. As the ship passed through the Straits of Gibraltar, the political news from Great Britain appeared to deteriorate further, as did the weather. When the ship finally neared the English coast, they were diverted first from Tilbury, then from Plymouth. Fog horns in the dark of night, emanating from the British Fleet manoeuvring off Portsmouth, added to a growing sense of foreboding. A pilot boat finally drew alongside near the mouth of The Solent and they eased their way up its headwaters and into the Southampton Docks.

The train journey took the team to Torquay, the fashionable seaside resort where the tourists were billeted in the Grand Hotel. The team gathered in the lounge to hear arrangements for their planned bus trip to London the following day when someone called for quiet and turned up the volume of the radio. It was the British Prime Minister, Neville Chamberlain. 'I am speaking to you from the Cabinet Room at 10 Downing Street. This morning, the British Ambassador in Berlin handed the German Government a final note stating that unless we heard from them by 11.00 a.m. that they were prepared at once to withdraw their troops from Poland, a state of war would exist between us. I have to tell you that no such undertaking has been received and that consequently, this country is at war with Germany.'

Everyone sat motionless in stunned silence. The consequences of the declaration were only too evident. If Great Britain was at

At sea on the Mooltan, September 1939, the Wallabies on deck in their Australian blazers. (Stan is standing in the third row, fourth from the right.)

war then, being part of the Empire, so was Australia. Like the rest of the team, Stan spent the day in a depressed state, racked by doubts and uncertainties. Would the tour continue, be postponed or, even worse, cancelled? How would Australia be drawn into the war? Even in the unlikely event that the tour could continue, perhaps to the USA, which at this stage was uninvolved, Stan was not sure that he could spend the next ten months playing football while Europe and the Empire were at war. On the other hand, however, there was a glimmer of hope. In the days following Chamberlain's speech there was talk of it only being a 'Phoney War', with neither side actually engaged in any fighting. Perhaps it was simply a case of brinkmanship by both sides. Hadn't Chamberlain invested too much time and effort into the peace process to allow it to be thrown away without one final push for a diplomatic solution? Hadn't he promised, 'Peace in our time'? Many others felt that even if fighting broke out it would be over before it had even begun. The debate raged in the bar of the Grand as the players and management all threw their opinions forward. While many of the Wallabies were in favour of abandoning the tour and enlisting in Britain, some argued against the rashness of this. How could they know how things would pan out? Would Australia really send troops? If a quick solution could be found, hasty action would mean all their work and effort would be thrown away for nothing.

News arrived the next day — the tour was definitely off. Some of the team wanted to enlist in England but this decision was taken out of their hands. Prime Minister Menzies cabled the Australian High Commissioner in London, Stanley Bruce, to say that an expeditionary force along the lines of that of the previous war could not be agreed to until 'the position of Japan has been cleared up'. It was made clear that if the players wanted to serve in the war, they would all have to return to their native country to do so.

Stan was naturally devastated by all these events. To have the experience of a lifetime dashed in such extraordinary circumstances seemed cruel. Then there was the confusion of what to do next. Like most Australians, he was a strong supporter of 'the Empire'. Only the year before, he had joined a militia company formed by Power House. Australia did not have a regular standing army at the time and the Australian Military Forces were made up of militiamen. It was almost impossible for Stan to come to terms with the sudden collapse of everything he had dreamed of for so many years, all for a war that might not even turn out to be a war at all.

Stan went to the bar of the Grand where some other Wallabies had gathered when the somewhat despondent hotel manager came into the lounge. 'I say, excuse me lads...' he began, 'we've been told that we need to sandbag our street-front windows. I mean, with all these air raids and things, and we were wondering if, um...' Steak Malone cocked an eyebrow quizzically at him as the manager asked 'if perhaps you chaps might lend us a hand.' He didn't look hopeful, but Andy Barr quickly broke the awkward silence and volunteered, as did Stan.

The response of the others was hardly overwhelming but some practical work would help to give them a sense of purpose and they shuffled outside. Three hours later they were still hard at it, some stripped to the waist, others in their training jerseys, piling row upon precarious row of sandbags along the Grand's street frontage. The Australians towered over the local team of sandbaggers and their work-rate was high. It was still tough work, however.

'Look what you've bloody got us into, Darkie,' muttered Malone, wiping the sweat from his eyes and inspecting his blistered hands. Stan was about to defend himself when the small cluster of Wallabies turned, distracted, to stare at two very new and very dashing-looking Cadillac saloons cruising slowly towards them. None of the men had seen machines like this at home.

The Grand's owner leant out of one of the rear windows. 'That might be enough for today, lads. What do you think? I thought we might go and have a pint.'

The boys rushed to their rooms for a quick scrub-down. Fifteen minutes later they were happily ensconced in the limousines, complete with chauffers, departing on a 'cider tour' of Devon and Cornwall. Stan's tee-totalling days had come to an abrupt end. The evening tour began with the newer, 'smooth' ciders in the pubs and bars of Torquay but ended with the older, more popular 'rough' versions in quiet Cornish village pubs complete with gin chasers. The smooth cider, Stan decided, went straight to his head, while the rough went straight to his legs.

A popular and mutually beneficial routine was established. The team would work all morning at the Grand, throwing its strength and fitness into the sandbagging job, and in the afternoon the grateful hotelier would lay on the limousines for anything the boys desired. In this first chaotic week of the war, fancy cars appeared to be readily available, but a dozen fit, young workers were an apparent rarity. Each team member received a pound a week spending money and even in 1939 it was a bit of a stretch to survive on this budget,

Torquay, England, September 1939. The Wallabies assisted in sand-bagging their hotel, The Grand, as protection against air raids. In compensation, the hotel manager provided chauffer-driven Cadillacs for countyside tours. (Stan is in the centre with a bag on his shoulder).

so the largesse of the hotel owner was greatly appreciated. The hard work and novelty of the tours went some way to taking the men's minds off the depressing reality of the cancellation of the tour and the uncertainty of what lay ahead.

Wally Matthews and Jeff Noseda organised travel to London so the team could fulfil some pre-arranged social engagements and have the opportunity to see some of the sights. As the train passed from the green fields of Surrey to the outskirts of the city, the drab industrial suburbs hardly fitted the images of the London everyone held so clearly in their imagination. When they alighted at Waterloo Station they were astonished to see weeping mothers hording hundreds of children onto a nearby train. Evacuations from the capital were already well under way. As they passed through the station's Victory Arch entranceway and strolled down to the Thames embankment, the great vista of the city opened up before them. Only a kilometre away was the City of Westminster and Big Ben itself, outlined against a grey evening sky that was already full of great barrage balloons, a deterrent to low-flying enemy aircraft.

In a very real sense, London was not a foreign city to this generation of Australians. They had been taught at school that this was their cultural and historical home. The names of the streets and the principal buildings were as familiar to them as Bourke Street or Pitt Street. They decided to assign their luggage to cabs and walk the short distance to their Park Lane hotel via The Strand, Pall Mall, Piccadilly and on to Mayfair. The lovely green of St James' Park was already criss-crossed by trenches and dotted with great gouges of raw earth formed by bomb shelters under construction.

The week was a whirl of activity: sightseeing, pub lunches, the theatre, and every evening a magnificent dinner. The sportsmen's clubs of London made a lasting impression, a total culture shock for all the players. Even Stan, who felt that he and Hal had had a rather good introduction to Melbourne's society as guests of Doc McAdam, was taken aback by their extraordinary opulence.

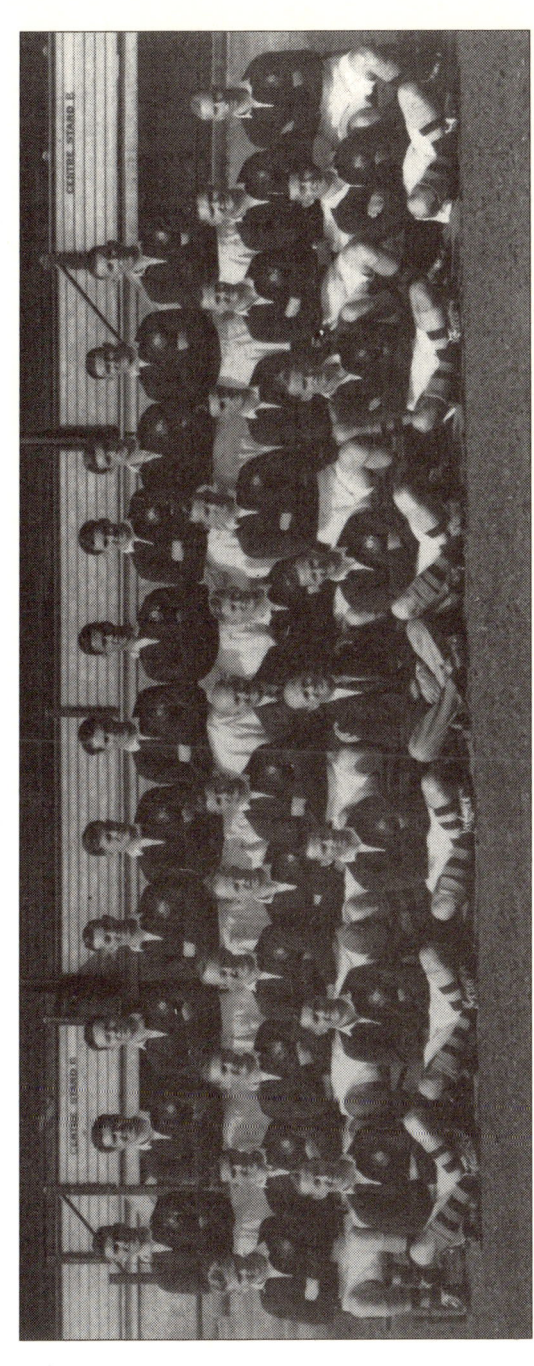

Torquay, England, September 1939. The Australian Rugby Union Team photographed at the Torquay Stadium where they would have played Devon and Cornwall in the first match of their cancelled British Isles tour. (BACK ROW, LEFT TO RIGHT): *George Pearson, Des Carrick, Jack Turnbull, Bill McLean, Mac Ramsey, Carrabo 'Bill' Monti, Stan Bisset, Boyd Oxlade, Brian Oxenham, Len Smith, Keith Windon.* (SECOND ROW, LEFT TO RIGHT): *Andy Barr, Ron Rankin, John McDonald, John Malone, Vic Richards, Vay Wilson (Captain) Wally Matthews (Manager) Eric de Courcy Gibbons (Vice-Captain), Aub Hodgson, Vaux Nicholson, Jack Kelaher, Alby Stone, Llewellyn Lewis.* (FRONT ROW, LEFT TO RIGHT): *Mike Clifford, Cecil Ramalli, Basil Porter, Jeff Noseda (Assistant Manager), Max Carpenter, Paul Collins, Winston Ide.*

The visit to the Lansdowne Club in Fitzmaurice Place, Berkeley Square, was a highlight. Originally the home of the Marquess of Lansdowne, it became a private club in 1930 and was fitted out in the Arte Moderne style by White Allom, the same firm that had fitted out the great Cunard liners like the *Queen Mary* and the *Queen Elizabeth*. There were social rooms, a swimming pool, squash courts, a fencing 'salle', bars, cafes and a fine dining room. Mr Bevan Whiteman, president of the Devon Rugby Football Union, had befriended the players at Torquay, and as he also had the privilege of being a founding member he had invited the entire team to a formal dinner.

There were other surprises in store. Weary Dunlop was practising in London. He had studied surgery at St Bartholomew's Hospital and had recently been admitted as a Fellow of the Royal College of Surgeons. Bart's was recognised as the world's leading surgical hospital and attracted students from every continent. Weary had recently gained a post at St Mary's Paddington and arranged to meet Stan and Andy Barr at the nearby Fountains Abbey pub, proposing that they 'drink great quantities of beer and solve the problems of the world'.

After they had groped their way along the darkened streets in the blackout, the three Melbournians had a riotous night on the town. Where they ended up, Stan has no idea. Weary managed to hail a cab to get the boys back to their hotel when something of a small disaster struck. Andy was half-way through complaining about the warm local beers when an inebriated looking gentleman stumbling out of a closing bar almost fell into the path of the cab. The cabbie slammed on the brakes, but the man was bowled up onto the bonnet before rolling down onto the roadway.

Fearing the worst, Weary and Stan dashed over to the figure lying in the gutter. The man was semi-conscious and Weary set about examining the extent of his injuries. Thankfully, nothing appeared to be broken. It was only as they helped him into the cab that they realised just how well-dressed this man was, bedecked with a top-hat, tails and white tie. Medals and orders of various descriptions adorned his chest and he carried a rather expensive-looking cane. He spoke in a thick, European accent and set about bestowing every blessing under the sun on Stan and Weary for their assistance. The character identified himself as a Belgian baron and insisted that they come to his home for a drink.

If the lads had been suspicious of the stranger's claim to aristocracy then they were proven wrong when the butler opened the door to his Chandos Street apartment. What appeared to be a relatively modest London townhouse was in fact the most lavishly furnished and decorated home they had ever entered. More significantly, the Baron had the best stocked private bar they had ever seen and he insisted that they be seated while he mixed cocktail after cocktail from his exotic collection of spirits. It was a happy conclusion to what could have been a serious incident.

The encounter with the Baron was not Stan's only bizarre brush with European aristocracy. At a team dinner hosted by the English Rugby Union on the evening of their visit to Twickenham, he was introduced to a Russian émigré, Prince Serge Obolensky, who had gained two rugby blues at Oxford and caused a sensation when he was selected to play for England in 1936, even though he was not a British citizen. He scored two tries in the game and was the key to the first ever English victory against New Zealand. Stan was saddened to learn that the Prince was killed when his Spitfire crashed only months later.

When the players visited Twickenham Stadium — affectionately known as the Cabbage Patch and the home of English rugby since 1907 — they fully realised what great experiences had been denied them. Instead of a stadium packed full of cheering spectators, the empty stands seemed to mock them with the echo of their own voices. The only onlookers were a handful of Air Raid Precaution volunteers who, together with the Auxiliary Fire Service, had taken

Twickenham, September 1939. Stan surveys the empty stands. The visit to this famous rugby stadium brought home to the team what great experiences had been denied them due to the cancellation of the tour.

over the stadium. The wooden benches were piled high with anti-gas overalls, gas-masks and decontamination equipment. It was truly a depressing experience.

Unquestionably the highlight of the Stan's time in London was the team's private audience with King George VI and Queen Elizabeth at Buckingham Palace the day before they sailed for Australia. The players were shown into a large hall where they were met by the King's equerry, Captain Sir Harold Campbell, and given a good-humoured tutorial on the 'dos' and 'don'ts' when in the presence of their majesties. Sir Harold told them to form a large circle and the King and Queen would move around and greet each player individually. He said there would be a five to ten minute wait and he then slipped out of the room. As the team waited Aub Hodgson insisted Stan give them a few verses of 'Why are we Waiting?' *sotto voce* and he duly obliged. Eric de Courcy Gibbons, known as 'Mike'

Twickenham Stadium, London, September 1939. Des Carrick (left) and Brian Oxenham inspect the turf, sporting gas masks. The stadium had been requisitioned by the Auxiliary Fire Service and contained stores of anti-gas equipment.

or 'Squirt' to all the team, was a cheeky, diminutive half-back from NSW, renowned for his on-field pluck and his off-field pranks. Not wanting to waste the moment, he sprang into the centre of the circle and pulled out two pennies and a two-up kit and began taking bets. The game rolled on for several minutes until the royal couple's arrival was announced by a knock on the door. Playing two-up in Buckingham Place is a claim not many Australians could match.

As Their Majesties entered the hall, the nonchalant attitude changed immediately. Even the most fiercely independent colonials amongst them could not help but feel honoured by this occasion. The King was accompanied by Wally Matthews and the Queen by Jeff Noseda, and they began to move separately around the circle as each player was introduced. Their conversations were friendly but formal, normally no more that a few polite words of congratulations on selection and condolences for the curtailment of the tour. When the King reached Stan and before he was introduced, he said, 'Now Mr Bisset, you're a member of the Lord Somers' Camp in Victoria, are you not?' Stan was taken aback but managed to reply that he had been a member almost since its inception. They chatted for several minutes and the King was obviously delighted to hear about the progress of his idea in Australia. The presence of three Power House representatives on the tour, he felt, was a great testament to the successes of the institution. The Queen, too, was keen to talk to Stan. She had heard about his singing, his time in the Melbourne Conservatorium and Stan's role as the team's 'choirmaster'. Sir Harold, the equerry, had clearly done his homework.

After an agonisingly short week in London the team was back aboard ship, this time on the impressive RMS *Strathmore*, bound for Sydney via Bombay. The mood at Tilbury Docks and the morose atmosphere on board were the absolute inverse of the buoyant mood that had pervaded their recent passage to England. Much of the discussion centred on enlistment in the forces upon their return to Australia. Andy Barr told Stan that he was intent on applying for the Air Force but Stan was slightly more hesitant. For him, the war at present existed in name only.

The facilities on board the *Strathmore* were a class above those on the *Mooltan* but nightlife was curtailed due to the blackout. At times the ship changed course alarmingly — presumably due to anti-submarine tactics — but be they real or imagined, no information was ever forthcoming. The despondent mood was momentarily alleviated when, on docking at Bombay, the team was invited to the Bombay Gymkhana on Azad Maidan for a match against the resident British Indian Army side. The Wallabies were impressed with the lavish decor and the hospitality with which they were received by a bevy of army officers and government officials. Obviously the players would not be capped for this game but it was the first and only time many of the squad would ever don their

RUGBY FOOTBALL

THE AUSTRALIAN R. U. TOURING TEAM *Vs.* BOMBAY XV

On Thursday, 5th October at 5-30 p. m.

COOPERAGE

AUSTRALIAN R. U. TEAM (Green & Old Gold)

M. A. Clifford

| B. J. Porter. | D. Carrick. | L. H. Smith. | V. M. Nicholson. |

P. K. Collins   E. De C. Gibbons.

| G. A. Pearson. | A. W. M. Barr. | J. E Turnbull. | B. B. Oxenham. |
| A. W. Monti. | S. Y. Bisset. | J. C. McDonald. | W. M. McLean. |

RESERVES :—

W. P. J. Ide.   C. Ramalli.   J. H. Malone.   K. S. Windon.

REFEREE :— R. W. Douglass.

K. F. Camp (B. G.)   Lt. Burnett (Suffolks.)   R. A. Low (B. G.)   J. R. Younger (B. G.)

Cpl. Sharp (Suffolks.)   R. H. Cowan (B. G.)   Pte. Unsworth (S. L.)   A. Mallinson (B G.)

A. G. Candlin (B. G.)   R. F. Walsh (B. G.)

J. C. Warren Boulton (B. G.)   J. G. Knott (B. G.)   W. G. Popple (B. G.)   H. W Witt (B. G.)

Lt. Campbell (Suffolks)

BOMBAY XV (Amber & Black)

Bombay Gymkhana, India, 5 October 1939. This is the program for the only match the Wallabies played during the entire tour — against a British Army XV during the return stopover in Bombay. For many team members it was the only opportunity to play in their national colours. Even though Stan had already played for Australia against South Africa, he felt greatly honoured to be selected in this side.

Wallaby colours and it was a proud and emotional moment for Stan as he took to the field with the starting XV. The local army side was keen but clearly outclassed, despite the Wallabies' long lay-off. The after-match function was most impressive and the British officers and opposing players were welcoming and generous hosts.

The Australians hugged the railings as the tugs guided the *Strathmore* down the Ulhas River estuary and the city of Bombay slipped slowly by on the starboard bow. One match out of twenty-eight — some rugby tour.

The petty rivalries that had soured the start of the tour were now a distant memory. With so much time together and all pretensions dropped, the team had bonded remarkably well. On this, the last leg of the home voyage, the team would invariably form a drinking circle on the top rear deck. When a latecomer wanted to join the

Fremantle, Western Australia, October 1939. The Wallabies returned to Australia on RMS **Strathmore**. *Following the declaration of the Second World War, the players faced an uncertain future.*

group, admittance would only be granted once he had sculled a glass of beer to the tune of 'Drink it down, down, down...' and they would all talk and sing under the stars till the small hours.

On the last night of the voyage a dozen or so of Stan's closest friends joined him in his cabin for a farewell party. Times had changed for this former teetotaller and the gin and tonic flowed freely while the party turned into a riotous talkfest and singing marathon. The purser sent to quieten them down was barricaded in the cabin until he agreed to chug-a-lug a full glass of gin. Accepting that his case was hopeless, he ended up joining the revellers. When they could just about stand no longer, Stan rendered a solo of one of his old favourites, 'Danny Boy', which touched a nerve with all present. The pent-up emotions of the last two months suddenly spilled over. Tears of frustration rolled down their cheeks; tears of missed opportunities, of friendships made and premature partings, of expectations raised and cruelly dashed, all mixed with fears of an uncertain future. They managed to gather themselves together after several minutes to make one last toast to everyone's good luck, future happiness and safekeeping before they all collapsed into an alcohol-induced slumber.

CHAPTER FOUR

Yellow and Blue

It is difficult to appreciate the impact the cancellation of the Wallabies' tour had on Stan. All the players in that strictly amateur era had sacrificed so much to be a part of the game. Stan had spent a huge portion of the last six years working towards the goal of international selection. He was fortunate to have had the support of the RACV, but training and time off for rugby had held him back from advancement in his profession. In fact, he had resigned before the tour commenced, recognising that it was untenable for his employer to keep a position available for him for such a long period of time. With the outbreak of war, Stan now found himself racked with uncertainty. Enlisting in the new AIF would mean more years of personal sacrifice for a war some still considered to be phoney.

Uninformed critics of Chamberlain's appeasement policy failed to appreciate that no hard evidence existed that Hitler had intended engaging Great Britain in war. In fact, Hitler saw Russian Bolshevism as a common enemy for the West and seemed bewildered at Britain's failure to fall into line with his views. It was Great Britain that declared war on Germany, not the other way around, and for eight full months after the declaration not a shot was fired. So it was not unreasonable for people to believe that it would only be a matter of time before cooler heads would prevail and this phoney war would end peacefully.

Still, many young Australian men rushed to enlist in the 6th Division, and with his strong sense of patriotism and background in the militia Stan was tempted to join them. But eventually, and after much reflection, he decided not to enlist for a war that was one in name only.

Stan returned to the RACV and tried to settle back into his normal routine of work and rigorous physical training, but he was restless and inexplicably lacking in motivation. Hal was still in Melbourne when Stan returned home from Britain, having made the decision to make his life in the city. The brothers had long chats about how they were feeling and both seemed torn between their strong work ethics and their bold and adventurous spirits.

At the outbreak of the war, Australia's regular army consisted of only 3000 staff and training officers with no permanent infantry or support forces. There was an all-volunteer army reserve of 80,000 men, referred to as the militia. According to Australian law, the militia could only serve in the defence of the homeland, be it on Australian soil or in its overseas territories such as Papua and New Guinea. In times of national crisis, the militia's numbers could be bolstered by conscription.

When faced with the prospect of sending a force overseas, the government could have changed the law to allow for an all-volunteer militia to fight anywhere the government chose. The formations of the militia were almost identical to those of the First AIF and they still carried their colours and battle honours. All that was required was an act of parliament and a name change to the Second AIF. Foolishly, the government chose to form a new, all-volunteer army in addition to the militia. This gave rise to the administratively complex and divisive situation where effectively three armies existed at the one time: a cadre of permanent army officers, the militia, and the new overseas force. There was an unseemly and disorganised rush of resignations and transfers. Despite the fact that most units ultimately fought with great distinction, the competition and uneven division of personnel and material bedevilled the army, or one should say, armies, for the duration of the war.

By late February 1940, newspapers and radios were full of stories of how volunteers had almost filled the ranks of the 6th Division and were now pouring into the newly formed 7th Division. At this time neither Hal nor Stan saw enough justification to do anything other than get on with life.

The brothers were not alone in their views. They had great respect for one of their friends, the lawyer Phil Rhoden. In 1939, Power House members formed C Company, one of the four rifle companies that made up the militia's 14th Battalion. Based in a drill hall in Commercial Road, Prahran, they soon had 250 members. Phil was second-in-command of the company with the rank of lieutenant. He advised the brothers to do as he was doing, that is, retain his occupation until there was greater clarity and sense of purpose.

Hal quickly established himself as the champion rifle shot of the company. One of the instructors was the headmaster of Melbourne Grammar, Mr Joseph Sutcliffe, who considered himself an expert shot. Hal obviously made some casual comment to the contrary and was immediately challenged to a shoot-out. After Hal fired off sixteen consecutive bulls-eyes in less than a minute, no one was left in any doubt as to who was the superior marksman.

There was a dramatic turn of events in April 1940 when Hitler's *Wehrmacht* struck at Norway and Denmark. German industry was heavily dependent on the importation of iron-ore from northern Sweden, most of which was shipped through the northern Norwegian port of Narvik.

By holding Norway, the Danish straits and most of the shores of the Baltic Sea, the Third Reich encircled Scandinavia from the north, west and south. To the east lay the Soviet Union, ostensibly Hitler's ally under the terms of the Molotov-Ribbentrop Pact, but clearly within his future sights.

These events dramatically affected Australia's strategic situation. Any remaining hope for a diplomatic solution ended with the appointment of Churchill as British Prime Minister following the resignation of Neville Chamberlain. For Hal, it proved to be enough justification for 'taking the King's shilling', and along with many of his friends he presented himself at Melbourne Town Hall for enlistment in the newly formed 2/14th Infantry Battalion, part of the 7th Division.

For Stan, the final straw came with the German invasion of France and the Low Countries on 10 May 1940 and the subsequent evacuation of the British Expeditionary Force from Dunkirk in early June. Stan's old footballing friend from Melbourne Old Boys' days, Keith 'Bluey' Truscott, was currently playing full-forward with Melbourne in the VFL as well as working for the huge meat processing company, William Angliss and Co. With Bluey's help, Stan had also found employment as a cost accountant in the same firm. Stan and Bluey were sharing a few beers after work on Friday 4 June when the news of Dunkirk came across the wireless. Stan was suddenly overcome with a strange sensation. It seemed that this piece of news instantaneously changed his perception of the world. For the best part of ten months he had drifted in a sea of mental uncertainly, lacking motivation and without a clear sense of direction. It was a state of mind that was so at odds with his former single-mindedness.

It was Stan's shout but he pushed his stool back and vigorously shook his old friend's hand. 'Another time, Blue,' he apologised. He donned his hat and coat and strode out the door, hopped onto a moving tram and headed uptown to the Town Hall and the AIF recruitment depot. After a day of further processing at Caulfield Racecourse he found himself aboard a troop train bound for central Victoria, a newly enlisted private in the 2/14th Infantry Battalion.

The army camp of Puckapunyal had only been established eight months previously but it had never bustled with as much frenetic energy as in the autumn of 1940. Throughout its thousands of acres, new encampments were springing up by the day. When Stan and several hundred other new recruits stumbled off the train at Seymour in the grey dawn, they were bundled into a convoy of trucks headed for the camp. Still in civilian dress they found themselves paraded in front of an encampment that had been named Passchendaele, after a famous First World War battle. A regimental sergeant major barked orders while under a nearby tent with rolled-up sides, a small huddle of officers and NCOs pored over lists of names. The recruits were to be allocated to a company that would

Puckapunyal, 1940. Hal (standing, far left) and Stan (standing, third from left) represented the Army rugby team when it played the Air Force. Cliff Lang (standing, far right) had partnered Stan in the second-row for Victoria and Australia. Sadly, Cliff was killed in action in Java in 1942.

become their virtual family for months, possibly years. Exhausted from his train ride, Stan was unaware that he was being scrutinized by one of the group in the huddle who promptly marched himself across the parade ground and paused in front of the squinting Stan. 'Private Bisset? You have been allocated to my B Company.' Stan looked up and a flicker of a smile ran across his tired face as he recognised the burly warrant officer who addressed him. It was Hal.

The original 14th Battalion was raised in Melbourne in 1914. During the four years of the First World War, more than 5000 men passed through its ranks. Given that the average strength at any one time was 850, these numbers give some idea of its rate of attrition. The unit's colours were 'yellow over blue', and in addition to Gallipoli its battle honours included such famous names as Pozières, Bullecourt and Amiens. One of the battalion's original members, Albert Jacka, won Australia's first Victoria Cross. The historian C.E.W. Bean called him 'the nation's greatest fighting soldier', and in typical Australian fashion the battalion then assumed the moniker of 'Jacka's Mob'.

After the war the 14th Battalion continued its existence as part of the militia, so when the Second AIF was raised, a new battalion called the Second 14th was formed. It was given the same colours but they were set within a silver diamond, to distinguish this unit from the militia battalion. This process of replicating battalions was repeated throughout the services. The Second AIF units wore their colour patches within a grey border and claimed to be superior in status to the militia as they were deemed to have inherited the honours and esprit de corps of their fathers' units. The militiamen were then derogatorily referred to as 'chocolate soldiers'. All available resources went to the newly formed units and the militia, stripped of its best officers and men and denied resources and material, was clearly weakened. When Australia subsequently faced invasion by the Japanese it was little wonder that many of the militia battalions were so ill-prepared to meet the threat.

None of these issues were at the forefront of Stan's mind when he arrived at Puckapunyal in early June. The process of training and transforming the thousand-odd recruits into a fighting force had only just begun. A small cadre of senior and non-commissioned officers had been in residence since early May in preparation for their arrival. Some were veterans but most were drawn from the ranks of the professional army or, like Hal, had transferred from the militia.

Hal had developed into a tall, powerful man. He was over six feet tall (183 cm), weighed thirteen and a half stone (86 kg) and was as tough as the karri trees he had spent years clearing. Yet Hal was still the product of a family with broad cultural interests and from a home where women played an active role in business as well as domestic affairs. It was as if his more masculine qualities developed in natural harmony with a refined and at times sensitive nature. He was as comfortable mixing with the refined guests at Doc McAdam's St Kilda home as he was around a drover's camp fire. It was a magnetic combination of personal traits.

There was no mistaking Hal at a party. He had a distinctive laugh and in all the written accounts of the man it is this laugh that seems to remain etched in people's recollections.

These qualities were immediately recognised at Puckapunyal and within weeks he was made a company sergeant major. His time on the land had stripped away any veneers or pretences when it came to personal relationships. His integrity allowed him to judge others quickly and astutely. If there was a need to convey these judgements, they were delivered without any element of harshness. It was just that there was no pussy-footing around. He went straight to the point. Even those who were on the receiving end of what they regarded as overly harsh orders still showed a respect for his honesty and willingness to stand by his convictions. 'Butch', as he was now becoming known, was described by Jim McAllester, his battalion's first intelligence officer, as 'a captivating figure, handsome, vital and inspiring'.

Puckapunyal could not be described as picturesque. Owing to the dry winter, the scanty grass barely covered the thin soil. Rushes, dogwood and prickly scrub struggled to eke out an existence and even the gum trees were low and stunted. There was ample room for teaching the basic principles of tactics, however, especially if one was preparing for the Middle East. No terrain could have been less suited to training for jungle warfare, had anyone yet visualised its need.

June and July were taken up with the fundamentals: use of rifles, bayonets and Lewis guns, grenade throwing, physical training, map-reading and fieldcraft, interspersed with parade drills and marching. Night training, bivouacs and fifty or sixty kilometre test marches were introduced in August as the weather improved. When the warning order for final leave was issued in September, an intensive two weeks of sports was organised. Athletics and inter-battalion

Melbourne, October 1940. Stan (left) and Hal joined the AIF 2/14th Battalion. Stan was rapidly promoted to sergeant and Hal to warrant officer. Both were selected to attend the Officer Cadet Training Unit in the Middle East and graduated as lieutenants.

boxing were well patronised, but it was Australian Rules football that drew the most interest. Even with a thousand men available in the 2/14th, Stan and Hal were automatic selections. The 2/14th beat the 2/2nd Field Regiment in the grand final in September.

After final leave, the battalion entrained on 18 October 1940 at Dysart siding bound for Sydney, where the men were ferried to the *Aquitania* that was waiting for them at Woolloomooloo Pier. With her peacetime paint removed, the old girl certainly showed signs of her long service. Her four funnels seemed too numerous and too tall compared to the more modern vessels of the day. In the bright sunlight of the spring afternoon, she sailed down the harbour together with the *Queen Mary*, escorted by craft of all descriptions with sirens blaring and flags waving.

The 2/14th was one of three battalions that made up the 21st Brigade. The second battalion was the 2/27th from South Australia and it was already aboard the *Mauretania*, standing off Cape Otway and ready to join the convoy. The third battalion was the 2/16th from Western Australia and it embarked on the *Aquitania* at Fremantle. These men made a distinct impression on Stan. They were big-boned and hard-looking and most sported shaven heads, which added to their tough demeanour. One company known as the Kalgoorlie Mob was made up of men from the minefields. The bitter rivalry between the two states would seem trivial after they were finally united as a composite battalion following the bloodbath on the Owen Stanleys.

A great deal of time was spent on drills in the event of fire, collision or attack from on, above or below the sea, and as the lifeboats looked to be in rather poor condition everyone 'bagsed' their own special life-raft. There was a wet canteen at nights but the NSW brew was judged by Stan as being only passable. When they crossed the equator there was nothing more than a brief announcement. Some of the days were taken up with cards and housie but the main distractions were sports, especially boxing.

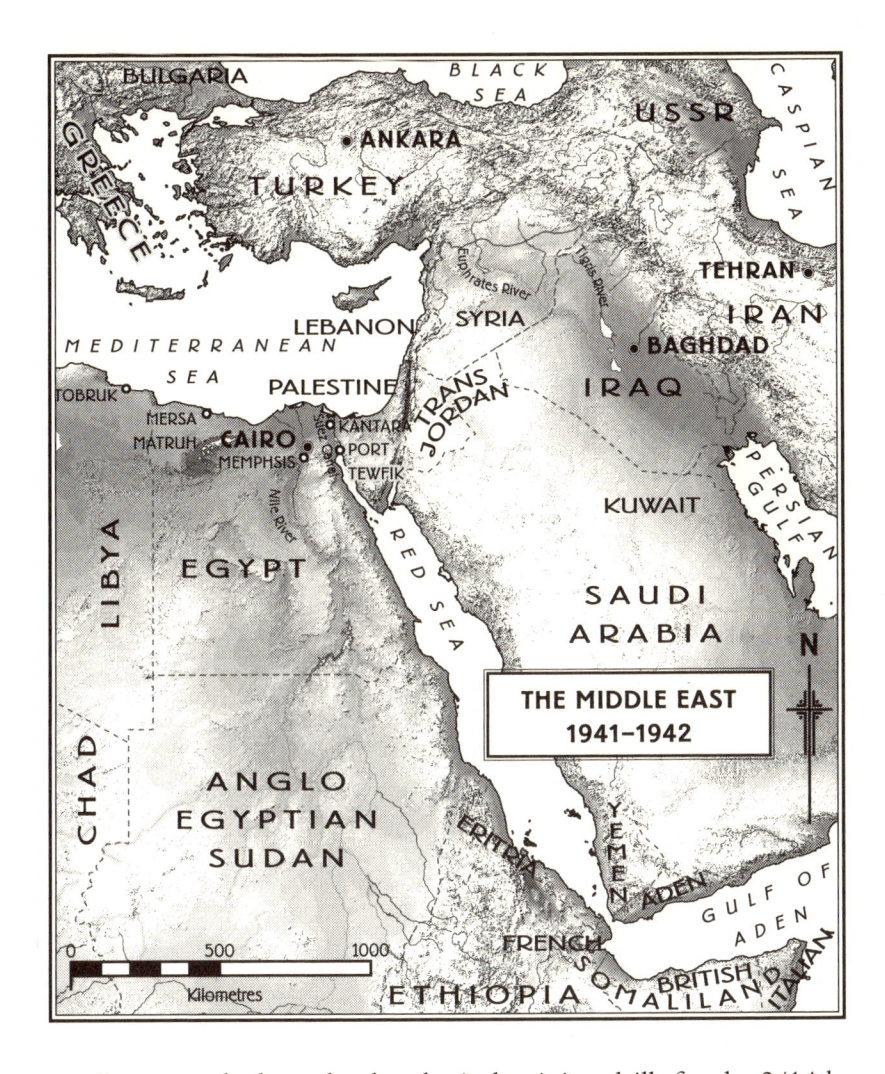

Stan was asked to take the physical training drills for the 2/14th. These became entertainment events in their own right, especially for the 2/16th who looked on with obvious sardonic pleasure. Stan was then asked to supervise special training for the officers, to be carried out on the upper quarter-deck, out of view of the masses.

After a two-week stopover in Bombay, some of which was spent at a British Army camp at Deolali, the battalion embarked on the *Dilwana*, a specially designed ship for carrying troops and their families to British tropical stations. The facilities on board were judged by Stan as excellent and the calm seas, good food and relaxation of physical exercises added to the enjoyment.

The *Dilwana* now made up part of an impressive convoy of eleven troopships, two armed merchantmen, three warships and an anti-aircraft sloop, the *Carlisle*. As they entered the Red Sea and came astride Italian East Africa, the *Carlisle* opened up on an enemy reconnaissance plane — the first shots Stan witnessed fired in anger. Stan was ordered to parade before Brigadier Jack Stevens the following morning. Stan worried that he might be in some form of trouble, but the brigadier told him he was good officer material. 'There's an officer cadet training unit in Cairo that I'd like you to attend. You'd rejoin us later, of course. What do you think?' Stan hesitated. He was only a corporal, and if he accepted the posting

Memphsis, Egypt, December 1940. Stan attended the Middle East Officer Cadet Training Unit (OCTU) for four months. He was made captain of their No. 1 rugby team. The team played weekly games and was undefeated against sides from many of the British regiments. (Stan is in the middle row, third from the left.)

he would be promoted over the head of many of the more senior NCOs. Brigadier Stevens reflected for a moment. 'I don't think that should pose a problem, *Sergeant* Bisset.'

The *Dilwana* steamed slowly up the Suez Canal to the entrance of Lake Timsah, where there was a large monument to the Anzacs erected in honour of their service in the Middle East during the First War. At 6.20 a.m. on 25 November 1940, the battalion set foot on Egyptian soil at Kantara. Four hours later, the battalion was en route to Palestine by train. Meanwhile, Stan was passing through Cairo's Ramses Railway Station on his way to Memphis, twenty kilometres south of Cairo. This was the site of the Middle East Officer Cadet Training School — his home for the next four months.

Before the outbreak of war most Australian officers were trained at the Royal Military College Duntroon in Canberra. The formation of the Second AIF in 1939, however, greatly increased the demand for officers and as a result a variety of Officer Cadet Training Units (OCTU) sprang up around the nation. The same was true in Britain, with the Royal Military Academy Sandhurst being unable to accommodate the demand for new officers. During the first few years of the war, OCTUs were established at overseas headquarters to accommodate men like Stan who were being chosen from the other ranks for commissioning.

When he arrived at the Cairo OCTU in the November or 1940, Stan was hugely impressed by the professionalism of the British regular officers who ran the course. The training of the 2/14th in Australia had been excellent, with the men emerging battle-ready and fit in a very short period of time, but the facilities at Puckapunyal had been basic to say the least. The small training cadre had struggled to make do with limited resources and, to some extent, limited experience. The British OCTU was an entirely different story, with career officers and NCOs who had spent years (or even decades) running similar courses at Sandhurst in the UK.

Australia had maintained only a skeleton standing army in the inter-war period and thus many instructors (like Hal Bisset) were essentially civilians with some experience as Army reservists. The British Army, however, had been fighting the whole time. British units fought against Bolshevik forces during the Russian Civil War in 1919, in the Turkish War of Independence in 1921, and against rebels in British Somaliland. They engaged in operations against the IRA during the Anglo-Irish War, and fought against Pashtun forces on the North-West Frontier.

It was little wonder, then, that Stan was amazed with the level of operational focus with which the Cairo OCTU course was run. For the rest of his military career Stan was continually praised not only for his personal courage and leadership, but also for his meticulous attention to detail in his administrative duties, which he attributed to the training he received from the British instructors in Cairo.

If Stan was impressed by the OCTU staff, the British officers were equally impressed by Stan. The primarily Public School, Oxbridge background of most staff officers resulted in sporting prowess being a key attribute of the British Officer Corps, and thus Stan's background made him something of a minor celebrity at the school. He captained the OCTU XV and when Hal was selected for officer training two months after Stan he joined his brother in the second row of the squad. The team remained undefeated throughout Stan's captaincy, playing weekly matches against teams from the British regiments in the area as well as Australian, New Zealand and South African units.

CHAPTER FIVE

Shifting Sands

Britain's colonial involvement in Egypt dated from 1869 when it took majority ownership of the Suez Canal while Libya, sometimes referred to as Cyrenaica, had become an Italian colony. When Italy declared war on Great Britain on 10 June 1940, the British promptly crossed the border into Libya and captured the Italian stronghold of Fort Capuzzo. This was followed by an Italian offensive into Egypt and then, in December 1940, a Commonwealth counteroffensive that virtually destroyed the Italian Tenth Army. This forced Hitler to dispatch the German Afrika Korps under Field Marshal Erwin Rommel to North Africa and the campaign then developed into a series of back-and-forth battles for the control of the southern Mediterranean coast.

After his graduation from officer training in late March 1941, Stan rejoined the 2/14th as a lieutenant in charge of 18 Platoon, part of Captain Brendan Noonan's D Company. Noonan was variously known as Steve or 'Uncle Diddy'. It was April Fools' Day 1941 when Stan arrived at the battalion's Dimra Camp, north of Gaza city, in Palestine. As far as the men were concerned the only fool on hand was the officer who ordered half the battalion to undertake one of the worst route marches in its history. It was a scorchingly hot day and while kitted-out in thick winter uniforms and full packs, the men were forced to trudge in deep, loose sand to the mouth of Wadi Hesi River and back, a trek of eighty kilometres. Some said it was 'to weed out the unfit' but not one man dropped out or even fell behind. Meanwhile, in a move that hardly engendered team spirit, the luckier ones in the battalion, Stan amongst them, were taken on a sightseeing tour of Palestine.

Palestine, March 1941. After completing his officer training, Stan returned to the 2/14th Battalion as a lieutenant in charge of 18 Platoon.

When everyone had returned to camp, news arrived that Rommel was on the rampage in Egypt. He sealed off a large garrison of Australian troops at Tobruk and the remaining Commonwealth Forces were in hasty retreat. The gloriously conceived but overly ambitious campaign in Greece was unravelling at the same time the whole British East Army appeared threatened. Cairo itself was considered to be in danger, so all available units then in Palestine, including the 2/14th, were called on to fill the void.

The massive movement of troops must have seemed impressive to the swarm of enemy agents in Cairo. At four-hourly intervals, trainloads of men steamed through Benha, north of Cairo, en route to the front. Convoys of vehicles and guns stretching in one continuous line for 800 kilometres poured into Egypt.

On 15 April the battalion reached Mersa (Port) Matruh, 450 kilometres west of Cairo. They formed part of a composite garrison that included such diverse units as New Zealand Engineers

Shifting Sands

Mersa Matruh, Middle East, March 1941. Hal on the beach after a refreshing dip in the Mediterranean.

Middle East, March 1941. Hal (far right).

and Indian Labour Companies. The latter helped load the destroyers that left the port each evening to take supplies to the Australians under siege at Tobruk. The men set to work digging, revetting and building wire entanglements — sweltering work in the extreme desert heat. Even the Indian labourers collapsed from heat exhaustion as they cleared sand from the tank trenches, and the Australians were ordered to take over.

The biggest threat came from land mines, some laid by the Egyptians and some by the British. Most of the charts showing their positions had been lost and many mines were so rusty they were likely to explode for no apparent reason. Charles 'Tiny' Faber became the first man from the battalion to be killed on active service when he stepped on one. The following day, while making his way along the wire with Steve Noonan, Stan suddenly halted with one foot poised over a barely visible mine. On retracing their steps and looking more closely at the ground, they realised that they had been neatly stepping on either side of mines for several metres.

On the night of 27 April, everyone was ordered to stand to as the battalion's mobile defence force reported that they had observed enemy tanks and armoured cars approaching from the west. They peered into the gloom all night, expecting all hell to break loose at any moment, but nothing eventuated. This nightly routine continued for two weeks.

The days were intolerably hot and at times visibility was reduced to zero by violent dust storms that sometimes lasted for two or three days. One day when the Khamsin, the famous 'east wind', was blowing its hardest, the mercury hit 125 degrees Fahrenheit (51 degrees Celsius). The only relief came from quick dips in the Mediterranean, a quota of Victorian beer supplied by Padre Whelan and some tobacco and coffee supplied by Albert Moore, the Salvation Army pastor. On 15 May, news arrived that the allied line had held and the enemy had pulled backed to Halfaya. No one was the least bit regretful when relief in the form of a South African battalion from the Transvaal arrived eight days later.

On entraining at Matruh the battalion, as usual, was not given any indication of its destination. By May 1941 the German *Wehrmacht* was fast overwhelming what was left of the allied forces in Crete, but a few men were still keen to wager that this would be their destination. The Abyssinian campaign was now drawing to a close and only the bravest gamblers were prepared to place their funds on that far-flung destination. The safest bets were seen to be Syria and Lebanon, and that is where Stan had his money. These territories were occupied by elements of the French Army still loyal to the Vichy Government and by default, Nazi Germany. Indeed, aircraft of the Luftwaffe had begun landing in Syria and were being engaged by allied aircraft.

The train journey from Matruh to Palestine was over 1600 kilometres. For Stan and his boys it was a particularly enjoyable one, in no small part thanks to the Pioneer Platoon's discovery of an entire trainload of beer at the Matruh railway station yard. As a result, a number of entertaining incidents occurred along the way, one of the most memorable being when Company Sergeant Major Les Tipton and young Johnny Stokes decided to leap from the train while it waited at Tanta Junction and engage in a neat bout of fisticuffs before the pair leapt back onto the cars and continued on with the their drinking as if nothing had happened. A further incident occurred once the train reached the far side of the canal when the 2/14th entraining officer, finding that the unit's cars had been left at the station without an engine, persuaded the Egyptian station master to give them the use of the engine of an apparently empty goods train resting on a siding. In fact the 'empty' goods train contained the entire 2/16th Battalion, the West Australian battalion that had accompanied them on the *Aquitania*, all of whom were fast asleep. The event did little to ease the animosity between the two battalions.

At the end of its mammoth journey, the battalion's train finally pulled into Benyamina station on the Palestinian coast, close to the border with Lebanon. If there had been any serious speculation as to the 21st Brigade's final destination, it ceased at this point. As hard as it was for the men to accept, their own unit, proudly displaying the names of Bullecourt and Pozières on its battle flag, was now about to actually fight the French. Stan's 18 Platoon was shocked at the prospect of going into combat against its former ally. In fact one of Stan's men, Les 'Pappy' Ransom, had fought in the First AIF. He had lied about his age to re-enlist in the Second AIF and still tried to keep the fact a closely guarded secret.

The battalion moved to a camp at Kefar Gidon, near Affula. Amongst its biblical associations it was home to the Hill of Megiddo where, according the Bible, the Armageddon, the last battle to end the world, would be fought. This foreboding image was not lost on Stan's men. Even at this time, well before the creation of the state of Israel, the area was already closely settled by Jewish Zionist immigrants who had established collective kibbutz farms. The Australians were allowed to spend free evenings in these settlements and Stan was astounded by the kindness and work ethic of the settlers. The men of his platoon were so overcome by the warmth and generosity of the Jewish communities that many vowed to return there after the war, whenever that might be.

It came as no surprise to Stan when Lieutenant Colonel Cannon informed the officers that they were destined to invade French-held Lebanon as part of an allied force of 18,000 men from General Lavarack's 7th Division as well as 9000 British, 2000 Indians and 5000 of De Gaulle's Free French. If Stan and his men were incensed at having to fight their former ally, how these Free French soldiers must have felt about fighting their fellow countrymen was beyond comprehension. Cannon next informed them that the 2/14th was to form the spearhead of the allied assault, crossing the border on the first day of the invasion. To regain some of the fitness the men may have lost in their time at Matruth, Stan led the platoon on some long route marches through the hills around Nazareth. If any of the boys had any doubts as to the mettle of their newly commissioned platoon commander, these were soon dispelled. Stan, in turn, gained immense confidence in his men.

In the first days of June, Stan and the other officers were presented with detailed orders for the unit's role in the upcoming invasion. Cannon informed them that General Wilson had set Sunday 8 June as D-Day for the operation. 'Ever since Gallipoli, everything has happened on a Sunday,' he added. 'And I bloody well know, because I've been there for most of them.'

Cannon went on to outline the role each company and platoon would play. Stan's D Company under the command of Captain Steve Noonan was to cross the border in the morning and attack the French garrison of Alma Chaab. Stan would be leading 18 Platoon, Harry 'Gerry' Dickenson 16 Platoon and Al Schultz 17 Platoon. They all planned to leave Hanita around 2 a.m. on 8 June and after crossing the border they would separate. Stan's platoon would approach Alma Chaab from the south and Dickenson would move in from the west, while Schultz would take 17 Platoon all the way through a second range of hills in the north to seal off the only line of retreat for the French troops who formed the village's garrison.

Stan and Gerry did a detailed map appreciation and set the start lines for their assault. Their platoons would covertly reach their form-up point just behind the start line where the men could silently drop their packs and check their weapons before the platoons would 'shake out' in line abreast. This was a typical attacking formation, giving the greatest frontage of fire without endangering other comrades. The designated H-Hour was set for 6 a.m.

Stan's sergeant, Ray 'Snowy' Lawley, was one of the most experienced men in the battalion and oversaw 18 Platoon's preparations down to the smallest detail. Exact volumes of ordinance

Lebanon, 1941. Stan (standing, far right) with 18 Platoon before leading them into action in the Middle East.

had to be sourced and issued. Men had to have the right number of rounds for their .303 Lee-Enfield rifles; the 'number one' on the Bren machine-gun in each of Stan's three sections had to ensure that he had enough magazines to keep his weapon active throughout the fight, and the assistant 'number two' had to source the gun oil and tools needed to keep the weapon operational. Mills bombs, smoke grenades and flares for signalling had to be issued to the men, as did combat rations and water. Bayonets had to be honed by the smithy and all the Thompson sub-machine guns had to be test fired and any faulty weapons seen to by the battalion armourer. Rucksacks and webbing were packed, and to ensure stealthy movement, were 'bounce tested'. A man would don his kit and bounce up and down. If something rattled in his pack or webbing pouches, the gear was emptied and repacked. Maps of the border were studied in detail, with routes and timings for various checkpoints planned and distributed to the men to memorise.

This intense activity served to distract Stan's men. For months they had trained and retrained, rehearsing procedures dozens of times, but now it was real. In a matter of days they would be in mortal combat, to kill or be killed by other young men. On the evening of 6 June when D Company was trucked from Jezeel to a staging post beside Azzib the reality of their situation began to sink in. The next morning they found themselves lying under a grove of olives, forbidden to move in the open and anxiously contemplating their future. Few could sleep that night and most were filled with a weird sense of fear tinged with an adrenalin rush of expectation. The area was clearly visible from the French-held ridges of Labouna, only a few kilometres away to the north. Once darkness had fallen, trucks again arrived to take D and B Companies up towards their objectives. They soon reached the end of a dusty mountain road and Stan and his men debussed and began the four-hour march to Hanita.

The narrow mountain track was covered with loose rock and scree and wound its way through olive groves and terraced gardens and they arrived at Hanita — a small Jewish kibbutz less than a kilometre from Lebanon — just before midnight. The company wasn't due to set off towards its start line for another two hours, so Snowy ordered the men take shelter. They took the opportunity to grab a quick feed from their haversacks and some even tried tilting down the brims of their slouch hats to grab some sleep. Stan took the opportunity to go over a set of confirmatory orders with Steve Noonan, Gerry Dickenson and Al Schultz. Alma Chaab was nestled in a valley just over a kilometre north of the frontier. Al and his 17 Platoon would have the longest march that morning while Stan's and Gerry's platoons had less distance to travel but would need to make the utmost effort to remain undetected as they approached the village through the fertile countryside of olives and carob.

The village itself was occupied by elements of the Foreign Legion. As Allied Command had hoped that the Legionnaires would lay down their arms rather than fight against their former allies, the Australians chose to wear their distinctive slouch-hats rather than helmets. Unfortunately, it was a forlorn hope.

As the first moment of combat approached, Stan was apprehensive, maybe a touch nervous. The tension all around him was palpable as each man pondered what the day ahead would bring. How would he react? Would he do his part? What would it feel like to finally be in action? It was not unlike the atmosphere in the change-rooms before a big game, but the thirty-odd men who would soon do battle had to sit quietly, waiting for the moment to take to the field. But this time, a loss could cost a man his life.

They were soon joined by their guide, a young Jewish lad from the settlement who would lead them over the ridge into Lebanon. Stan gave Snow Lawley the nod. The men slipped their arms back into their webbing, shouldered their packs, gripped their weapons and heaved themselves to their feet. The Jewish boy indicated the way towards a narrow goat-trail to the north and at 2 a.m. on 8 June, less than two weeks after receiving their orders, they set off for the border.

Stan set the pace up the thickly wooded hillside. It was immediately apparent he had lost none of his fitness and there was no doubt that the men's preparation had been first-class. As the lead men of the platoon reached the crest of the ridge, their guide paused and gestured for Stan to come over to him. The platoon propped on one knee, facing out for protection, and the guide gestured towards the stony forest floor under Stan's feet. 'Lebanon,' he whispered.

The war between the British and the French had only recently come to this range of mountains, and soon it would be gone, but this Jewish boy knew these trails and frontiers as a result of his own war. While Lebanon had a large Christian population there were many Muslim and Druze enclaves. Hanita was a fortified settlement with its own palisade and tower and this young fellow had grown up over the past few years accustomed to living close to hostile Muslim settlements. Ten Jewish settlers had been killed in the first week of the kibbutz's life and conflict had raged ever since.

As Stan and his men began making their way down the steep slope of the ridge, the terrain was revealed in the pale pre-dawn. Immediately below them a road snaked its way to the west through the mountains to the Mediterranean. Away to their left was another cluster of hills through which Allen Schultz would now be making his way. Directly ahead, partially hidden by the easternmost spur of these hills, lay a cluster of small white village houses: Alma Chaab. Stan felt a knot tighten is his stomach.

The men silently picked their way down the ridge and across the last few hundred metres of flat ground towards the village, over ancient dry-stone walls and carob groves. Immediately ahead a low ridge marked the edge of the village. Stan glanced at his watch: the time for Dickenson's 16 Platoon to assault the village from the west was approaching. Directly in front of Stan's men was a large, two-storey fortified house that presumably housed the town's main garrison. Away to the left a smaller fortified building faced the west in the line of Dickenson's advance. Beside this building Stan could see a fortified machine-gun nest and as he crept closer to the edge of the village he could make out a sentry post manned by four Legionnaires complete with their distinctive kepi blanc caps.

Through his binoculars, Stan could make out several figures approaching the French sentry point. These were, he later discovered, men of 17 Platoon led by Corporal Gil 'Bluey' Lee, who had decided to try to silently neutralise the Legionnaire's sentry post prior to the main assault. Suddenly the crawling, half-hidden figures exploded into life and Stan could see the shimmer of four well-honed Australian 12-inch bayonets. Two of the Legionnaires fell lifeless but the other two gave fight and a scuffle ensued. The Legionnaires were subdued without a shot being fired but they had made enough noise to alert the garrison. The French

THE ATTACK ON ALMA CHAAB MORNING 8 JUNE 1941

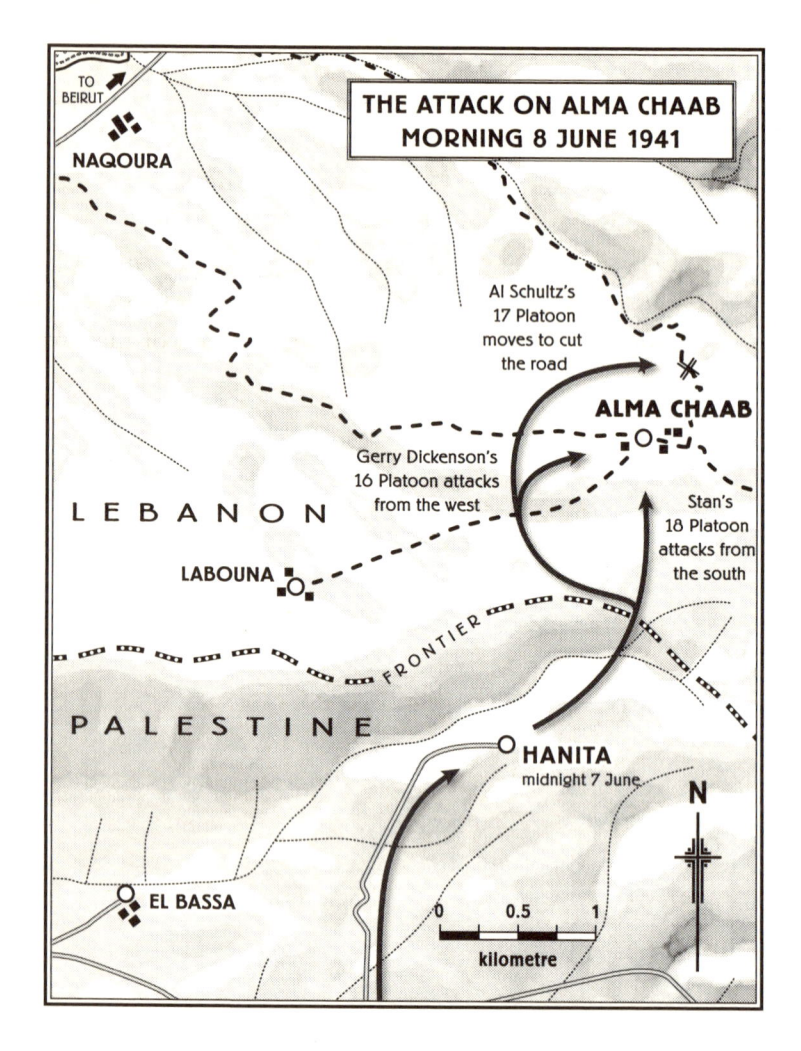

machine-gun position burst into action and at the same moment Gerry Dickenson and his platoon broke cover and began to rush towards the western blockhouse.

Stan had a conscious thought: so this is war and now I am really a part of it. He continued to watch, spellbound, through his field-glasses. On breaking cover, Dickenson's men had immediately come under fire from both the fortified houses and their assault began to falter. Stan and his men had to knock out the larger of the two houses if Dickenson's men were to have any success in their advance. He yelled out a set of snap orders to Snow Lawley and his other two NCOs, Tom Pryor and Dickie Wintour. 'The blockhouse! Shake out!' he yelled to the platoon. Well drilled, the men fanned out in an extended line for the attack.

The Bren gunners began to put down heavy covering fire on the blockhouse and the nearby gendarmerie, identifiable by the tri-colour insignia above its door. His three sections of men were well versed in 'fire and movement' and no further instructions were necessary. Some men laid down fire while others bounded towards the next piece of protection, then they began to fire as the others came forward. Stan had directed one section to concentrate on the machine-gun position that was pinning down 16 Platoon. He loosened a few shots into the windows of the gendarmerie. With the enfilading fire provided by Stan's platoon, Dickenson's attack regained some momentum. Some of their leading men reached the smaller blockhouse and began to clear it with grenades. Stan's platoon was advancing in line but as he glanced towards his right flank he saw a figure lying motionless behind a low stone wall with an upturned slouch-hat by its side. It was Snow Lawley.

With a heavy volume of fire from the Brens right at the critical moment, and with additional fire from Thompson guns and Lee-Enfields raining down on its doors and windows, the platoon was able to make the final rush to the blockhouse. A few Legionnaires, black Senegalese troops, rushed out to challenge the Australians but they were met with a point-blank volley and slumped back against the blockhouse walls. They were immediately followed by a white French officer with major's tabs on his epaulets. With a pistol in one hand, he was busily trying to button his shirt with the other. Only an aristocratic Frenchman would worry about his dress in the middle of battle. He stood stock still with no attempt to raise his pistol — he had little option as he faced Stan's .38 service revolver and Wink Wakefield's bayonet poised only centimetres from his throat. The Legionnaire laid down his weapon cautiously amid the broken bodies of his compatriots. Stan left the shaking major with Wakefield and ran to the other side of the building just in time to see a group of Senegalese Legionnaires mount horses in a yard some distance away and ride to the north at the gallop.

As suddenly as it had begun, the fighting in Alma Chaab was over. Gerry Dickenson and his men had carried the western blockhouse and machine-gun positions just as Stan's men had done to the south. Stan checked for other casualties. Pappy had a bullet wound to the knee but it appeared not to have done major damage. Stan had pushed the sight of the motionless body of Snow Lawley out of his mind during the assault, but now he had to deal with the loss of a friend. He had little concept of how many more times he would have to confront such a situation in the years ahead.

The Foreign Legion had a reputation for toughness and ruthlessness, but these legionnaires had broken and run in the face of the determined Australian assault. Stan could not have asked more of his men. He then reflected on his own performance. Would he have done anything differently? Probably not. He was only recently commissioned but was now confident he could live up to the responsibility that had been placed upon him.

The various platoons of Stan's company regrouped after the fighting and pushed on north towards Tyre. It was a long, tough march of approximately thirty kilometres and as they reached their destination on the evening of 9 June the other companies of the battalion were also arriving. Most of the men had had no sleep for several days and had been in and out of combat, with all their objectives carried. The men collapsed in the town and got a few hours much needed rest. For A Company, however, there was to be no such relief as they were told they had been seconded to the unit's sister battalion, the 2/16th. They left immediately for their next objective, the formidable French defences on the Litani River, eight kilometres further north.

Shifting Sands

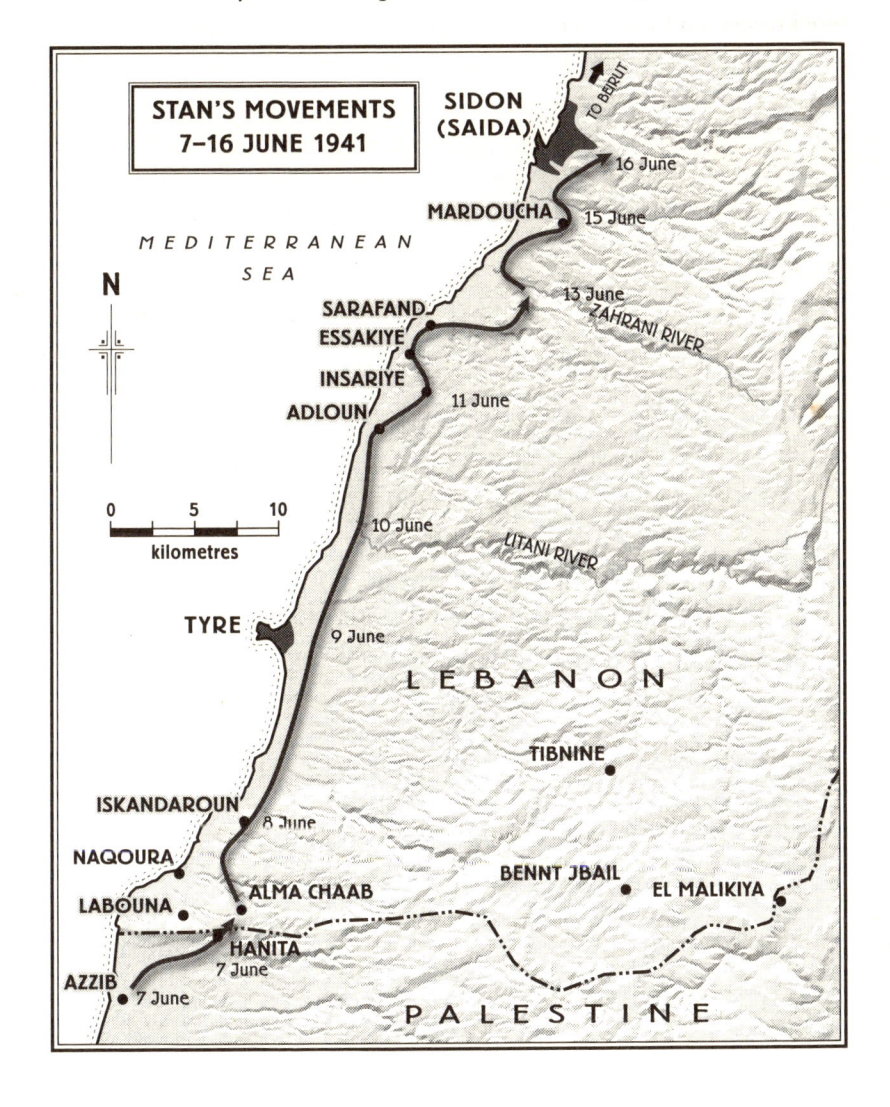

In Tyre, Stan met up with Jim Kyffin, who had been given charge of one of the most daring operations of the invasion — a raid on the village of Isakandaroun where the allied command believed the road north had been mined for demolition by the French. Led by Palestinian guides, Kyffin and a select team of soldiers had marched fifteen kilometres during the night and attacked the small but heavily defended post. A chaotic fire fight ensued in the darkness and although the position was eventually captured the mined road was still destroyed. Jim was later awarded the Military Cross for his actions. His native guide, like Stan's, had been a young Jewish settler. Despite his supposedly non-combatant role, the young man proved to be astonishingly courageous and a face wound he sustained resulted in the loss of one eye. The lad was Moshe Dayan, who went on to become a famous Israeli General. Dayan was later awarded the British Distinguished Service Order for his actions that night.

Stan and his men spent the afternoon getting some much-needed rest. The ancient city of Tyre was as pleasant a place as one could find in the midst of a campaign and the sea-breeze blowing in from the shimmering azure of the Mediterranean made a welcome reprieve from the dust of the desert. Only a few kilometres to the north, the Australians were engaged in a bitter fight to force a crossing over the Litani River and push north towards Sidon. The sound of heavy gunfire was audible right through the night. Stan later learned that his friend Allan Haddy, whom he had met on the way to the Middle East, had played a key role in the battle. As the Western Australians rushed to secure the last remaining bridge over the river, the French destroyed it with carefully placed charges. The attacking companies had been pinned down without cover and were taking heavy casualties from French machine-gun fire from prepared positions. Realising the need for drastic action, Allan dropped his rifle, seized a rope and dived into the fast-flowing river. By the time he had reached the far bank he had been wounded twice. He barely had enough energy to fasten the rope to a tree before collapsing with shock and loss of blood.

By dawn the sound of fighting had died down and reports came back to Tyre that the 2/16th had crossed the river, still under French fire, in boats pulled by hand along Haddy's rope. They then drove the French from their positions. The 2/14th and 2/27th would now push forward through the exhausted 2/16th and take up the

Shifting Sands

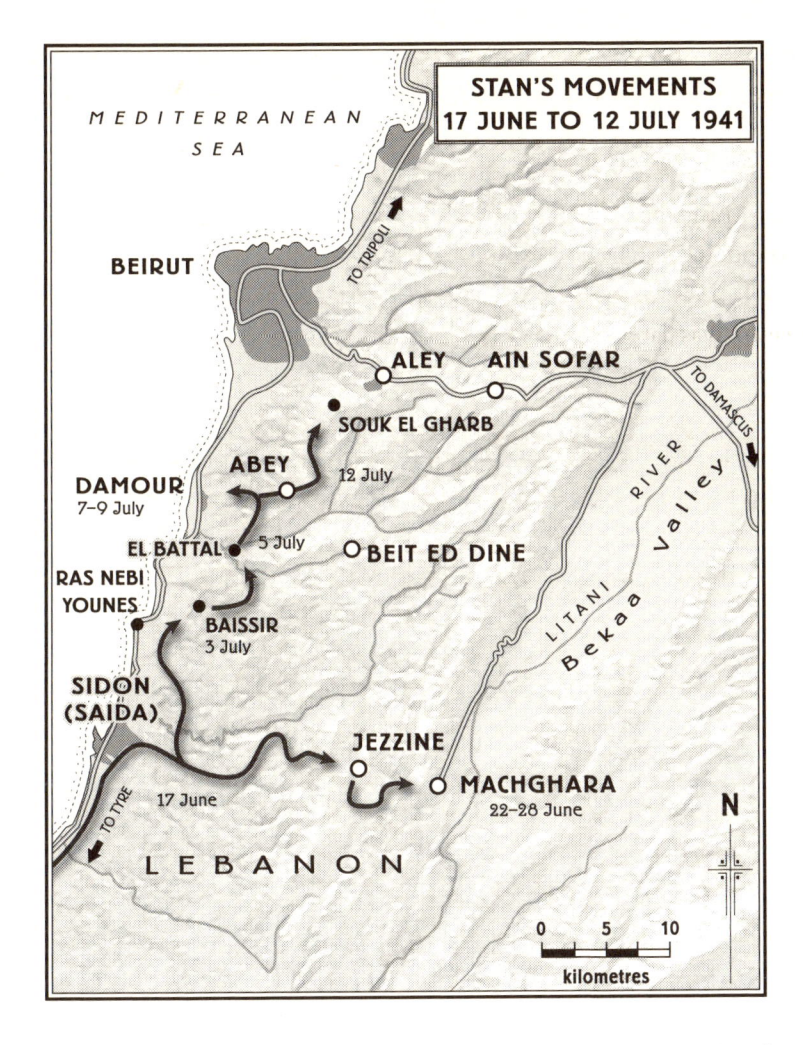

advance. Stan's 18 Platoon took the point position, at the head of the battalion. The men marched all day, fording the Litani in small boats, and then continued up the coast road to the north. The 2/27th Battalion was ahead of Stan and the plan was for the South Australians to go into the attack that night and seize the French positions at Adloun. The 2/14th would then move through them and continue the advance. That evening, in the stony fields on the outskirts of the village, the 2/27th prepared for their midnight attack.

The Victorians were just to the rear of the 2/27th. The ground under their backs was rough with coarse lumps of stone and shale but most collapsed into the deep sleep of the utterly weary. Stan was suddenly awoken on the stroke of midnight by the roar of gunfire. The Victorian 2/4th Field Regiment artillery was pounding the enemy. It was the first time Stan had observed an intense barrage at such close quarters. This was a sound and light show of awesome magnitude. Sheet lightning winked and flared across the sky while the fierce crack of the firing to his rear and the explosions of the shells ahead of him pounded in his ears.

Some of the men in Stan's company crawled forward to watch the start of the battle.

This campaign in which so many Australians lost their lives was to be expunged from history for many decades. The 7th Division was to become the 'Silent Seventh', unable to speak about their experiences in Lebanon and Syria for the duration of the war. The machinations of international politics saw to it that most Australians would never know that so many of their young men had died fighting against France. In the post-war era the relatively negligible contribution to the war effort of De Gaulle's Free French forces was always vaunted in the public sphere but the far larger and more significant collaborative actions of the Vichy forces who fought against the British and Australians in the Middle East and Africa, and who assisted the Nazis so vehemently in the rounding up of French Jews for the concentration camps of Europe, were virtually erased from history. The bitter irony was that despite the Lebanese and Syrian Campaigns, Australia and America maintained full diplomatic relations with the Vichy state until the end of the war.

Before dawn, Stan shook his men awake. The battalion formed up on the road and pushed north towards Sidon. The 2/27th had seized the French defences at Adloun, but as Stan and his men wound their way through the shattered village the occasional chatter of gunfire was heard as the South Australians fought to silence the last pockets of resistance.

Immediately to the north of the village the battalion fanned out. Cannon felt sure there would be enemy positions covering the road itself. The other two battalions in the brigade had exhausted themselves and it now fell to the Victorians to take up the vanguard. Stan's D Company under Steve Noonan moved far out to the right into the foothills and narrow gullies to the east of the road. They had only just taken up patrol formation when the sound of machine-gun fire became audible. Some French soldiers were obviously still in the area. The heavy exchange of fire lasted for some time before the enemy was silenced by Australian artillery support.

After an hour of patrolling under the burning sun, Stan began to doubt whether there were any of the French left in the hills. He took a swig of water and glanced over at Tom Pryor, who raised his eyebrows at his platoon commander. At that moment a volley of rifle fire rang out from the crest of the gully. The men threw themselves to the ground. Muzzle flashes were evident on the flat ridge and in the gullies, and rounds were pinging and fizzing past their ears. It only took a few moments, however, for D Company to regain its wits and soon the sections' Bren guns opened up on the French. The heavy cascade of Australian fire seemed to momentarily stun the enemy and it gave Captain Noonan the opportunity to move the company forward to push the French down out of the hills. Stan's men moved forward in bounds with supporting fire. The French Legionnaires would retreat to the next ridge or wadi and the Australians would attack yet again. It was hard and dangerous work. The sharp-edged shale on the wadi floors tore their knees and elbows to shreds but they had no option at times but to crawl towards the defenders.

Soon Stan saw a white flag being waved from the French position. 'Cease fire! Hold your fire!' he yelled. As they lowered their weapons the Foreign Legion Company filed down from the hills. Stan counted around forty-five prisoners, who Noonan sent to the rear. A later sweep of the area confirmed that nine of the enemy had died in the brief but savage contact.

Not many accounts of this campaign survive beyond the battalion's diaries, so few will appreciate the strength of the forces arrayed against the Australians. They were bombarded by French destroyers off the coast. The French were equipped with armoured vehicles and tanks whereas the only forms of transport available to the Australians were commandeered local vehicles or mules. The French had heavier artillery and mortars. For the first two weeks of the campaign, French planes ruled the skies. At first there was confusion over the identity of the planes. The design of the French roundels was a blue dot with a red circle while British planes sported a red dot and a blue circle. There should not have been any confusion — the only planes in the air were French. As the advance continued, Stan came under intense aerial attack for the first time and was forced to take shelter in the dry creek beds and the stone terraces that ringed the hills.

As they approached Sidon, the battalion was ordered to take an inland route and attack the town from the east. By the time they arrived, it had already fallen to the 2/27th. The last two days marching had been particularly gruelling but the inhabitants of the outlying settlements did their best to make up for men's parched throats by offering them draughts from 'guzzle jars' full of arak, an anise-flavoured liqueur made from grapes and 'other things'. Stan remembers it as a witch's brew that made everyone's head swoon, especially given their state of dehydration.

As they perched on the hills overlooking the Mediterranean, their first view of Sidon almost made the climb worthwhile. Within its beautiful harbour, guarded by an old Crusader castle, lay three ships that might well have carried Ulysses on his Odyssey and were surely similar to the ones that James Elroy Flecker observed when he wrote his famous poem: 'I have seen old ships like swans asleep, beyond the village which men call Tyre, with leaden age o'ercargoed, dipping deep.'

Unfortunately there was little time for literary musings and the men were ordered down from the hills and onto the road that led to Jezzine, their next objective, some thirty kilometres inland. Miraculously, a motor transport convoy appeared from nowhere to truck the bulk of the battalion to a point ten kilometres from their new forming-up position. Stan can still visualise the scene that unfolded from the tailgate of the lorry that morning. The road wound upwards through thick pine forests. Then the wooded hills gave way to bare rocky outcrops that fell away towards the green plantations of the coastal plain.

The enemy held two commanding peaks referred to by their height in metres — Hill 1284 and Hill 1332 — just beyond Jezzine. The town itself was not occupied by the enemy but the road that led into and out of it and most of the surrounding area was dominated by these enemy-held peaks, obliging any vehicle or troops approaching along the road to run the gauntlet. These fire-swept stretches became known as 'The Mad Mile' or 'The Mad Minute'.

The enemy's right flank was almost impregnable, as it dropped away in sheer cliffs. Attacks already carried out by the 2/31st Battalion from the front and enemy left flank approaches had failed at considerable cost. Two more days were therefore spent on intense patrolling to gain a fuller understanding of the terrain. The only other possible approach was from the left rear flank. It was from that direction that Lieutenant Colonel Cannon decided to mount a two-phase attack that would exploit a hill called Mount Kharatt that rose behind the enemy positions. At 4 a.m. and under the cover of darkness, B Company would attempt to capture a machine-gun-swept flat section of land at the base of the enemy positions. At dawn, under the cover of an artillery barrage, C Company would attack up Hill 1332 while B Company would go for Hill 1284. The attack was set for the morning of 23 June but was postponed for twenty-four hours due to the heavy fog.

Stan's role before and during this attack was to lead patrols further inland, to the east, as enemy reinforcements were expected to come from that direction. The intelligence section reported that the next village, Machghara, housed an entire battalion of Foreign

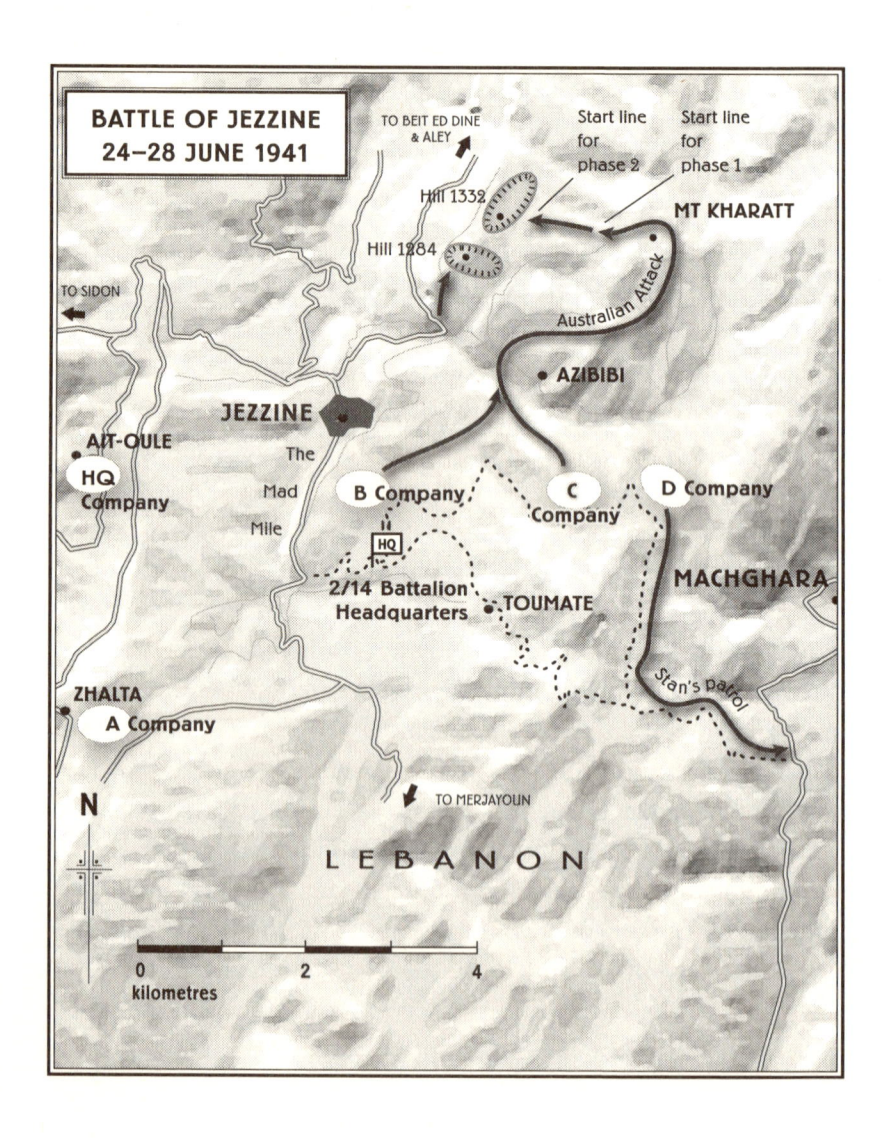

Legionnaires who had just arrived from Damascus. Working with patrols led by Alan McGavin, Stan was able to keep this enemy force at bay. The road from the east passed through a narrow defile and Stan's patrol intercepted and bombed several armoured vehicles, preventing any substantial movement from that direction. They were on the move for five straight days and nights. It was bitterly cold after sunset and the men were dressed in nothing more than shirts and shorts. An hour or two's sleep could be had during the day while the rocks retained some heat, but at night sleep was virtually impossible.

While the main attack failed to take its objectives, sustained pressure by the Australians over four hard days of intense fighting finally forced the enemy to withdraw from its main positions on 28 June. The battalion had sustained heavy casualties and all that day and the next, search parties combed the battlefield to bring in the dead and wounded. When Stan returned from patrol he met his old Power House mate Bob Dougherty, who had somehow managed to keep going for another two days and nights leading the stretcher parties. When Bob handed over the last of the wounded he fell sound asleep in the frozen grass and Stan had to carry him to shelter. Another to distinguish himself in this heroic work, not for the first or last time, was Con Vafiopolous, a medical orderly and stretcher-bearer. Known to everyone as 'Vappy', he was universally liked and respected for his huge heart and big smile. Throughout the battle he tended to the wounded under intense mortar and machine-gun fire until he himself was severely wounded in the chest. Fortunately he survived and stayed with the unit right through the New Guinea campaigns. A rock on the Kokoda Track where he assisted in emergency surgery was named after him.

In the last days of the battle welcome reinforcements arrived, including Stan's brother Butch, who had just returned from the Officer Cadet Training Unit. Albert Moore, the Salvation Army padre, later recalled how the company had passed through the jaws of death and had been strained to near breaking point. That particular night, as the men tried to snatch some sleep, the inevitable wits began to crack jokes. Out of the still night air, Moore heard peals of laughter coming from someone he couldn't recognise, which seemed to relieve the tension of the day. The following morning Moore heard the laughter again and realised it belonged to Butch. From that day on, Moore, along with every other man in the company, seemed to hold a special place in their hearts for Butch — he was such a unique and special character.

At 2 a.m. on 2 July 1941, the battalion was trucked to Ain Maya, a small coastal village north of Sidon. The day was spent among the date palms and olive groves, with some men washing clothes and cleaning gear while others were unable to raise themselves from a deep slumber. Sixteen kilometres to their north lay Damour, the next Australian objective, and they knew they would be on the move again at any moment.

Palestine, 1941. Hal (far right) shares a drink with some of his platoon in a Tel Aviv café.

Shifting Sands

Middle East 1941. After officer training at Memphis, south of Cairo, Hal returned to the 2/14th Battalion as a lieutenant in charge of 10 Platoon.

Hal's B Company received unexpected orders to move immediately to the town of Baissir in preparation for a flanking role in the upcoming battle. Two of Hal's men, Jim Marsh and Cornelius Dillon, had gone absent without leave in Sidon and made merry at several well known haunts. They were rounded up just in time to join the trucks and sang in joyous mood until they had to alight to cover the last several kilometres on foot. By the time they reached the hills, they were done-in. In typical fashion, Hal only laughed, took their rifles and packs and carried theirs as well as his own.

The Battle of Damour was to be conducted on a large scale, involving close to 2000 men and requiring the support of destroyers off the coast, land-based artillery and strafing and bombing from the air. Tanks would also be used to a limited extent for the first time. Approval for the attack came from divisional headquarters but planning and execution would fall to the dynamic commander of the 21st Brigade, Brigadier Jack Stevens.

The French had made the best of their natural defences. Two kilometres south of the town the Damour River flowed into the sea. Its banks were exceedingly steep and considered impassable and the only bridge crossing on the main coastal road had been demolished by the defenders. North of the river lay a coastal plain, about 800 metres wide, covered with banana trees and date palms interspersed with many stone houses, all excellent defensive positions. The inland approaches were dominated by a series of hills. The dominant ones were Hill 560 and Hill 903 and these afforded the defenders excellent observation of any approach from the east.

After several days of careful consideration, Stevens devised his plan. Heavy fire would be directed towards the defenders along the flatlands north of the river to keep them pinned in their positions. The river would be forded well inland under the cover of darkness, via a narrow, single-file, zigzagging track that led down into a 500-metre-deep gorge. This movement would commence at 8 p.m. and by morning the bulk of the attacking infantry column would be hidden out of sight in the hills, north of the river. This attacking force would be supported by mule trains.

The crossing of the river took place on the night of 5 July. By midnight of the following day, Stan had reached El Boum, a village less than a kilometre north of the river. The terrain was so rugged that it was almost impassable for even the mules. One team of fifteen attempted one of the climbs but only three succeeded — the others had to be left behind. Several mules had fallen into deep gorges with swift flowing creeks. One of them fell ten metres into the water but miraculously neither the mule nor the load of bombs it was carrying was damaged. After four hours rest, the company continued on and reached Daraya, another small village inland from Damour, at 8 a.m. on 7 July.

By this stage the bulk of the brigade was holding positions on a north-south line in the hills parallel to the coast. At a given signal, they all turned to face the sea and in a series of well-planned attacks they stormed the French defences. Some of the hill positions were heavily fortified and only fell after intense engagements. However, because the French had not expected an attack from such mountainous terrain, some sectors were not fully manned and the Australians were able to overwhelm the startled defenders.

D Company attacked along the north bank of the Damour. Stan led his platoon across the river. Their job was to clear the northern bank of any resistance. By 5.15 p.m. Stan had not only done that but found himself at the outskirts of the town, seemingly unopposed. He relayed this information to Captain Noonan, who promptly formed up the remainder of the company in two lines and they marched down the road towards the town in column of route.

The enemy was still about but Noonan's approach was so outrageously brazen that the French assumed the advancing column was their own reinforcements and held their fire. As the leading Australians turned into a road that led to the town centre, they found themselves staring down the muzzle of a French machine-gun at virtual point blank range. Everyone dived for cover, but after a few grenades were tossed in their direction the five French defenders waved a white flag.

Spasmodic exchanges of fire continued throughout the day and that night Australian six-inch howitzers shelled the town. The remainder of the town was occupied on 9 July and the Battle of Damour was effectively over. Stan was ordered to move forward and hold the small village of Kfar Matta, several kilometres to the north-east, and await further orders.

The audacious plan of Jack Stevens involving encircling and outflanking movements from the hills had been a resounding success. Given the size of the opposing forces, the loss of thirteen Australians was considered exceptionally light. The capital and major port of Beirut lay virtually defenceless only thirty kilometres to the north. Another embarrassing loss by the French seemed pointless and at 12.15 a.m. on 12 July Stan received a message to say that an armistice had been arranged to take effect as of midnight, that is, fifteen minutes earlier. The following evening, Stan gazed down on Beirut from the hills. It was the first fully lit city he had ever seen in the Middle East.

The situation was still tense, however. The question remained of how to safely deal with the 40,000 prisoners, many of whom still retained their weapons. The French Army of the Levant was composed of a variety of units, most coming from the mainland's regular army while others were made up of men who had volunteered for overseas service and were called 'colonial troops'. 'Special Troops of the Levant' was a term used for indigenous units from Syria and Lebanon or the French colonies in Africa. The infantry, together with mounted and mechanised cavalry, totalled over 35,000 men, supported by artillery, tanks and armoured cars. Theoretically, this force should have overwhelmed the Australians.

Stan's unit was assigned to guard a petrol supply dump on the coast. Their proximity to Beirut was a bonus when it came to leave. Only a week or so after the armistice, Stan was called to a meeting with the battalion's intelligence officer, Jim McAllester. Jim was being promoted to brigade headquarters and he told Stan that he had nominated him as his successor. This meant another stint in Cairo, this time at the Middle East Intelligence School. Stan greeted the news with mixed feelings, but he could not pass up an opportunity for promotion and enhanced training. If the war was to drag on, the more training he received the better for him and his men. In fact, of all the units of study he undertook the one that proved to be the most practical was that of direction-finding by the stars. There would be many a night when he and his men would fall back on this specialised skill.

When Stan returned to his unit they were on garrison duty at Tripoli, about a hundred kilometres north of Beirut. Winter snows were limiting all movement and the Australians were feeling relatively calm and confident. It was to be short-lived, however. In early December 1941, on a clear but freezing day, the most unbelievable news reached the front. In the space of twenty-four hours Japan had made simultaneous attacks on the United States at Pearl Harbor and its territories of Guam, Wake Island and the Philippines, and on the British colonies of Hong Kong and Malaya. The British Commonwealth and the United States had immediately declared war on Japan. Although it was not obliged to do so under the terms of the Anti-Comintern Pact with Japan and Italy, Germany also declared war on the US on 11 December. In a single day the war had become a truly global conflict.

For the Australians holding their positions in northern Lebanon, the implications of these events took little time to sink in. For the first time in history, their homeland was under threat of foreign invasion. The Japanese offensive in the Pacific affected Stan in a way that the war in Europe and the Middle East had never done. Over the coming days, a sense of frustration began to build in the Australian camp. The desire to return home became overwhelming. The dubious gratitude of the Lebanese civilians at being 'liberated' from the French only served to heighten their sense of frustration. How long would they be kept here on the other side of the world in some god-forsaken range of hills when their own homes and families could, at any time, come under attack from the marauding Japanese?

That night around the fire, Stan and Hal talked of home. Hal reminded Stan that Doc McAdam, with his typical foresight, had pointed to the threat posed by the Japanese. Contrary to the accepted wisdom of the day, Doc had explained that it was the threat from Japan and not Germany that had been the motivation to form Power House's own militia unit. Hal hadn't believed him at the time.

'Well, he always seemed to know what was best for us,' said Stan. 'Hell, he knew straightaway that you needed to come home from the bush and join Power House, and he hadn't even met you!' Hal nodded at the thought of it and chuckled. They reflected on how very different their lives would have been had it not been for their association with Doc. They also talked at length about the dark shadow that was now cast over them and their loved ones at home.

In his new role of intelligence officer, Stan had command of the 'I' section that formed part of the unit's headquarters company, which in turn came under the command of Phil Rhoden. His section was comprised of ten men including Sergeant Geoff Woodley and Lance Corporal Roy Watson. When the battalion next went into action, Stan's role would be twofold. Firstly, he would command his section in the field, gathering intelligence on the battlefield itself. This would involve the section conducting its own patrols or setting up outlying observation positions in an attempt to monitor enemy movements. Much time would be spent debriefing other returning patrols. The second element would be to collate the information, make a decision as to what was relevant, and then brief the commanding officer. This might involve such diverse topics as the disposition and tactics of enemy forces, the nature of the terrain and the forecast climatic conditions. Needless to say, the position came with a huge workload and great responsibility, but at the same time it was incredibly rewarding. One of the great frustrations of being a private or a junior officer was not having access to the bigger picture. Stan would now be responsible for many key operational decisions.

By the end of December 1941, the battalion was well and truly dispirited as boredom and staleness were mixed with the frustration of not knowing what was happening back in Australia. Stan, however, was amazed at how little impact Japan's entry into the war had on the bulk of the men in the battalion. Japan was an unknown quantity as far as its war-making capabilities were concerned. And at that time 'Fortress Singapore' still stood as a bulwark between the aggressor and the Australian homeland. The idea that this huge British base could fall was simply inconceivable to most Australians. It was not a case of intentional brainwashing by the government, but more the fact that for generations Britain had held the position of an unassailable superpower. This role had been reaffirmed by its extraordinary defiance of the Germans during the Battle of Britain. Besides, weren't there almost 100,000 Allied soldiers under the command of Lieutenant General Arthur Percival on the Malayan Peninsula?

In early January 1942, the battalion was relocated to its old training camp in Palestine. One hundred and eighty reinforcements arrived in addition to masses of new equipment. Rumours abounded of an imminent move, but to where? Finally, orders were received for the battalion to move to Port Tewfik on the Suez Canal and on 29 January, in full marching order, wearing greatcoats and carrying sea-kits and weapons, the 1024 strong battalion marched to the Shell Wharf to embark on the *Ile de France*. This was a fine ship, a former French Compagnie Générale Transatlantique liner that had been commandeered by the British Admiralty. She set sail at 10 o'clock the following morning with all 3000 men of the Australian 21st Brigade on board.

After a short stopover in Bombay, the battalion re-embarked onto a smaller ship, the Ellerman Line's *City of Paris*, and joined a convoy of eight other transports, escorted by four destroyers and a British battleship. They headed south into the Indian Ocean but still no one had any idea of their destination. A series of chance happenings, victories by Japan on the battlefield and decisions taken by the world's leaders all combined over the following weeks to have a dramatic impact on the men's fate.

Chance was the first factor to come into play, as not long after leaving Bombay several of the transports experienced engine trouble, delaying the convoy for three days. The men were not aware of it but their destination had already been agreed upon by the Australian Government — it was to be Java, part of the Dutch East Indies, one of the main islands of what we now know as Indonesia.

After the delay, the convoy got under way again on 15 February. This happened to be the very day that the impossible happened — Singapore fell to the all-conquering Japanese. This capitulation represented the greatest single military defeat in the history of the British Empire. More than 90,000 Allied soldiers, including 17,000 Australians of the 8th Division, fell captive to the Japanese. Had the transports not broken down, they most certainly would have landed the troops at Batavia (now Jakarta) and they would have faced annihilation in battle or spent the remainder of the war as prisoners. As an example of their possible fate, some other Australian troops had left Suez on the Orient Line's *Orcades* nine days after the *Ile de France*. Travelling fast and unescorted, the *Orcades* had passed Stan's convoy and landed its troops at Batavia. All these Australians were taken prisoner and many perished on the accursed Thai-Burma railway.

Stan's convoy was still en route for Java when another dramatic event took place. On 19 February the Japanese First Air Fleet under Admiral Chuichi Nagumo bombed Darwin, rendering it useless as a supply and naval base to support further operations in the Dutch East Indies. This was the last straw for the Australian High Command. At 8 a.m. on the following morning, the men heard a long, shrill whistle blast from the leading destroyer. In an extraordinary manoeuvre, every ship in the convoy lurched to starboard and ploughed a broad, 180 degree turn without dropping a knot of speed. For two full days they steamed back in the direction from whence they had come. No one on board had any idea of what was happening. There was not a skerrick of information to alert them to the dramatic machinations taking place in Whitehall, Washington and the humble offices of the Australian Prime Minister, John Curtin, in Canberra.

When Singapore had fallen to the Japanese, Curtin made a statement to the Australian press: 'The fall of Singapore can only be described as Australia's Dunkirk. The fall of Dunkirk initiated the Battle for Britain. The fall of Singapore opens the Battle for Australia. What the Battle for Britain required, so the Battle for Australia requires. Our honeymoon has finished. It is now work or fight as we have never worked or fought before.' Curtin, speaking from a hospital bed, stated that 'this blow at Darwin, and the loss it has involved and the suffering it has occasioned' must make Australians 'gird our loins and nerve our steel'. Against this backdrop, Curtin and Churchill had engaged in a war of cables concerning the control of the two divisions of Australian troops then returning from the Middle East. While Curtin was adamant that these troops should return to Australia to take part in the defence of their homeland, Churchill, supported by the US President Roosevelt, wanted at least one of the divisions to be diverted to Burma. Curtin refused to bow to this concerted pressure. Initially, he sent the convoys to Colombo and allowed some of the 6th Division to remain there to await events unfolding in the Dutch East Indies, but the 7th Division, of which the 2/14th Battalion was a part, was committed to return to Australia immediately.

When the *City of Paris* entered Colombo harbour, Stan was presented with an amazing sight. Hundreds of ships were moored in long lines, mostly in twos and threes, with all lights blazing as if taking part in some exotic eastern carnival. Even at this late hour there was an audible buzz of activity on board all the transports as well as on the wharves and in the town itself. The *City of Paris* slid alongside another transport and secured itself to her with lines. With no shore leave given, some of the men took matters into their own hands, lowered the ship's life rafts and rowed themselves ashore. Others slid down the mooring cables and boarded native boats.

Evidently chaos reigned on the docks and no rations had come aboard by the time the ship slipped her cables on the morning of 1 March 1942 and headed out into open waters. The intolerable heat, a boring diet of bully beef and beans and shockingly cramped conditions were about all Stan could recall of the next two weeks until the beloved homeland finally came into view on 15 March. He will never forget, however, the two hours he spent with his mates at a pub at Fremantle where an unbelievable feed of meat pies, tomato sauce and peas was washed down with ample quantities of cold Emu

Draught lager, before re-embarkation that afternoon for the next leg to Adelaide. It was also the first time in the war that Stan had encountered Americans. They were everywhere. US warships lined the harbour and there was the reassuring sight of dozens of sleek Gato-class submarines, moored in pairs along the quay.

After three weeks of training in camp at Springbank in the Clare Valley, the battalion arrived in Melbourne on 16 April for seven days' home leave. Memories of this period are a heady mixture of the joy of seeing family and friends again, together with the gut-wrenching suddenness of their parting.

Forty-eight hours after entraining at Watsonia, the battalion was in Glen Innes in northern NSW, and then on 11 May it arrived in Yandina, north of Brisbane. The eleven weeks it spent there, marred as they were by the lack of leave and the threat of an imminent move into battle, proved to be happy and fruitful. The camp was pleasantly situated. The warm winter days were followed by clear frosty nights, many of them spent singing around blazing camp fires

Spencer Street Station. Melbourne, 16 April 1942. Stan (second from left in officer's cap) returns to Melbourne after service in the Middle East. After a week's leave, the battalion moved to Queensland to prepare for the New Guinea campaign.

with the company beer barrels always close at hand. Training was conducted all along what is now known as the Sunshine Coast. There were Saturday night dances at nearby towns and many a weekend was spent at Tewantin, just upriver from Noosa Beach. The Tewantin pub opened at 8 a.m. on Saturday mornings and stayed open till the last man was carried to his swag, well past normal closing hours.

The battalion's commander in the Middle East, Bill Cannon, was assigned to a new post and was replaced by Arthur Key. Key was already something of a legendary figure before he was posted to the 2/14th. Like many of the war's successful battalion commanders, Key was not a professional soldier, but that was not to say that he was a novice in military affairs. He had served as an officer in the 52nd Militia Battalion before enlisting in the AIF. As a company commander with the 2/8th Battalion, Key had fought through the entire Libyan conflict against Rommel's Afrika Korps and at the Battles of Tobruk, Bardia, Derna and Benghazi. In Greece he was appointed second-in-command of the battalion as it fought its desperate rearguard action against the Germans at the Monasir Gap. The SS *Costa Rica*, upon which Key and some members of the 2/8th managed to secure a passage across the Mediterranean during the evacuation from Kalamata, was sunk by German Stukas. Key had a lucky escape when the party was rescued by a patrol from the Royal Navy.

After surviving the hell of Greece, Key went on to command a detachment of the 2/8th in Crete, fighting a series of battles at Perivolia, Suda Bay and Sphakia. Stan describes Key as having a gentlemanly manner and an air of quiet efficiency. Their relationship was an important factor in the development of the battalion's battle readiness and obviously high esprit de corps. The battalion's first adjutant, Major Bill Russell, later commented on Stan's 'sound judgement and high sense of duty' which were 'matched by his mighty physique and resolution under fire'. In Russell's opinion,

Australia, 1942. Stan became the intelligence officer for the 2/14th Battalion.

when Stan was subsequently promoted to adjutant, his role was just as important as Key's command while 'the individual excellence of each man was enhanced by their splendid teamwork'.

Despite the volume of office work associated with his intelligence work, Stan never missed an opportunity to oversee the training of his section. Each morning he would rouse his section early and take them for a punishing run up the steep slopes of Mount Ninderry. And every morning he would make the same comment, that a gentle jog might 'clear our lungs' before the real day's work began.

Shifting Sands

In addition to training, weeks were spent on defensive works along the coastal roads and beaches. These works gave rise to the infamous 'Brisbane Line' controversy. This secret plan to abandon the northern half of Australia in the event of a Japanese invasion had been initiated by General MacArthur. This proposal first came to light when a Labour politician, Eddie Ward, received confidential information from public servants in the Defence Office.

At the time, Stan felt there was a distinct possibility he would see out the war in Australia. The Japanese were thought to be planning an invasion, so together with all the other AIF units then being withheld in Australia, the 2/14th would probably be called on to hold this major defensive line. Weeks passed devoid of any news from the outside world and the war in the Pacific seemed to recede into the distance. Then, late on 4 August, an order arrived for all the brigade's officers to attend an urgent conference at

Queensland, 1942. Stan was one of the first officers asked to test the Australian Owen sub-machine gun. It was designed by Evelyn Owen from Wollongong and championed by the steel manufacturer Lysaght at Port Kembla. Lighter than the US Thompson sub-machine gun and more robust than the British Sten, Stan believed it was ideally suited to jungle conditions and rued their limited and delayed production.

divisional headquarters. The brigadier himself was on leave and many of the 2/14th's officers' whereabouts were unknown. There was great confusion as dispatch riders were sent roaring off on their bikes, scouring the countryside for anyone sporting pips on their shoulders.

By noon on 6 August the battalion, together with all its stores and equipment, was at sea on the Liberty ship, the *James Fenimore Cooper*, en route to New Guinea. Conditions were so cramped that if Stan got up during the night to go to the crude temporary latrines on deck, there was no way he could find his way back to his bunk through the mass of bodies. There was only one fresh water tap for drinking, so washing was done courtesy of a saltwater sea-hose. Meals had to be prepared on deck, drawing on the battalion's own supplies.

On the morning of 12 August the brooding, cloud-covered mountains beyond Port Moresby Harbour came into view. As the ship drew near to the coast, men got their first glimpse not of the palm-fringed beaches they had expected but of black volcanic soil and drab, brown, grass-covered hills. The bombed wreck of the Burns Philp ship, the *Macdhui*, sunk on 17 June, lay on its side in the harbour. At least the Japanese submarines that had sunk three other ships during the previous week allowed them to pass by unmolested. As they hove to in the harbour, an Australian Navy corvette ran alongside and commenced ferrying the troops ashore, whereupon they were immediately trucked inland. One hundred and fifty kilometres away, directly to the north, fresh Japanese troops were landing at the beaches near Gona and Buna and making their way inland, heading towards the Owen Stanley Range.

CHAPTER SIX

The Bloody Track

When Stan and Hal first embarked for war it was to farflung lands unknown to many of the young soldiers. They fought in towns, valleys and mountains whose names they could not pronounce. In truth, it had been something of an adventure, the chance to participate in a historical event.

When they departed Australia for a second time in the August of 1942, they sailed into a very different war. On this occasion they were not headed for some far-flung corner of the globe to fight for British Imperial interests, but were instead embarking on a campaign to defend Australia itself from the now frighteningly real threat of invasion.

Japan's concept of the Greater East Asia Co-Prosperity Sphere — through which it planned to control the South-West Pacific — was formally announced by the Foreign Minister Yosuke Matsuoka in a 1940 press interview. However, Japan had long coveted an empire that would provide the raw materials its homeland so evidently lacked. In pursuit of this goal, it made the first of many incursions into China as early as 1931, and finally a full-scale invasion was launched in 1937.

Wattle Park, 1942. Like many mothers whose sons were overseas on active service, the war years were lonely and anxious for Olive, pictured here with the family dog, Kim.

Japan's expansionist policies were met with steadily increasing concern by Western powers, who imposed embargoes and sanctions on Japanese imports. In 1940 the US suspended shipments of aircraft parts, machine tools and aviation gasoline. Following Japanese expansion into French Indochina in 1941 further embargoes were placed on iron, steel and oil, and all Japanese assets in the US were frozen. The oil embargo, above all, was seen by Japan as a provocative act and enabled extremists to gain control of the Japanese government, led by the fiercely militant Tojo Hideki who became Prime Minister in October 1941. With no rubber and with iron and fuel supplies almost exhausted, Japan concluded that war in the Pacific was inevitable.

The belief that a pre-emptive strike against the US would weaken its sea power in the Pacific led to Japan's attack on Pearl Harbor on

7 December 1941. Simultaneous assaults took place on Guam and Wake Islands, Hong Kong, the Philippines and Malaya.

The sinking of the British capital ships *Prince of Wales* and *Repulse* in the South China Sea on 10 December was the first of many major shocks to Australia. By January 1942, only six weeks after the declaration of war, the Japanese had pushed as far south as the Solomon Islands, seizing Bougainville and Rabaul in New Britain. They defeated the British and Australian forces on mainland Malaya and laid siege to Singapore, which surrendered on 15 February. Now there was little protection, if any, between Australia's mainland and the all-conquering Japanese.

The Japanese Army and Navy High Commands next debated whether they should invade mainland Australia. The navy contended that Japan should not switch to a defensive policy, as this would invite a prolonged stalemate during which the US would grow in strength. As well, Australia could be prevented from becoming a base for a US-led counter-offensive and Japan would acquire vast stocks of wool, wheat and minerals. The army argued against this, contending that the invasion was in excess of Japan's capabilities. The necessary ground forces for such an invasion were estimated to be twelve divisions, which would strip other vital fronts of manpower. The army also believed that available shipping was incapable of providing the logistical support for such a force.

The views of the army held sway. Plans for a direct assault on Australia were held in abeyance and the Japanese turned their attention to New Guinea. Port Moresby, with its large harbour and airfields, was close to the major Japanese base at Rabaul, so a sea-borne invasion was planned. Thanks to allied intelligence reports, the Japanese invasion fleet was intercepted by a US carrier force mid-morning on 7 May. The ensuing Battle of the Coral Sea, a clash of air power without direct surface ship contact, was concluded by the afternoon of 8 May and the invasion convoy was forced to return to Rabaul.

With a direct sea-borne invasion thwarted, Japan's Imperial General Headquarters focused their attention on a land-based thrust towards Port Moresby from the north coast of Papua, pushing south over the Owen Stanley Range. The main force was to be the South Seas Detachment, part of the 17th Army, commanded by Major General Tomitaro Horii. The majority of this 14,000-strong force was deployed for the drive towards Port Moresby in mid-August, only days after Stan and Hal disembarked from their Liberty ship.

As Stan's battalion was driven the seventy kilometres north-east from Port Moresby to its base on the Sogeri plateau, its path snaked through dun-coloured hills that more closely resembled north-west Queensland than the tropical foliage the men had envisaged. The trucks stirred trails of ochre-red dust that mixed with the haze from fires around the airstrip at Seven Mile following a Japanese air raid. The road then ran through lightly wooded grasslands for another twenty kilometres before winding its way up the precipitous Rouna Pass. They finally debussed at a well-established rubber estate, Itiki Plantation.

Maps were issued to Stan's intelligence section but they were on a pitifully small one-inch-to-the-mile scale that rendered them almost worthless. On 15 August, three days after their arrival, Brigadier Arnold Potts addressed the battalion and gave them their orders. Enemy troops were thought to number approximately two to three thousand. Unfortunately this was a woeful under-estimation — the total was more than 14,000. The brigade's task was to wipe out the Japanese at Kokoda, or to push them back over the Kumusi River. Potts was confident that this was a realistic goal — an optimism that was shared by most of the men.

The main road-head leading to the ranges terminated at a plantation owned by Percy McDonald, who personally doled out hot tea to the passing troops. The start of the walking track was marked by a single signpost pointing north: 'To Tokyo'. The jeep

The Bloody Track

track twisted up and down scrubby slopes for another ten kilometres and as the men crested a small hillock they were met by a most astonishing sight. The four-wheel-drive track ended abruptly at a precipice, beyond which extended a vast vista of emerald green. Range after range of jagged, jungle-shrouded mountains stretched as far as the eye could see. The escarpments were so steep that in parts they were just vertical shafts of rock. Beyond the first range ran another, and then another, each one higher than the last. They were separated by deep, twisting gorges. The narrow valleys were shrouded in swirling mists, so it was impossible to tell how deeply they ran.

From the end of the jeep road, known as Owers' Corner, a bush-covered trail slipped off the edge of the escarpment and plunged towards the valley below. The track was narrow, just wide enough for a single man. There was no way the battalion's 546 infantrymen could move along the trail as a single entity. Stan watched as one man, then another, filed off the road to be seemingly devoured by the jungle. For the first time, the extraordinary challenges they faced became evident. He thought of all the principles of warfare that had been drummed into him at officer's school — maintenance of contact, control of fire, concentration of force. How could any of these military tenets be applied in this alien environment?

Stan and his commander, Arthur Key, waited behind on the side of the road with Albert Moore, the battalion's Salvation Army officer, in case the last of the men coming forward brought any new intelligence on the situation at Kokoda. There was nothing, of course. How could there be? The twelve kilo backpack wireless sets with which they had been issued were almost useless, and many had already been discarded. The signallers were laying wire behind them to keep in touch with headquarters, but there was no way of knowing what was unfolding on the far side of the ranges. Stan set off with Key and Moore, the three rear-most men of the entire battalion, on what they called the Kokoda Track.

From Owers' Corner, the trail wound steeply down to the first valley where the Goldie River ran through the small native village of Uberi. It was only a short descent but it had taken them an hour, far longer than expected. The jungle floor was saturated and the hundreds of men before them had churned the narrow track into a snaking line of boot-sucking mud. They emerged from the half-light of the tree canopy and waded across the cold, fast-flowing river, clinging onto a line the leading men of the unit had strung up earlier.

When Stan and Arthur Key reached Uberi, the battalion was in the process of establishing a night location in a small jungle clearing. The native settlement was no more than a cluster of grass-thatched huts. A handful of bemused natives sat and watched the Australians drop their heavy packs and webbing and start erecting shelters. Key immediately convened a meeting of his senior officers to discuss the next day's march.

Kokoda Track, Papua, 16 August 1942. Lieutenant Colonel Arthur Key, Commanding Officer 2/14th Battalion (left), Stan, the battalion's intelligence officer (centre), and Albert Moore, the Salvation Army padre, commence their trek over the Owen Stanley Range.

The Bloody Track

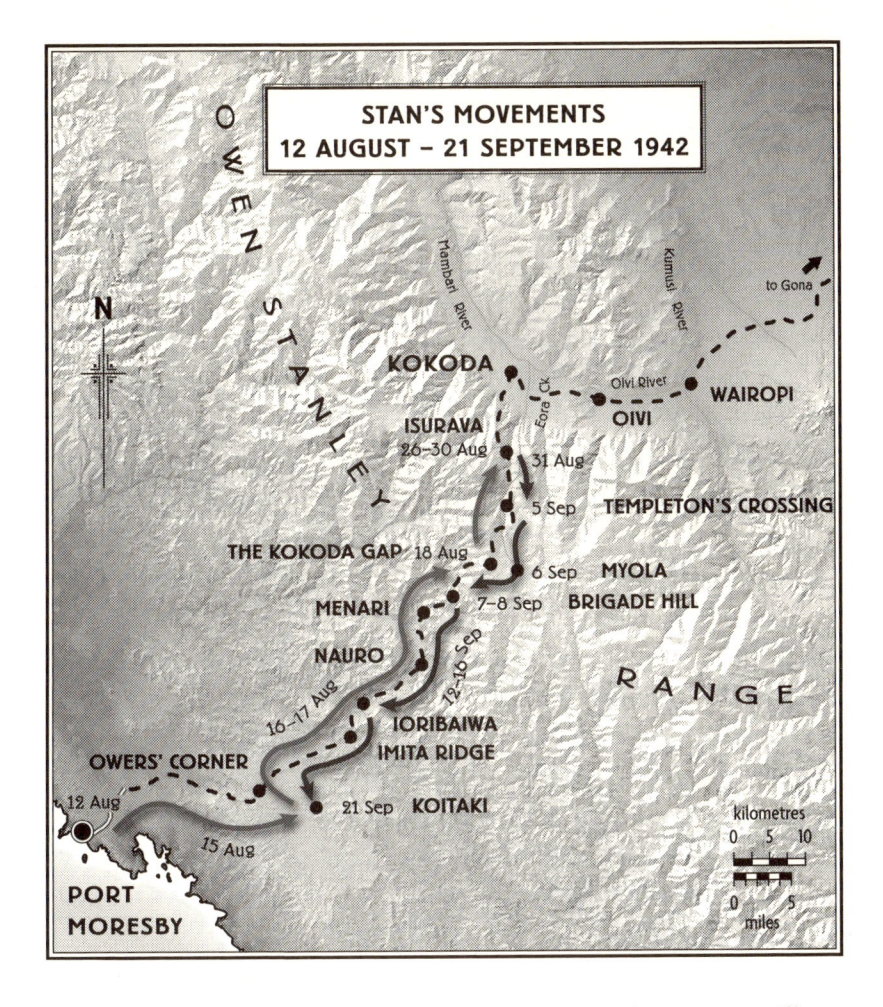

**STAN'S MOVEMENTS
12 AUGUST – 21 SEPTEMBER 1942**

Their pre-arranged destination was a similar native village, Ioribaiwa. Although it was only around nine miles away 'as the crow flies' on their pre-war survey maps, after their first short descent on the trail the men had to seriously re-assess the next day's march. Key turned to his company commanders for advice. 'What do you think?' he asked Hal's B Company commander, Captain Claude Nye.

'The march from Ilolo had been fine along the old road', Nye told him. But once they left the road-head things slowed to a standstill. 'And that was only going down', he said. 'Look at these ascents tomorrow.' There was a general murmur of agreement. No one had expected the trail to be so treacherous and by the time the platoons were in their evening positions, they were completely exhausted.

Key thought on this for a moment. He too had noticed that the last thing the men needed to do after the day's march was try to organise their positions and light fires in the perpetual damp. Eventually he told Stan to take the 'I' section at first light and get on the trail before the rest of the unit. 'I know you and your boys can set a good pace', he noted. 'I want you into the night location at least two hours before the rest of the unit. Speak to the villagers and try and rustle up some food, get some fires going and a brew on, and try to map out a rough battalion perimeter.' Stan nodded in agreement. Key thought for another moment, then told Stan to take Bert Lane and some of the cooks with him. This kind of task was a typical role for the intelligence officer, but Stan couldn't help but feel that he had been chosen partly in recognition of the physical fitness of his men.

Stan found Hal and his 10 Platoon boys erecting crude tents out of the canvas ponchos that the men carried. The ponchos could be clipped together and lashed between a few trees, and two together provided just enough protection to keep the rain off two men. Since they were so far from Kokoda and the Japanese, Key and Stan allowed each platoon a small fire to heat up some bully beef stew or a pot of tea. Hal thrust a mug of steaming tea in his younger brother's direction and the two men sank mercifully to the ground. Hal's boys, he saw as he looked around, were in what the sergeant major would describe as a 'right bloody state'. They were covered in mud and their boots, gaiters, and webbing were still soaked from the river crossing. He was about to chide his brother when he realised that he, too, must have been in the same state. Stan chatted with Hal and his men and shared the culinary masterpiece of bully-beef-and-biscuit stew for which 10 Platoon had become famous in Lebanon, before wandering off to find the intelligence sergeant and erect his own poncho for the evening.

None of the men would ever forget that first night in the jungle. Stan and Hal were used to sleeping rough, but nothing had prepared even them. As the last light of day faded away, so did its lingering warmth and they were gripped by the cold chill of the early evening. The men had no groundsheets or sleeping mats and simply lay on the damp jungle floor. During the day they sweated heavily and they had been wringing wet after the river crossing. Now they lay shivering in their saturated clothes. Eerily silent during the day, the jungle erupted with noise as the sun set. Crickets and cicadas kept up an incessant drone and mosquitoes hovered around their bodies. The most unnerving phenomenon, however, was the fireflies. In the rear of the campaign area, the battalion had posted sentries and the men took their turn in pairs for the long vigils. In the eerie darkness of the jungle the mind played tricks on the eyes. Weird shapes seemed to appear and disappear, then suddenly, in the distance, a light would flicker through the trees, only to go out and then reappear in another part of the murky gloom. These fireflies were so bright that many a nervous sentry would open fire on a 'Jap patrol', only to realise that he had been wasting his ammunition on insects.

In the first few hours of this night, few of the men slept. A 'twenty-five percent watch' had been posted and there was no movement at all in the company localities. But as dog weariness began to overcome cold discomfort, some began to sleep. Then the rain came. Stan had drifted off into a fitful doze when his sergeant, Geoff Woodley, shook him awake. 'Jeez, Stan,' he muttered. 'What the hell is *that?*' The noise sounded like a steam-train ploughing through the forest, growing louder and louder until it burst onto the tree canopy above. A great gust of wind ripped the ponchos from their fastenings and the rain lashed their exposed bodies. Then came great streaks of lightning that cracked against the trunks of distant trees, followed by thunder that boomed in the valleys like artillery battery. The high, rugged ranges pushed the moisture-laden air from the Pacific up into the troposphere to create these strange, unstable weather patterns. Small, localised rain storms rolled through each valley then swept up and over the escarpments. The stars might then appear for a time before the weather gods chose to repeat their grand performance.

It was still dark when Stan assembled his small party and they pushed off the moment it was light enough to make out their footings. Stan wanted to complete a good portion of the day's march in the cool of the morning.

Up until this point, the trail had been relatively easy going, but from Uberi the track climbed steeply to Imita Ridge along a section euphemistically called the 'Golden Staircase'. These stairs turned out to be little more than a series of log steps held in place by stakes. The entire hillside was soaked from the rains and each log held a pool of muddy water behind it. A few of the stakes had worked loose and when a log gave way completely, one of the boys went careering in cartwheels off the side of the track. After twenty or so metres he was suspended well off the ground in a thick matting of lawyer vines, what the men called 'wait-a-whiles', much to the entertainment of the whole section.

The hills were less amusing. Each one seemed to consist of a series of false peaks. Just when they thought they had reached the summit, another winding ascent appeared through the jungle. In addition to their thirty kilo packs, everyone carried spare ammunition for the Bren-gunners. They all carried extra mortar rounds weighing three kilos each. It had been impossible to prepare physically or emotionally for this kind of punishment, so when they finally reached a ridge summit they collapsed in absolute exhaustion.

The next few days were extraordinarily tough and as the enormity of what they faced began to weigh on Stan he became concerned about morale. The reputation of the Japanese was

The Bloody Track

formidable enough, but few had given much thought to the fact that they might also have to face another, equally potent enemy: the jungle itself. As the days of climbing wore on, however, the battalion seemed to find a rhythm to the day's march and each night all manly pretensions were done away with as they huddled together for warmth and the sleep their bodies craved. By the time they reached Efogi on their fourth day of walking, they had regained some of their earlier self-confidence. Efogi lay in the shadows of Mount Bellamy, just below the Gap over the highest part of the ranges. From there, the steep-sided Eora Creek valley would lead them all the way down the far side of the ranges. Nestled in the flatlands were the small village of Kokoda and the Japanese. After tonight, Stan knew there would be no more camp fires, no more sleeping under the relative comfort of their ponchos in village clearings. The war was getting closer.

After the evening's briefing with Key and the headquarters staff, Hal found Stan chatting to his sergeant. Some of Hal's boys were having a sing-along, and he asked Stan to give them a song or two. Everyone fell quiet as Stan sang the beautiful Irish melody 'Mountains of Mourne'.

'...Well, if you believe me, when asked to a ball, faith they don't wear no top to their dresses at all.' The men whistled and cheered at the reference to the 'ladies of London'. One of Hal's NCOs handed Stan the last drop of his whiskey in an old army mess-tin. They asked for another song and Stan figured he would continue with his Irish theme and sang 'Danny Boy'. By now the entire camp had fallen silent and Stan's clear baritone voice floated through the night air.

'The summer's gone, and all the roses falling, 'tis you, 'tis you, must go, and I must bide.' It might have been the song, Stan was never sure, but when he finished and looked at his brother chatting to his friends and sharing a joke in the flickering light of the fire, Stan had a strange premonition that, perhaps very soon, they were going to be parted. He had never felt like this before. They had thought about death, but rarely spoke of it. They carried with them an air of invincibility, typical of most young men. As he lay there, however, staring at Hal, he began to grow more and more concerned that this coming battle might not just take the lives of his friends, of the soldiers under his command, but his own brother. He silently repeated the words of the song…

'But when ye come, and all the flowers are dying, if I am dead, as dead I well may be, you'll come and find the place where I am lying, and kneel and say an Ave there for me.'

As they climbed out of Efogi the next morning, the terrain began to change. The thick, sweltering jungle gradually gave way to open grasslands. After another hour they entered a tall-timbered forest, different yet again to much of the jungle through which they had passed. Here was a ghostly landscape of trees so tall that the canopy was lost in a sea of green, hundreds of feet above. Branches were draped with tendrils of pale green vines that hung down over the trail. There were great thickets of impenetrable bamboo. Everything was covered in moss — the trunks and buttress roots of the trees, fallen logs, and the forest floor itself. Eeriest of all was the phosphorescent moss. The men felt like dwarves in a fantasy world populated by weird, supernatural phenomena.

When they finally arrived at Myola, Stan was shocked to learn that the aerial re-supply they had been expecting from Moresby had not eventuated. He later learned that the Japanese air raid that had struck the Seven Mile airstrip the day they left Moresby had almost completely destroyed the only squadron of DC3 'biscuit bombers' that was available to supply their force. The planes had been parked wingtip to wingtip on the apron of the strip. This made for easier protection against sabotage on the ground but left them woefully exposed to aerial bombardment.

The senior officers met with Bert Kienzle, an administration officer who was in charge of the native carriers. Bert owned a plantation in the Yodda Valley, not far from Kokoda, and at the commencement of the campaign had volunteered to organise a native carrier force responsible for supply. Bert's plantation had an airstrip, as did the village of Kokoda, a fact that now gave the area obvious strategic importance, and he had been flying over the ranges for years. Bert had observed a strange geographical feature on top of the ranges to the east of the main track — two broad, flat expanses of grassland in the middle of the jungle. It was presumed that a prehistoric out-pouring of volcanic lava had left behind an acidic soil that prevented tree growth. Realising that his native carriers had no way of maintaining sufficient supplies if forced to man handle everything up the track, Bert convinced the high command in Moresby to attempt re-supply by air. Bert had taken it upon himself to cut a track to these 'grass lakes' and had given them the name 'Myola'. If indeed supplies had been dropped here by the small number of aircraft remaining, they had evidently been lost in the boggy marshes of the grass lake or in the surrounding jungle. It was also possible they had never arrived at all. The supply planes were flown by American civilians under contract to the US Air Force and some of the pilots were regarded as unreliable cowboys, more interested in their own safety than the admittedly hazardous task they had been assigned.

Continuing their march without sufficient supplies was not an option, so Lieutenant Colonel Key conferred with his brigade commander, Arnold Potts. They ordered all the men to assist the native carriers in searching the marshes and nearby jungle and enough rations were eventually gathered for one company to be able to continue its advance. Potts decided that the bulk of the force would have to wait at Myola until more supplies arrived by whatever means. It was by no means an ideal situation as no commander would have chosen to feed his forces piecemeal into battle, but there was no viable alternative.

Early in the afternoon, a runner found Stan and summoned him to a meeting with Key and Potts. Again he was tasked with leading the advance of the battalion. Potts was going to move forward and establish his brigade headquarters at Alola, two kilometres south of another small village called Isurava, where the 39th Battalion was known to be digging in and preparing for the latest Japanese advance. Stan would wait at Alola for Potts. Once the headquarters was established, Stan and his section would go forward to Isurava. There, Stan would meet with Lieutenant Colonel Ralph Honner, commander of the 39th Battalion, to gain an appreciation of the forward dispositions of the Australian troops and the presumed location and strength of the enemy. Stan would then be required to return to brigade headquarters at Alola and meet with, and brief, each of the companies of the 2/14th as they moved to take up their positions at the front.

Stan shook his section awake before dawn and they quietly shouldered their packs and rifles and set off north, away from Myola and down into the valley of Eora Creek. As the small patrol made its way along the steep, northern escarpments of the ranges, the track literally fell out of the clouds. A gust of warm air that surged up from the valley carried with it the sound of the foaming cascade of Eora Creek that ran roughly parallel to the track. They dropped down to the valley floor and forded the stream where the carriers had established a small ammunition dump. Stan's men pushed on to Templeton's Crossing, a track intersection named after Captain Sam Templeton, the Officer Commanding B Company of the 39th Battalion — the first Australian unit to pass this way several weeks earlier. The trail then wound upwards again before descending to another crossing several hours later. After more than a week in the mountains they had become more accustomed to the conditions and found themselves making good time up what only a few days ago had seemed like impossibly sheer inclines.

Once Brigadier Potts was well established in his headquarters at Alola, Stan and his section set off for Isurava. The small party was now well and truly in enemy territory. Their senses were alert to every sound and possible movement in the undergrowth. After an hour and a half of cautious advance, their watches told them they were drawing near to the Australian perimeter at Isurava. They were now under as much threat from twitchy Australian listening posts as they were from the enemy.

They stealthily made their way down to what they guessed was their last creek crossing when Stan thought he saw movement behind one of the large boulders in the middle of the stream. A single raise of the arm sent his men into contact drill formation. They immediately spread out on either side of the track and, while maintaining visual contact, crouched down and moved forward as quietly as possible. Stan hoped any noise they made would be shielded by the rushing waters of the creek. He slipped off the safety latch on his service revolver and kept steady aim at the boulder as they drew to within twenty paces of the creek. Was he hearing things, or was that someone whistling? They were startled to see the head of a man, staring into a hand mirror, emerge from behind the rock, his face a lather of shaving cream. Without looking in their direction, the man called nonchalantly, 'If you're looking for the boss, he's waiting for you at BHQ. He was expecting you two hours ago.'

Once Stan spoke to Honner he immediately got the impression that operations were beginning to diverge drastically from what he and the other AIF units had expected. Honner's summation of the situation was clear and concise. Maroubra Force, as the Australian units in this sector were now referred to, had been tasked with 'preventing Japanese penetration of the ranges', 'the recapture of Kokoda' and then 'the conduct of offensive actions' that would throw the invaders back into the sea. The reality at the front made a mockery of headquarters' thinking. Honner's unit of several hundred militiamen had been in the ranges for five weeks and had confronted the leading elements of the Japanese force, at that stage numbering in excess of 3500 men. The Japanese force, Honner explained, was far larger and far better supported than anything Stan had been led to believe. Stan looked at the 300 men, all who were left of Honner's battalion: tired, haggard, sick and emaciated, scraping weapon pits into the jungle floor with their tin hats and bayonets. Orders calling for 'offensive action' were clearly a nonsense. 'Isurava could yet become Australia's Thermopylae,' Honner told Stan. This was startling language, coming from an Australian battalion commander, but as Stan listened to the patrol reports coming in from Honner's constant reconnaissance it was obvious that the severity of the situation was not being exaggerated.

Had the Japanese chosen to attack the 39th Battalion immediately and in force, the Australians would have been overrun within hours. Honner was not yet aware of it, but the bulk of the Japanese Force, known as the South Seas Detachment, would not land until 20 August, and as it would take them up to a week to make their way inland the 39th Battalion was to have several days reprieve. Meanwhile the 39th Battalion continually sent out reconnaissance and fighting patrols.

Over the next few days, Potts and the 21st Brigade Headquarters established themselves at Alola while Stan and the intelligence section were free to make their own reconnaissance patrols. The one positive element of Stan's observations was the excellent geographical nature of the defensive position Honner had chosen. It lay astride the main track that ran along one side of the valley, parallel to but well above the main creek. As one approached the perimeter from the rear, the high ground was on the left and the low ground on the right. A tributary creek that ran at right angles to the track formed the rear of the perimeter. Another tributary creek that also bisected the track formed the 'front line'. Over the millennia, what came to be known as Front Creek had gouged twenty-metre almost vertical banks, which any attacker would find difficult to scale. To the right, the ground fell away sharply to the valley floor.

The Bloody Track

There was one weak spot, however, and that was on the high, left flank of the perimeter. Here it was possible for an attacker to look down on the defenders. 'He who holds the high ground, holds the advantage' is one of the 'Principles of War'. Nonetheless, Honner had fallen on a stroke of good fortune that lessened the natural disadvantages of this sector. Well before the war, the local villagers had cut a patch of jungle for a native garden on a relatively flat section of ground that now lay just beyond the defensive perimeter. Honner had his men slash the gardens to ankle height with their bayonets. He was absolutely certain this was where the Japanese would concentrate their attacks, but now they would have to do so over open ground, devoid of protective cover, in full view of his defenders who positioned their pits strategically within the thick bush just inside the perimeter boundary.

It was a good defensive locality, but as Stan spoke to the officers and soldiers of the 39th Battalion and gathered what intelligence he could about their past month of fighting, a grim picture emerged. When the Japanese had landed at Buna on the north coast of Papua five weeks earlier, the 39th had only one company of 120 men on the north side of the ranges. Under the command of Captain Sam Templeton, the men had fought a series of patrol actions and ambushes, delaying the Japanese advance as best they could. They fell back on Kokoda just as the rest of the battalion, under the command of Bill Owen, had come forward over the ranges. Owen concentrated his force on the small plateau where the Kokoda government station was located. They were soon engaged in a pitched battle with thousands of crack Japanese troops. Owen, a veteran of earlier battles on New Britain, was among the first to be killed.

Outnumbered, the battalion fell back to the foothills of the ranges where Major Alan Cameron temporarily assumed command. Lacking sound intelligence on the Japanese, Cameron unwisely ordered the battalion to retake Kokoda. One company managed to do so unopposed, but it was quickly pushed out of its position. Thirty men were killed in these brief but intense encounters. On hearing of Bill Owen's death, Port Moresby sent forward Lieutenant Colonel Ralph Honner to take command of the 39th.

Nobody could be better placed than Stan to make a judgement on Ralph Honner as both a man and soldier. Stan observed him on the Kokoda Track and at Gona, and later fought beside him in the Ramu and Markham valleys. Honner was born in Fremantle. He played senior Australian Rules football for Claremont and represented his university in rugby and athletics while completing his law degree. He worked as a solicitor and barrister before serving in Libya, Greece and Crete as an officer with the 6th Division. Stan thought Honner was 'quiet and unassuming in appearance and manner' and an outstanding commander of great personal courage. Above all, he had a great understanding of, and genuine affection for, his men. Stan could attest to all this. Only once did he have cause to criticise him. Honner was normally a meticulous planner, and thorough and unhurried when it came to reconnaissance. On one occasion, however, in the Markham Valley, he refused to heed Stan's warning of the need for more caution and he was seriously wounded in an ambush.

Stan had to leave the 39th to its own fate while he returned to Alola to brief Potts at brigade headquarters. He had barely passed through the rear of the perimeter when the boom of ranging mortars and Japanese artillery rained down on the Australian positions. The wounded of the 39th had been evacuated to a regimental aid post at Alola and immediately identified the sound as that of the much-feared Japanese mountain gun, which had been dragged all the way from the coast and reassembled on the jungle spur overlooking the Australian positions. These guns weighed an amazing 540 kilos. The roar of gunfire was complemented by the chatter of the Japanese Juki 'woodpecker' heavy machine-guns raking the 39th's pits above

The Bloody Track

Front Creek. Of a larger calibre than the Australian Brens, they carved their own fire-lanes through the thick jungle. After a day of intermittent fire, the once thick foliage immediately before the Australian pits had been torn to shreds. The Australians had been forced to leave their heavy Vickers .303 machine-guns and their specialist crews in reserve in Port Moresby, as the allied command had been convinced that it would be impossible to carry them over the ranges. Consequently, the defenders at Isurava had nothing to match these lethal Japanese weapons.

Stan felt greatly pained to be in Alola, so close to the drama unfolding over the ridge but not being able to help. The men in Alola knew how drained the 39th was at this point, but Stan and Roy Watson had their orders and their own important role to fulfil. They set about preparing themselves to brief the advancing companies of the 2/14th as they arrived along the track from Eora Creek. Roy Watson was part of Stan's intelligence section and the two men had made detailed notes and sketches of the topography and the Australian dispositions as well as the likely direction of Japanese attacks. This enabled them to build a three-dimensional mud-model on the earthen floor of one of the native shelters. It sounded somewhat crude but it was becoming an accepted method of situational briefings.

Roy was just pushing the last mounds of earth into place and Stan was distributing the markers that represented the Australian and Japanese positions when the first 2/14th troops, C Company, under Captain Gerry Dickenson, clambered up into Alola over the lip of the steep rise from Eora Creek village. Stan had only just begun to present an overview of the situation when there was an eruption of rifle and automatic fire from the direction of Isurava, obviously signalling the first of the Japanese attacks. Knowing the desperate state of the 39th, Dickenson was sorely tempted to forgo the briefing and move forward without delay, but Potts insisted that the briefing continue.

At Isurava, the Australians established a roughly circular perimeter about the size of a city block. The border was defended in depth. That is, it was not a single trench-line but a series of two-man pits extending back up to fifty metres. The pits had interlocking arcs of fire, whereby the rearmost pits covered the outer-lying pits. The regimental aid post and the battalion headquarters were roughly in the centre of the locality. The headquarters was in touch with each section of the perimeter by telephone wire or by runners. Reserves were on hand to reinforce any sector under threat. After Stan had presented his intelligence update to the company commanders, Potts gave a brief outline of his orders for the relief of the 39th Battalion. The companies of the 2/14th would 'superimpose' over their respective units in the 39th, and once the entire unit was established on the perimeter the survivors of the 39th could pick themselves up and make their way back to Alola.

The first 2/14th company to move forward through the last few kilometres of jungle to the besieged village would be Claude Nye's B Company, in which Hal was serving as the commander of 10 Platoon. They would relieve their corresponding militia company, which had established its weapon pits in the canefield high on the uppermost parts of the ridge where the defences were most in danger of being encircled by the Japanese. Gerry Dickenson's C Company would move up behind Nye and take up positions inside the 39th's C Company perimeter, to the lower right of the track, in the thin grove of native gardens that separated the village from the gorges of Eora and Front Creek.

Stan had been thoroughly briefed by Don Simonson and Bob Sword, two of the more experienced lieutenants of the 39th Battalion. He gave the troops an overview of the situation at the forward positions. The Australians had been conducting their rigorous schedule of patrolling operations in the thickly wooded ridges and valleys that surrounded the village. From 22 August,

The Bloody Track

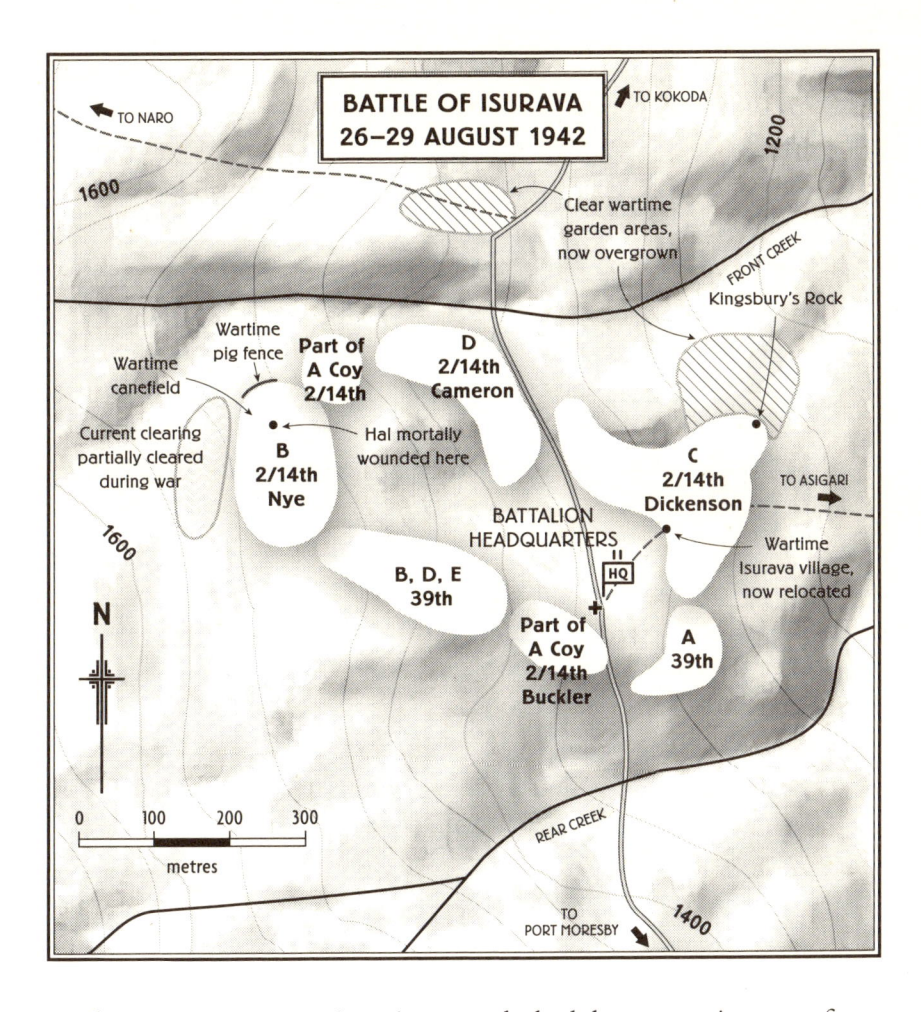

BATTLE OF ISURAVA 26–29 AUGUST 1942

eight to ten man section-size patrols had been moving out for twenty-four or forty-eight hour periods to monitor the movement of Japanese troops. These had primarily been standing patrols, where the section would move out into the jungle and occupy a small 'harbour' for one or two days to observe any enemy movement while remaining unobserved. Several other patrols had been either cut off or annihilated by the Japanese. Stan gave brief recommendations on the composition of these patrols in terms of numbers and weaponry, timing of rotation and the best tactics to avoid detection. They could not afford a repeat of the losses suffered by the 39th.

Stan then went on to talk about the likely timing of attacks. European armies had traditionally marched through the day, prepared through the night, and attacked at dawn. The Japanese would group at two or three assembly areas and rest all day. Attacks would often start after dusk, or at any unpredictable hour of the night. In fact, they preferred night attacks on areas where they believed the terrain was important or vulnerable. While these attacks were obviously harder to coordinate, the Japanese clearly felt that the darkness made their banzai-style massed charges more effective.

Despite reports to the contrary, the Japanese did not commence all their offensive operations with massed, full-frontal assaults. These would come later. Like the Australians, they conducted a rigorous schedule of patrolling and probing with small attacks designed only to determine the strength and disposition of the defences. Ideally, the Japanese were seeking avenues through which their force could encircle the defenders and attack from the flanks or the rear, and these initial, feigned attacks were designed to draw fire from the Australian defenders. The intensity and direction of this fire would then enable the attackers to assess the strength and depth of the defences. One of the hardest lessons that had to be conveyed to the commanders, and then drilled into the infantrymen, was to hold their fire even when the enemy was clearly in view and well within range. If it proved to be a feigned attack, and the Australians gave away their positions too early, they could expect a later assault with ten times as many attackers.

The Japanese used the crudest of ruses to draw fire from the Australians, from bugle calls to combined chants or blood-curdling yells. When the mass attacks did come, the Australians referred to them as Banzai charges as the Japanese actually yelled 'Tenno Heika banzai!' meaning, 'May the Emperor reign for ten thousand years' as they rushed towards the enemy. The nerve-racking effect of these charges on the defenders was considerable. In the dark of night and through the thick, swirling mists of the jungle, these cries had an understandably disconcerting effect on the Australians.

Stan knew that he was talking to professional soldiers, hardened by months of fighting in the Middle East, but he chose to recount two anecdotes to ram home his message. The first related to an officer from the 9th Division whom he had encountered in Palestine before the officer and his unit had been rushed into action in Libya. The officer had been captured earlier, but had escaped. The officer recounted how General Rommel had inspected the prisoner-of-war camp and spoken individually with each prisoner. When asked about treatment and conditions, several Australians had stepped forward to complain of maltreatment. Rommel interrogated the German officers responsible and ordered the issues be adequately redressed. Germany was a signatory to the 1929 Geneva Convention covering the treatment of prisoners, and complied with it. Suffice to say that Japan was not a signatory.

Stan then went on to relate an incident that had been recounted to him at Isurava. One of the men from the 39th had been wounded in the withdrawal from Kokoda and captured. The Australians formed a defensive perimeter at the small village of Deniki, and the Japanese commenced their probing attacks. When the Australians had maintained their discipline and withheld fire, they were then exposed to a terrifying experience. The captured Australian had been dragged to within earshot of the Australian positions and was subjected to some unimaginable torture. His screams tore at the Australians, whose natural instinct was to rush the Japanese positions.

This was exactly the reaction the Japanese had wanted to elicit. To attack recklessly would have been suicidal. This was an example of the vicious nature of the enemy. This was no longer a war with rules of engagement. Western concepts such as honour and chivalry among combatants on the battlefield were unknown to the Japanese. This was a savage fight to the death. Anyone who was captured was liable to be subjected to torture. In fact, no prisoners would be taken on either side as the Japanese would not surrender under any circumstances, and in the unlikely event that the Australians captured a wounded Japanese, if they did not kill him he would kill himself. At the conclusion of Stan's briefing, no one spoke for a full minute.

As the first of the 2/14th platoons set off to relieve 39th Battalion, the volume of fire from the battle intensified yet again. All through the previous day and night, the Japanese had probed the Australian perimeter, expending a great deal of ammunition and making as much noise as possible, without launching a full-scale attack. Hal, as part of B Company, took his platoon up to their position on the high ground on Thursday afternoon, 27 August, reinforcing the 39th Battalion's B Company sector, and immediately came under enemy attack. D Company took up its position covering Front Creek. Gerry Dickenson's C Company took over the low ground on the right flank. During the night the Japanese continued with their usual ruses, calling out in English and making a great deal of noise. One C Company man was bayoneted through the arm without seeing his assailant approach.

At daybreak on 28 August the Japanese mountain gun and mortars commenced a barrage that everyone knew heralded a major attack. The shells burst in the treetops and sprayed shrapnel over a radius of forty metres. Then the Juki machine-guns opened up, chopping off the trunks of small trees and ricocheting bullets off the larger ones. Amid wild yelling from Japanese not even taking part in the attack, the enemy swarmed towards the Australian lines. There were few bespectacled midgets among them. They were generally battle-hardened tall men of fine physique, coming mainly from the mountainous Kochi Prefecture on Shikoku. Never having faced such concerted opposition, however, the Japanese soldiers must have been stunned by the reception they received. Those who survived the enfilading arcs of Bren gun fire were met with rifles and Tommy guns, followed by a hail of grenades. Those who still came forward were met with bayonets. Attack after attack was driven back and the anticipated weak spots failed to materialise.

In the B Company area, which everyone referred to as 'the cane field', 11 Platoon, under Lieutenant George Moore, was subjected to particularly fierce and continuous attacks, probably because the enemy had determined that this was a junction of two Australian companies and there were no physical impediments to their advance. Towards evening, Hal and his platoon took over this hot-spot and George moved his platoon slightly closer to his right, to tighten the link with the D Company positions. By nightfall, enemy casualties were estimated to be 350 while the brigade's official minimum estimate was put at 300.

The Japanese 1st Battalion commander, Colonel Tsukomoto, withdrew his remaining men to their holding position, but the following day he was joined by another two full battalions. Given that a full-strength Japanese battalion totalled 1100 men as opposed to the 550 that made up an Australian battalion, and even with the 39th Battalion making up a reserve, the 2/14th was outnumbered by about six to one.

From first light on 29 August the pattern of the previous day was repeated, but this time the attacks were in far greater number and intensity. The thirty men of Hal's 10 Platoon repulsed eleven concerted attacks during the day. When the Australians reoccupied the area two months later they counted 250 enemy dead in front of this position.

Stan was constantly moving about the perimeter, reporting back to Arthur Key on where reserves needed to come forward. As he inched his way along the track that marked the perimeter between C and D Companies, he surprised a Japanese patrol darting across the track directly in front of him. He let fly with a volley of shots from his service revolver, felling two of the enemy while the others dissolved into the undergrowth. Even though the jungle was incredibly thick and the foliage so dense along the main track that it was like walking through a tunnel, the Japanese had obviously been able to determine that this was a junction point between two companies. Their ability to discern possible weak spots was quite extraordinary. On Stan's advice, Arthur Key sent 9 Platoon forward to strengthen this position and these reinforcements arrived only minutes after the Japanese had hurled themselves at the C Company perimeter and achieved a significant breakthrough. Lindsay Bear took up a Bren gun and killed fifteen of the enemy at point blank range. For his gallantry and leadership during these engagements he was awarded the Military Medal.

More reserves were called upon and Sergeant Bob Thompson from the signals platoon came forward with a party of his own platoon as well as some men from the headquarters company. Lindsay Bear, Alan Avery and Bruce Kingsbury attached themselves to Bob's party. Lindsay had been badly wounded by this stage and could not carry on, so this left Bruce as the only Bren gunner in the party. Bob led the men in a clearing patrol formation outside the C Company area, spreading them out in an extended line. As they advanced at a slow walking pace, Bruce swept the ground in front of them with his Bren gun, scattering the enemy who still lurked in the bush.

The party completed an arc, right across the front of the C Company perimeter. As they neared the end of their sweep they passed a large boulder on top of which were perched several C Company men who had been bypassed by the attacking Japanese. Bob's party paused momentarily to talk with them and at that moment, perhaps as Bruce lowered his guard, he was shot and killed by a sniper. Bruce was posthumously awarded the Victoria Cross, the first for an Australian in the Pacific and the only

Victoria Cross ever to be won on Australian soil, as Papua was a territory of Australia at the time.

Enemy pressure continued to mount throughout the day and Lieutenant Colonel Key decided to pull the Australians back under the cover of darkness as part of a phased withdrawal, but everywhere the enemy pressed at their heels. If it were not for men like Charlie McCallum who provided covering fire for the men carrying the stretchers, many wounded men would not have survived. Stan remembered Charlie as a good-natured farmer from the Tarra Valley in Gippsland. A big, barrel-chested man and a local wood-chopping champion, Charlie was firing his Bren gun from the hip. He had also acquired a Tommy gun from a wounded comrade and when his Bren gun magazine ran out he swung the Tommy gun forward with his left arm and fired this while he reloaded the Bren gun with his right hand. For this action he was awarded the Distinguished Conduct Medal. Charlie was killed just over a week later at the Battle of Brigade Hill.

It was evident that the Australians could not hold the area much longer. Key ordered Stan and Ralph Honner to scout back along the track and reconnoitre another fall-back position. This meant that Stan had to leave the rear of the battalion perimeter in the semi-darkness and enter the jungle that was infested with Japanese soldiers. About 500 metres beyond the rear creek, the track rose sharply up to a clearing where, on the edge of an escarpment, there were three native huts. This was known as the 'rest house' area as the huts had been used as shelters in pre-war days by Australian Government patrol officers, who called them by their pidgin English name of 'kiaps'. It was hardly an ideal position but it was the best that Stan could find, given the time that it would take to coordinate the movement of the entire battalion. He moved about the whole area in the dark, guided by a mist-shrouded moon that cast ghostly shadows in the clearings. On at least two occasions he was certain he passed within metres of Japanese patrols.

It was impossible to recognise anyone in this environment and they probably assumed he was one of their own.

After a nerve-racking three hour recce, from 6 to 9 p.m. in the eerie jungle darkness, Stan was able to report back to Key. After making radio contact with Brigadier Potts, Key ordered the general withdrawal to commence that Saturday night, 29 August. It was a nightmare manoeuvre and it took more than five hours to complete. Stan and the other men from his intelligence section had to act as guides, moving back and forward in the dark, leading every unit in the battalion to Stan's pre-determined fall-back positions.

The evacuation of the wounded was extraordinarily difficult. Stretchers had to be constructed out of poles and vines. Almost every man in the battalion took his turn at carrying although the regular stretcher-bearers, mainly men from the band, bore the brunt of the work. Captain Don Duffy, the regimental medical officer, and his team of orderlies battled ceaselessly against the mud and rain, trying to prevent the wounds from becoming infected. Assisted by a medical orderly, Con 'Vappy' Vafiopolous, and using a bare rock as an operating table, Don amputated one young soldier's almost severed foot. Many wounded men could barely walk but they refused to be carried and half-crawled and half-dragged themselves on vines and bushes back along the boggy track.

Some time between 10 and 11 p.m., a young private from Hal's platoon, George Woodward, came stumbling up the trail to find Stan. Although George took a few moments to catch his breath before passing on his message, Stan took in his ashen face and bloodstained uniform and immediately supposed the worst, steeling himself for the news he had hoped he would never have to hear. Hal had been wounded during the night's fighting, hit in the stomach by a burst of machine-gun fire as he had been moving between his foremost pits distributing grenades. The fighting in the cane field in front of 10 Platoon's position had been so vicious that the unit had exhausted its supply of Mills grenades and it was testament to the dire state of affairs in which the platoon had found itself as well as Hal's tremendous personal courage that, as platoon commander, it was necessary for him to move through the front pits during a fire-fight with a resupply.

Immediately behind George struggled four other men from 10 Platoon, Col Blume, Murray Bolitho, Bill Bray and Roy Howe. They clambered up the muddy slope with a prostrate form on a makeshift stretcher on their shoulders. George explained to Stan that, despite the volume of fire the platoon was receiving when Hal had been hit, his men had pushed forward to the edge of the perimeter to drag their wounded and much loved platoon commander to safety.

Don Duffy, the unit's medical officer, was meeting every stretcher case as it came into the new perimeter. The concept of triage nursing dates from the Napoleonic Wars when wounded soldiers were separated into three categories: the not-so-severe, the severe and the hopeless. A similar system operated in New Guinea. The medical officer would look at a wounded soldier and say to his orderly, 'one', 'two' or 'three'. This referred to the vials of morphine to be administered. One injection would dull the pain. Two would render a man with a severe wound semi-conscious. Three shots was a lethal overdose for a case considered beyond care. In the rigours of war, the Hippocratic Oath could not be applied in its traditional form. It was inhumane to keep a man alive when he was obviously going to die and might fall into the hands of the enemy who might murder or torture him. Likewise it would be immoral to endanger the lives of up to eight carriers who would be delayed unnecessarily and might themselves fall into enemy hands.

Don pulled back the blanket covering Hal and looked at his stomach. Stan was by his side and turned away in horror. It was all he could do to stop himself from retching. 'Will you stay with him for a few hours, Stan?' Don asked. Stan nodded. Don turned to his orderly. 'Make it a "two" then.'

Stan helped carry the stretcher several hundred metres back along the track and then the small party made its way into the bush and set the stretcher down in a small clearing. They nestled Hal against a sapling, loosened his webbing and made him as comfortable as possible. Stan sat beside him and held his hand. They talked of family, of childhood pranks, of times together in the bush. Stan sang quietly as Hal lapsed into periods of unconsciousness that became longer as the night wore on. Hal died in Stan's arms at 4 a.m. on 30 August 1942.

After Stan and Don Duffy had buried Hal in a shallow grave, Stan allowed himself a few moments of peace and solitude, those most rare and valuable of commodities in war. He sat in the tiny clearing beside the rough-hewn wooden cross as the first grey fingers of dawn began to probe through the thick canopy and tried to regain the composure that he knew would be expected of him. This day was to prove to be one of the most demanding and challenging of Stan's entire life. He stood and lingered over Hal's grave before wrenching himself away and striding back up the hundred metres of track to the rest house to find Key and Honner and help facilitate the extraction of the battalion from a position that was fast becoming untenable.

CHAPTER SEVEN

Retreat

By first light, the 2/14th Battalion, together with the remnants of the 39th Battalion and a company of the 53rd Militia Battalion, had formed a new, tight defensive position in the rest house area. Their right flank was secure because the land fell sharply. A frontal attack, up a sharp spur, would be easily contained. The high ground on the left flank was a different matter. Given that it had taken nearly all night for the battalion to relocate, there had been insufficient time to send out patrols to give warning of enemy movements from that direction. The Japanese had kept up constant harassing mortar fire on the Australian positions and a further withdrawal could not be delayed much longer. At 3 p.m. Key ordered C and D Companies to form up on the track and move back some distance to facilitate the withdrawal of the remainder of the force. A and B Companies would hold the front line until the last possible moment. Every unit would have to be formed up on the track by 5 p.m., the time set for the general withdrawal.

Stan moved about the units to ensure they had received and understood their orders. The wounded had to be assigned stretcher parties. All weapons and stores that could not be carried had to be rendered useless to the enemy. He barked orders at a group of young militiamen from the 53rd Battalion but they simply ignored him. This unit had been decimated by the fighting on the far side of the valley. They had lost several keys officers in the first days of action and sustained terrible losses. Discipline had obviously suffered and they were now in a state of disarray, masking their fear and fatigue with an air of listless distain. The signallers of the 2/14th had lost several men and Stan needed to find extra hands to carry their equipment. There was a genuine sense of urgency in everything Stan was doing and when he repeated his orders to the militiamen no one moved. Stan paused, drew himself upright and slowly walked over to the biggest of them — a young lad of no more than nineteen, sitting on his haunches. Their eyes met. With deliberate movements, Stan flicked the cover off his holster and drew out his Webley revolver, slipped off the safety catch, checked the weapon was loaded, cocked it, and pointed the barrel at the boy's ear. There was no need to repeat the orders for the third time.

During the previous night and all that morning, the 2nd Battalion of the Japanese 144th Regiment had worked its way around the high ground so that by 4 p.m. almost 1000 Japanese were lying in concealed positions in a rough line running parallel to the track, only a hundred metres or so above where the Australians were waiting for the signal to move. At precisely 4.55 p.m. a Japanese bugle call split the air. The Australians were then subjected to the most intense fire that any of the survivors could ever recall.

Everyone in the battalion, from private to colonel, was firing every weapon at his disposal as the Japanese pressed home their attack. It would only be a matter of seconds before the unit was wiped out if something wasn't done. Over the roar of the battle Stan yelled to the men around him to withdraw from the low side of the track, and all up and down the line small groups of men were doing the same. In ones and twos, sections and platoons, the Australians were diving for safety into the thick jungle as hundreds of Japanese swarmed onto the track from above. Any semblance of an ordered withdrawal was impractical. They literally jumped three to four metres down into the tangled web of undergrowth. The thorny leaves of the koporupoka jungle vines tore at them as they thrashed about trying to free themselves and find their footings.

Stan saw Jock Greenwood, a British Grenadier officer posted to the unit, grab the branch of a small sapling as he vaulted off the track. As he swung clear, a burst of automatic fire blasted the branch from its trunk and Jock tumbled over the edge of the escarpment, the branch still firmly in his grasp. Stan glanced around and saw Bill Lynn and the regimental sergeant major, Les Tipton, behind him, showered with shredded foliage. They half-ran and half-fell down the almost sheer jungle slope and after twenty minutes managed to reach the relative safety of the thick bush along Eora Creek, almost 800 metres below the track.

Just as Stan caught a glimpse of the waters below, his foot slipped on an exposed rock shelving. His feet went from under him and he was pitched forward. As he crashed to the ground, the small of his back took the full weight of his body. The pain was excruciating and he lay motionless, possibly blacking out for several minutes. Bill and Les tumbled down to where he was lying but could do nothing to help as they were too exhausted. A good ten minutes passed without a word. Stan rolled onto his side and tried to ease himself onto one elbow. The shooting pain up his spine was almost unbearable. Sitting up would be a challenge, let alone walking. They began checking one another for other injuries. Nothing other than cuts and abrasions. Stan took mental stock of their situation. In only a few moments, the 2/14th had been effectively wiped out as a fighting formation. They were obviously out of contact with their commander, Arthur Key, and the adjutant, Tommy Hall. Everyone must have been in a similar situation.

*Kokoda Track, Papua, 16 August 1942. (Left to right):
Lieutenant George Moore (killed in action 28 August 1942),
Lieutenant Hal Bisset (killed in action 30 August 1942),
Captain Claude Nye (killed in action 8 September 1942), Lieutenant
Lindsay Mason (severely wounded 29 September 1942), Lieutenant
Maurice 'Mocca' Tracey, MC (killed in action 29 November 1942).
The loss of these experienced commanders in such a short period of time
demonstrates the vicious nature of the fighting in Papua.*

Stan, Bill and Les checked what supplies they had between them. None of them had been wearing a backpack when the Japanese struck. Other than their weapons, ammunition and bayonets or knives, the only supplies they had were carried in small pouches attached to their webbing. Each had an emergency field service ration tin that would keep them going for several days and some basic first aid materials and field dressings. They had no protection against the weather other than the clothes they wore.

They agreed there was no point in trying to find a way back up to the tracks anywhere in this area. There was no option other than to follow the creek upstream in the hope of outpacing the Japanese.

There were definitely Australian units up ahead of them who would attempt to hold the main track, giving all those cut off as much time as possible to regain the Australian lines.

Stan was not particularly worried about Japanese patrols. The bush was too thick. Moreover, the Japanese would concentrate on moving forward, clearing any resistance and opening it up for the bulk of their force still coming up from Kokoda. Stan also knew that they were bound to come across other members of the battalion in the same situation as themselves. In the remaining hour of light they came across eight others including three walking wounded.

The pain in Stan's back was still agonising. All elite footballers suffer serious injuries at some time in their careers. They have to learn how to differentiate between injuries that are so serious that rest and recuperation are the only options, and those they need to ignore and play through. Learning how to manage pain is part of this process. In other circumstances, Stan's injury would have hospitalised him. It took all his physical and mental strength to stand upright and keep moving. That wasn't sufficient, though — he had to set the pace, and a cracking one at that. He was the senior officer in the party and it was obvious everyone else was looking to him for leadership.

As he walked, he began to think through other options that may be open to them. Going bush in the hope of finding a native garden as a food supply and laying up was a possibility, but what then? Besides, to find gardens meant climbing to higher ground. There were tracks on both sides of the valley but they were now in the hands of the Japanese. The possibility of detection would be much greater. Capture meant death. He dismissed these thoughts almost at once. They had no real option but to push on, whatever the cost. The pain was so bad that his head spun, and he felt nauseated and disoriented.

Several kilometres up the valley, above them to their right, would be Alola. Via the main track, it would have taken them less than an hour to get there, but deep in the jungle the hours dragged by as the small group cut its way with bayonets and bush knives through the thick tangle of vines and foliage in the darkness. With no more than instinct and dead reckoning, Stan felt confident they were close to intersecting a major track that ran from Alola to the village of Abauri on the other side of the valley. It was certain to be in use by the enemy. Stan and Les crept forward to investigate. Sure enough, after fewer than fifty paces the pair emerged onto the native pad before they'd even seen it.

For a moment they knelt in the darkness by the edge of the track, listening in silence. Les thought he could hear voices being carried to them on the breeze. Stan knew there was an Australian supply dump on the track up near Alola, where this track intersected the main one. Was there a remote possibility that Alola was still in Australian hands? Was there a chance that the Japanese had not continued with their advance but waited till the bulk of their force caught up to their leading elements? Highly unlikely. If the Australians were still at Alola, they would be sure to maintain absolute silence. The voices they thought they heard were bound to be Japanese, but Stan could not resist the temptation to investigate. Besides, there was a chance of finding abandoned stores on or near the track. Concealed in the foliage, the two men crept closer to the village. They dropped to all fours and crawled over a small rise just short of the junction. Their navigation had been spot-on, as had been their assumptions: they could now see around sixty Japanese troops about twenty metres away — talking, laughing and feasting on tins of bully beef, courtesy of the Australian Government.

Stan and Les held a short whispered conference. 'I've still got two grenades,' Les said. 'Why don't we sort these bastards out?' Stan was silent for a moment, seriously considering the proposition. They had the opportunity of wiping out nearly all the Japanese clustered around the pile of stores, but getting away undetected would be near impossible. Stan was still suffering the psychological trauma of Hal's death. The recurrent memory of tossing the earth over his brother's body in the shallow jungle grave, not twenty-four hours previously, brought such anguish that the desire to die here in an act of bloody revenge was unnervingly strong. Les pulled the grenades from his belt and handed one to Stan. Stan was astonished to see his hand trembling. He had been in so many life-threatening situations during the past year and had prided himself on his coolness, self-control and sound judgement. Now his head was spinning and he was sweating. Perhaps a minute passed, he was not sure, but for some reason he became so conscious of his pounding heartbeat that he put one hand to the side of his neck. It felt as if the carotid artery was just about to burst under the pressure. He started to breathe deeply, and without any conscious will the heartbeat slowed within a matter of moments and a calmness and sense of self-preservation returned.

Les was loath to give up the opportunity of doing such damage to the enemy, even if it cost him his life, but he knew Stan was right. Stan had been in Alola a week before the rest of the battalion and his knowledge of the jungle and the trails was vital if the small party was to regain the Australian lines. Silently, and without further discussion, the pair crept back to the rest of the party with the news that Alola was now in Japanese hands.

It was now 5 a.m. and Stan had not slept for more than two days. This night had been spent in combat and attempting to coordinate the chaotic fighting withdrawal, and the previous night he had been awake, caring for, and burying Hal. The events of the past forty-eight hours had been unbelievably physically and emotionally draining, but the task that lay ahead was no less daunting. Stan told the men to grab an hour's rest before dawn, but most of the group found it difficult to get any real sleep. At first light Stan assembled his party and told them his plan. They would bush-bash through the jungle, find a way to cross Eora Creek and then try to pick up one of the small native trails in the jungle on the eastern side of the valley. They would make for Eora Creek village and then push on to Templeton's Crossing if the village was held by the Japanese.

Stan tasked Bill with doing a stores check and discovered that the ad hoc patrol had less than one emergency ration per man, and no groundsheets or equipment of any kind other than their weapons, ammunition, and the clothes they stood up in. Their green ration tins contained three meals, each sealed in a bituminous paper carton protected by a covering of wax. A typical meal was a three ounce (85 gram) packet of biscuits and a four ounce (110 gram) tin of stew. The three meals were normally for a twenty-four hour period. Stan and his men had already consumed one meal. From now on their daily consumption would be two biscuits and less than half a small tin of stew, washed down with a cup of cold tea with half a teaspoon of sugar and powdered milk.

Three of the men had been wounded the previous day but were able to walk. Stan asked Bill to dress and re-bandage the wounds. At dawn the party set off down the steep slope to the stream. Eora Creek was less than a kilometre away but it took the group the better part of the day to reach it as they had to pick their way down the almost vertical hillside while making every effort to conceal themselves from any Japanese patrols.

When they reached Eora Creek in the early afternoon it was running high, roaring and foaming as it cascaded down the narrow valley. In dry weather one could ford the creek almost anywhere, but now it ran so high and with such ferocity that it would be impossible to wade or swim across. Stan's party needed to find a crossing but they knew the Japanese would be using and observing all the main crossing points. Throughout the afternoon, making every effort to remain unseen, the small group ranged up and down the steep bank of the creek looking for a reasonable place to cross. Late in the day they found a spot where a recent storm had felled a great tree in the valley. If one could balance, one could walk across the log to the far bank. The problem, however, was that anyone on the log would be perilously exposed to any Japanese patrols that were almost sure to be in the valley. Still, Stan had no option. The party *had* to cross the stream, so one by one the men edged their way across the roaring waters.

Luckily the party was not spotted by a Japanese patrol, but when they reached the far bank they realised that someone had indeed been observing their crossing. 'Hey, boys,' a hoarse whisper hissed from the thick foliage. 'In here.' Stan crept into the thick jungle on the southern bank and found two soldiers from the 2/16th Battalion hidden in the bush. Stan recognised one as Captain George Wright, a company commander he had known in the Middle East. He and another young soldier were in a similar position to Stan and his men, cut off from their unit and with scarce food and supplies.

Les told the Western Australians they were making for Templeton's and suggested Wright do the same. Wright agreed, but 'on one condition'.

Stan's heart sank as he felt sure Wright was going to insist on his seniority to lead the party, but he insisted that Lieutenant Bisset take command. 'He'll do a better job of getting us out of here than I ever bloody will.' There were laughs and murmurs of assent from the men. Stan nodded in agreement. After a brief conference, they continued after dark up the far side of the valley to a small native footpad that Stan had reconnoitred when stationed in Alola. The men marvelled at Stan's ability to navigate in the jungle. He could find bearings by the stars and the mossy sides of the trees and knew the area better than anyone in the brigade. Despite his back pain, his physical fitness was also beginning to set him apart. With almost no food or sleep, most of the party struggled to remain conscious, let alone put one foot in front of the other, but Stan navigated through the dark jungle, cutting a path for the group with his bayonet. To the astonishment of all, he brought the group to the small native track he knew to be in the area. Stan then found a concealed spot for the party to rest. Bill and Les organised sentries for the night while the small group collapsed into a fitful sleep on the jungle floor.

The winter and spring of 1942 were the wettest in history in the Owen Stanley Range and that night, like every other, the cold rain poured down through the canopy. Stan's party lay huddled together on the sodden floor in shirts and shorts with no ponchos or groundsheets. Some of the troops began shivering uncontrollably in the cold mountain air. Several of the party had contracted malaria, as every Australian soldier eventually would during the campaigns in New Guinea.

Over the coming days, Stan set a tough regimen for his small party. Every morning before dawn he would wake those who had been able to sleep in the freezing night and got everyone ready to set off at first light. He had learned from George Wright that Eora Creek village was now held by the Japanese so he decided to head further up the valley to where the Kokoda Track forded the creek at Templeton's Crossing. The Australians would be attempting to slow the Japanese advance by setting up defences along the track but Stan knew that it would be only a matter of days before Templeton's fell to the enemy and then his group would have almost no hope of survival. Thus, Stan set a cracking pace for his poor men. Navigating by the sun and the stars and using his extremely poor survey map, he led the party through thick jungle and down native footpads, through re-entrants and small streams, all the while keeping off the main track that was undoubtedly being used by the Japanese.

By the third day, the party was nearing total exhaustion. Stan, forging ahead as usual, suddenly found himself alone. The others, it appeared, had been unable to keep up. Stan could hear them labouring up the jungle slope behind him. 'Lieutenant Bisset,' Les Tipton boomed out in his RSM's voice, 'You need to damn-well slow down. One of these poor bloody boys is going to die if you keep this up.' Stan knew that Tipton was correct. The men were in such a state that surely they could not survive this torment much longer. Nonetheless, he refused.

Stan insisted that none of them could slow down. 'We're *all* going to bloody die out here if the Japs get to Templeton's before us. We need to keep moving fast. Faster than this.' The rest of the party now gathered around, silently watching the confrontation. The thought of keeping this pace up seemed scarcely possible, but dying from exhaustion and exposure was preferable to falling into the hands of the Japanese. They knew what their fate would be then.

'Right, that's enough talk. Let's go.' Without another word Stan turned, bayonet in hand, and continued cutting a meagre path through the tangle of vines. Bill, Les and the others, squatting on their haunches gasping for breath, glanced at each other before dragging themselves to their feet and stumbling after Stan.

That night was the worst so far. The rain was heavier than Stan had experienced so he helped the party make a rough shelter out of vines and pandanus leaves. It was almost useless against the monsoon but it made some impact on the men's morale. The party of thirteen huddled virtually on top of each other in an attempt to keep warm. 'Damn,' whispered George Wright, 'What the hell is that stench?' Initially, Stan could barely detect the odour but it grew and grew over the next few minutes and became almost unbearable.

'It's the wounds,' said Bill Lynn, who had been tasked with dressing and tending to the bullet wounds of the three injured members of the party. They were festering and there were no new shell dressings. Each man had one emergency shell dressing in his pocket as per procedure, and after three days in the jungle Bill had used them all, but still the wounds festered and suppurated. The party had no other first aid equipment: no antiseptic, no spare bandages or stitches, and certainly no anaesthetic. The pain from the wounds had been bad enough for the three young soldiers over the past days but now that the wounds were infected and were festering with pus, the pain was becoming much worse. With the stench of the rotting wounds from the men lying on top of him, the biting cold and the torrential rain, Stan did not sleep that night.

The condition of the party deteriorated even further the following day, but by their fifth day in the jungle Stan was confident they were close to the main track and Templeton's Crossing. They were still unsure of the location of the Japanese forces, who perhaps already occupied the crossing, so Stan gave the order that absolute silence be adhered to as the tiny group made its way down the last slope to where the trail crossed back over Eora Creek. Every so often Stan would silently signal for the group to halt and the men would pause and listen to the sounds of the jungle. At one such pause, Stan and Bill heard rustling in the jungle immediately below them. The group froze. Stan quietly fixed his bayonet to the rifle he was carrying and crept forward. As he reached out to part the foliage before him, it was whipped away from the other side and Stan found another bayonet directly in front of his face. He froze and it took him a moment to focus. He had been expecting a Japanese soldier but instead found himself staring into the blue eyes of Allan Haddy, the Western Australian boxer he had fought and then befriended on the voyage to the Middle East. 'G'day Stan,' said Haddy. 'They were wondering where you had got to.'

Most of Stan's party collapsed from relief, too weak to even walk. Haddy's 2/16th troops, the Australian rearguard holding the track directly above Templeton's Crossing, had to assist the exhausted men down and across the stream. Stan, to Haddy's surprise, was in remarkable shape and the first thing he did was bombard Allan with questions on the situation of the brigade. Haddy was impressed by Stan's focus after so many days without food or sleep and it added to the respect the pair had for each other. During the Lebanon campaign, Stan had been immensely impressed by the fact that Haddy had swum the Litani River with a barge rope in his teeth under French machine-gun fire, being wounded twice in the process. The brigade had then been able to ford the river in boats, pulled by hand along the rope Alan had secured to the far bank.

Most of the 2/14th, Stan discovered, had been forced into the bush but small groups had drifted in over the past few days and were concentrated on the far side of the valley. The 2/16th had fared somewhat better in the withdrawal from Alola and was holding the track and the crossing so the rest of the brigade could regroup. Haddy had patrols out up the track, putting in ambushes, but warned that the Japanese would be with them that day. He was correct. Only half an hour after Stan had met Haddy and crossed the creek through the 2/16th's defensive positions, the Japanese burst out of the jungle across the narrow stream and attacked the exhausted Western Australians holding the crossing.

From the defences at Templeton's, the old wartime mail-route ran south-west up the steepest section of the Naro Ridge and down to Kagi village. By the time Stan and his intelligence section had advanced up the track a fortnight earlier, a new track had been cut from Myola down through the moss forest along the slopes of Mount Bellamy. It was along this trail that Stan and his beleaguered party now made their way. Those men of the 2/14th who had been able to regain the Australian lines were currently resting at Myola and Stan and Les were determined that they should reunite with the battalion as soon a possible. The steep climb up Mount Bellamy was challenging for any man, but for Stan and his thirteen followers it was even more demanding. Still, the tired men pushed on until they arrived, spent, at Myola on the afternoon of 2 September.

The first thing on Stan's mind was to report to the battalion commander and bring himself up to speed on the condition of the unit and the state of the fighting. 'Where's Lieutenant Colonel Key?' he demanded of the first 2/14th troops he found resting in the open, sunny expanse of the Myola lakebed. The troops, boots off for the first time after weeks of fighting, declined to answer the question directly. The reason soon became obvious: Key was missing in action along with a considerable portion of the battalion. Much of the unit had been pushed down off the trail because of the Japanese attack during the retreat from Isurava. While some men, like Stan's small group, had been able to regain the Australian lines before the Japanese stormed into Templeton's Crossing, many had not been seen again and Arthur Key was amongst that group. Les Tipton, who had been so angry with Stan for pushing the party beyond exhaustion, began to realise that without the lieutenant's demands to move ever onwards, the men's chances of survival would certainly have been slim.

Some of the groups that had been cut off, like a party under Captain Ben Buckler, eventually made contact with allied forces weeks later, but most either died in the jungle or perished at the hands of the Japanese. Arthur Key was one of the many in the latter category. With the loss of their commander, Stan's old Power House friend, Phil Rhoden, assumed temporary command of the 2/14th Battalion. In Stan's absence, Roy Watson had assumed his role as battalion intelligence officer, a big job for a young lance corporal but Roy had performed admirably.

The 2/14th was a depressingly depleted unit when Stan rejoined it that afternoon. Of the 546 men who had left Owers' Corner for Isurava three weeks earlier, the current strength of the battalion was down to around 150. Some men were lost in the jungle; many were so sick with dysentery and malaria that they had to be evacuated. The lack of native carriers had meant that men with all manner of horrendous and debilitating wounds had to walk on their own torn and bloody feet all the way back down the track. Lindsay Bear walked all the way from Isurava to Owers' Corner with two bullets lodged in his spine, all the time helping a friend who had been shot through his Achilles tendon. Aside from the huge losses due to injury and illness, eighty men from the battalion had been killed in action. Most had fallen in the battle at

Isurava and the subsequent withdrawal; some had died from their wounds and others had succumbed to starvation in the jungle. Stan knew at this point that some of the captured troops had been tortured before their deaths. He desperately hoped that Arthur Key had been spared this fate.

After the hell they had just endured, Stan and his small party were able to enjoy a few hours blissful rest. The camp at Myola, almost devoid of provisions when Stan and his section had left it on their way north, had been resupplied by a constant trickle of native carriers. Now the 2/14th had access to unheard of luxuries such as one poncho per man, a bowl of hot stew and a pair of fresh socks. Stan had not been able to take his boots off for well over a week and when he finally had the chance to do so he discovered the socks and the soles of his sodden feet had been fused together in an indeterminate, rotting mass. He was not the only one. The whole battalion exposed their puffed and leprous-looking feet to the sun. Ken Clark, who had taken on the most unenviable role of the battalion's chiropodist, worked incessantly, paring the rotten tissue. They washed in the creek and changed into clean clothes, discarding the stinking rags that they had been wearing. They ate to the full, but were careful not to gorge. They stuffed their packs, though, with everything they could carry. Whatever was to be left behind would be destroyed or fouled. If they weren't able to shoot every Japanese soldier, they hoped to give all those who survived a good dose of dysentery.

The day after their withdrawal from Myola the 2/14th and 2/16th Battalions filed up a narrow, open spur out of Efogi village valley and passed through new defensive positions that had been prepared by the 39th Militia Battalion. The 39th had scraped out new company positions astride the track facing into the valley and stood guard as the 2/14th and 2/16th withdrew up the spur-line. It was the first time in Australia's military history that a militia unit had covered the withdrawal of the AIF and the significance of the fact did not escape the teenaged militiamen whose faces bristled with pride. As soon as Potts had his AIF brigade in position, Honner would withdraw the 39th back to Menari and then on to Moresby. The long ordeal of these young militiamen was almost over. Before the campaign, no one would have believed the militia could have performed the way it had done under such intense and sustained enemy pressure.

Mission Ridge, the main spur up which the track wound out of Efogi, was relatively open, with good fields of fire to either side. There was no alternative track to the south: anyone wishing to move towards Moresby would have to head straight up the steep, grassy slopes into the new Australian defences. Stan marvelled at Potts' selection of the site to make a stand against the Japanese. He knew the brigadier had been under immense pressure to try to hold the enemy at Myola, but any attempt to do so would have been suicidal. The Japanese could have easily bypassed the small Australian force and moved straight on to Port Moresby. The spur on which the Australians were digging in was the first locality where the brigade could stand without reasonable fear of encirclement. Away to the west, the ridgeline was steep and the jungle thick. To the east, the Australian positions on the high ground could dominate the valley in front of them and prevent any flanking Japanese attack.

At the top of the open spur the trail again entered the jungle and worked its way around the side of the steep ridge. Phil Rhoden was with Stan as they came to the tree-line. 'Potts wanted the battalion up in there,' he told Stan, gesturing to the jungle track behind him. 'Brigade HQ's about half a mile back. I wouldn't mind having your boys forward though, to keep an eye on things up front.' With the remainder of the battalion back in the thick woods, away from the fighting, Rhoden would obviously want to know what was happening when the battle broke into full force on the open spur.

Thus Stan and the intelligence section installed themselves in a small observation position, or OP, on the forward slope where they had a good view down into Efogi and the valley below. Al McGavin, who had been with Stan that first dawn when they went into combat in Lebanon, was also acting as a forward observer. Later that day, the first elements of the 2/27th Battalion arrived to relieve the 39th. The militiamen left all their automatic weapons, ammunition and grenades with the fresh unit as it filed down the open hillside to occupy the pre-prepared weapon pits. The unit was at full strength: almost 600 fit, tanned, healthy infantrymen. Stan found it difficult to conceive that only a few weeks ago his own unit had been in the same condition. Now they more closely resembled vagabonds than riflemen. Their uniforms hung off shoulders gaunt from privation and illness and their once tanned faces now bore the deathly pallor of the sunless jungle. Arnold Potts had come forward to inspect the defences with the 2/27th's commander, Lieutenant Colonel Geoffrey Cooper, a scion of the family that had founded the famous South Australian brewery. Cooper was a competent and experienced officer and he and Potts cast a critical eye over the South Australians' forward positions. They soon decided to pull the battalion back further up the hillside, closer to Stan's position in the tree-line, to shorten the brigade's lines of communication and to force the enemy to advance an extra 200 metres over the open ridgeline under fire.

It was a good decision that reinforced Stan's immense respect for Potts. This veteran of Gallipoli and Pozières was a soldier's soldier to the last and he had made all the tough decisions necessary to safeguard his men and keep them between the Japanese and Moresby, even when it involved directly disobeying his orders. He placed tremendous value on the lives of the men in his charge. Stan felt that there were far too many officers in the AIF who would callously risk the lives of their troops for their own ends.

Kokoda Wallaby

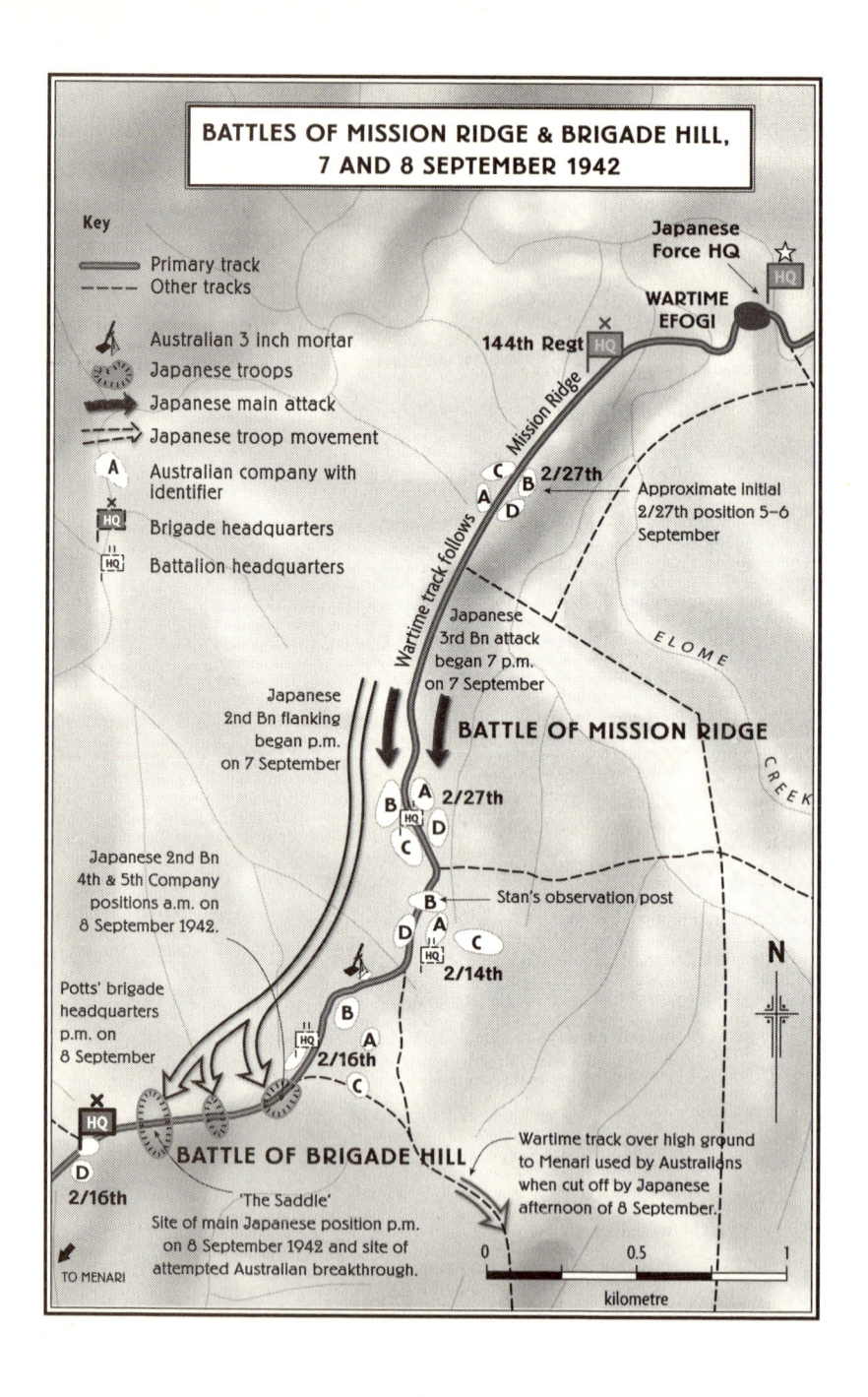

BATTLES OF MISSION RIDGE & BRIGADE HILL, 7 AND 8 SEPTEMBER 1942

Key
- Primary track
- Other tracks
- Australian 3 inch mortar
- Japanese troops
- Japanese main attack
- Japanese troop movement
- A — Australian company with identifier
- HQ — Brigade headquarters
- HQ — Battalion headquarters

Japanese Force HQ

WARTIME EFOGI

144th Regt

Mission Ridge

2/27th

Approximate initial 2/27th position 5–6 September

Wartime track follows

Japanese 3rd Bn attack began 7 p.m. on 7 September

Japanese 2nd Bn flanking began p.m. on 7 September

BATTLE OF MISSION RIDGE

ELOME CREEK

2/27th

Stan's observation post

2/14th

Japanese 2nd Bn 4th & 5th Company positions a.m. on 8 September 1942.

Potts' brigade headquarters p.m. on 8 September

2/16th

BATTLE OF BRIGADE HILL

'The Saddle'
Site of main Japanese position p.m. on 8 September 1942 and site of attempted Australian breakthrough.

Wartime track over high ground to Menari used by Australians when cut off by Japanese afternoon of 8 September.

2/16th

TO MENARI

0   0.5   1
kilometre

198

As darkness settled, the order came for complete silence and no movement in the locality. The men on the forward slope of the hill began to see the shimmer of strange lights on the far ridgeline where the trail descended from the moss forest into the Efogi valley. The lights looked just like the fireflies that frequented the jungle at night. They shimmered ghostly reds and blues in the darkness and flickered ethereally as they wound their way through the foliage. Were they really fireflies or had the jungle conjured up some other paranormal phenomenon to taunt them?

The whole position could see them now, flickering in the distance. Roy Watson spoke first: 'Jeezus, they're bloody lanterns.' General Horii's enormous force was making its way down the track into the village of Efogi. In addition to their own lanterns, the Japanese had cut sections of captured signal wire which were coated with a thick, green plastic that burned slowly and brightly. At times, the flickering lights went flying in all directions in the darkness, testament to the difficulty of negotiating the greasy, muddy slopes that the Australians had encountered only the day before. The sight brought a chuckle to the Australians but the good humour did not persist as the lights kept coming and coming, seemingly without end. Stan made the intelligence posts stay awake throughout the dark night, trying as best they could to assess the size of the enemy force massing in the valley. Even at dawn, the lights were still filing down the far slope. Stan reckoned he counted fifteen hundred, and that would represent only a fraction of the total.

Just before first light, the 2/27th was ordered to stand to in their pits. The Japanese were unpredictable, but the hour before dawn was the one when any static position was most vulnerable to attack. The darkness gave an assaulting force the ability to approach unseen and the defenders were invariably lethargic after their mind-numbing night-watch. To counteract this, the last watch of the night shook all their comrades awake and the whole position spent a silent hour in their pits, weapons at the ready, peering into the jungle.

Only when the day had fully broken could the men go about their morning ritual of re-checking weapons and scrounging a meagre dry biscuit breakfast.

After stand down, Phil Rhoden came forward to see Stan, who was still intently scanning the valley with his binoculars trying to make an appraisal of the enemy strength. His estimate was that at least a brigade, well over 3000 men, had entered the valley, and that they were still coming. Phil went through the same process with Al McGavin and was given the same estimate: 'a brigade or more'. Phil had some good news — Potts had ordered an air strike and thought it may well come in that day. He also asked Stan if he could borrow Roy Watson for the morning. Roy had obviously made a good impression during his brief stint as battalion intelligence officer and Phil wanted someone to recce an alternative trail to Menari. Establishing alternative routes to their rear was standard procedure, as the Japanese tactics of envelopment were by now well understood.

Roy was able to find an alternative trail back. An old native footpad wound off the main track up the steepest part of the range and down a different spur-line. It had obviously not been used for years, so Rhoden and Cooper detailed a dozen men to clear as much of it as they could. When Roy returned to Stan he was not particularly enthusiastic about the new trail. It was horrendously overgrown, almost impassable in parts, and would be very slow going. The main track down the other side of the range was clear and steep and one could reach the village in less than two hours. This alternative route would take at least a day and would be almost impassable for stretchers.

Stan had not forgotten that terrible six days spent trying to cut a path through the jungle after the battle at Isurava, all the while praying that the Japanese would not beat him and his small party to the Australian lines. The men of the unit were surely not in a condition to survive another such ordeal. Being surrounded and cut off would have to be avoided at any cost. For once, however, the Australians had topography on their side. The cliffs to the west would force the Japanese straight up Mission Ridge into the defences of the fresh 2/27th.

Phil's predictions of air support proved well founded. The silence of the jungle morning was broken by the roar of Pratt & Whitney aero engines as eight Martin B26 Marauder medium bombers, escorted by four Kittyhawks, burst into view — skimming above the canopy as they swooped down over Efogi where General Horii's force was concentrated. The Marauders climbed, circled and dived, time and again, until they had each delivered their 1800 kilo payloads onto the newly formed Japanese camp. As each bomber pulled up from its dive it was the turn of the Kittyhawk fighters. They came screaming down the valley on repeated strafing runs with all six 12.7 mm machine-guns blazing at the enemy. As each wave passed overhead, cheers rippled up and down the Australian lines. The amount of damage the air raid inflicted on the Japanese was never fully determined but there was no doubting its morale-boosting effect on the beleaguered Australians. After so many weeks in the mountains, Stan and his men had begun to feel they were fighting their own private war. Even if the morning's raid achieved little, it at least demonstrated that they were not alone in the world and cut off from the wider conflict.

Despite the damage it must have caused the enemy, the attack did little to slow the pace of the Japanese advance. They had dragged their Juki machine-guns, mortars, and their 70 and 75 mm mountain guns to within range of the Australians on Mission Ridge and commenced a bombardment that could not be construed as anything but preparation for an assault. Stan's 2/14th escaped this fire relatively unscathed, with only Hec McDonald and two others being wounded. The brunt of this fire fell on the newly dug defences of Cooper's 2/27th, which sustained ten men killed and many more injured.

In the darkness of the early hours, Cooper and his South Australians heard for the first time the strange battle-cry that invariably preceded a Japanese assault. While Stan, Al McGavin and the small handful of other 2/14th soldiers recognised the eerie call-and-response screams that flowed like waves up and down the hidden ranks of Japanese before they burst from the foliage for an attack, the 2/27th were momentarily shocked. They were no newcomers to combat, having fought the French all through Lebanon just like their counterparts in Stan's unit, but this was the first time they had faced the terrifying prospect of a Japanese bayonet charge. Stan was never able to determine if these chants were primarily designed to spur the attackers on to greater deeds or to scare the hell out of the defenders. They proved to be highly effective on both scores.

At precisely 0430 hours on the morning of 8 September the mortar and mountain gun barrage that had denied the Australians any sleep suddenly ceased and the first wave of attackers emerged from the turbid light. While the spur was devoid of trees and should have provided the defenders with clear fields of fire, the kunai grass was so thick it enabled the Japanese to crawl perilously close to the Australian perimeter. Covered with thick camouflage and with their wickedly honed bayonets fixed to their rifles, the enemy burst out of the long grass so close to the 2/27th defences that many were able to leap straight into the Australians' weapon pits, fighting with bayonets, boots and fists.

The attack was launched from all angles and every company of Cooper's battalion was engaged at once. Such was the intensity of the battle that the battalion expended its entire supply of grenades, as well as the brigade reserve, and six of the unit's precious Bren guns were knocked out of action. Cooper's men took heavy casualties — thirty-nine were killed and forty-six seriously wounded — but they inflicted a horrendous toll on their attackers, roughly ten times this number. Numbers given for Japanese losses throughout the campaign often appeared to be exaggerated, but they were not. Whenever the opportunity presented itself, Stan's job was to do a body count of the enemy. While this was clearly difficult during the withdrawal, experience gave the intelligence section the capacity to make accurate estimations.

Most of the Japanese soldiers came from peasant stock, and recruits were subjected to intensive indoctrination in the tenets of bushido and Shinto religion. This meant their lives were dedicated to the Emperor. Defeat was viewed as shameful, surrender unthinkable, and a defeated enemy was held in utter contempt. Military discipline was maintained by a culture of extreme brutality and compassion was seen as nothing but weakness. When these elements were combined with the belief that it was a great honour to die in battle, the net result was an army of near fanatics who sacrificed their lives without hesitation.

Stan and the intelligence section watched these events unfolding from their position on the forward edge of the hill up which the trail from Mission Ridge wound its way south to Menari. Just after daybreak, three hours into the battle, Stan and Bill Lynn suddenly heard a most astonishing sound: from behind them to the south, far to the rear of the battle along the track to brigade headquarters, the unmistakable sound of grenades and rifle fire had suddenly become audible. 'Bloody hell,' someone said, 'what the heck is *that*?'

A sensation of shock, if not panic, quickly spread amongst the 2/14th positions. The battle to the front was dire enough, but if the track to the rear had been cut, getting the wounded men out in a withdrawal would be almost impossible. Only moments later a runner arrived along the track from the 2/16th positions with news for them. Their fearful supposition was correct. A Japanese force of at least battalion size had somehow worked its way around the Australian flank, scaled the almost vertical hillside during the night, and lodged itself on the track in the saddle between the rearmost 2/16th positions and Potts' brigade headquarters. The full details of the first contact that morning were only told to Stan several days later. Brigadier Potts had awoken at dawn and along with his aide John Gill had moved to the edge of the position to answer a call of nature. The brigade headquarters was in a small clearing astride the track and as the two men stood by the edge of the jungle and relieved themselves, the sharp crack of a Japanese rifle tolled out and Gill collapsed dead beside Potts.

The brigade headquarters was immediately subjected to sustained and accurate fire. Potts, more than a kilometre behind the front and supposedly in a strategically safe position, suddenly found himself fighting for his life. His entire brigade was forward of his position and with their sole line of withdrawal now cut, their chances of survival were slim. The enemy had pursued the same tactics all along the track, but Potts' assumption that the cliffs and jungle would secure the Australian flanks for a few days was entirely reasonable. The 2/14th and 2/16th had not been expecting to engage the enemy at all and had not made any concerted attempt to dig in.

A brief emergency conference was held between Phil Rhoden and the 2/16th commander, Bert Caro, both of whom found themselves cut off from brigade headquarters. They were still in intermittent radio contact with brigade and Potts sent them an unequivocal order. Caro was to organise an attack south along the track in an attempt to clear the Japanese from the trail.

The Japanese force on what became known as Brigade Hill consisted of three companies, more than 500 men, and the Australians were fully aware of how difficult a task it would be pushing them back off the trail and into the jungle. The Japanese had the entire night to prepare defences — some members of the 2/16th claimed to have heard the sound of digging and the chopping of logs from the area now known to be in enemy hands. In the early morning a group of West Australians had cleared the first hundred metres of the trail to their rear where the track ran along a knife-edged spur through the forest. But the main Japanese force was dug in further to the south where the spur-line broadened and the Japanese could position themselves on a front of at least 200 metres astride the main track. There was no opportunity for the 2/14th and 2/16th to surround them on the track and whittle them away over a matter of days. The only option would be to attack on a broad front.

Despite being separated from brigade headquarters, Caro and Rhoden kept in constant contact with Potts via their 108 wireless sets. The 108 had acquired a reputation for being astonishingly ineffective in the jungle environment, but throughout 8 September the long-suffering signalmen of the brigade managed to keep the forward positions in constant contact with Potts, and this link was to prove vital.

Stan assisted Phil Rhoden with preparations for the attack that was to go in early that afternoon. One company of the 2/14th was to participate and the task fell to Claude Nye and his B Company. Nye was an impressive officer and it was his company that had held the high ground to the west of Isurava when Hal had been mortally wounded. The 2/16th's B Company was to attack directly astride the track and C Company would be on their left.

By this point in the campaign, B Company of the 2/14th had been reduced to about half strength. The two companies of the 2/16th Battalion, who were also to participate in the attack, had fared no better. In a typical but unavoidable irony of war, this most onerous of tasks had yet again fallen to these exhausted men who had already endured more than any man could reasonably be expected to endure. The 2/27th, fresh and at full strength, was still so heavily engaged on the Mission Ridge front that it was impossible for them to assist. Their fight was still going to be a close-run thing.

As Stan and Roy watched Nye's B Company in their final preparations for the attack at Brigade Hill, they knew, just as the men themselves must have known, that their chances of ever returning were slim. But their task was unavoidable. As dim as their prospects of survival might be, to have to take to the jungle at this point would present an even slimmer chance of emerging from it alive. If the rest of the brigade was to have a chance of survival, then no matter how many lives it cost, this section of the track needed to be regained. It was as simple as that.

Despite the gravity of the situation there was no drama, no histrionics, amongst the troops. They stood by the fringe of the jungle without making any effort to conceal themselves. They sensed that the Japanese in the lodgement were under orders not to fire and reveal their positions prior to the commencement of an assault. The Australians smoked, bickered and laughed. Throughout the campaign the men of B Company had attempted to out-do each other with off-jokes at the most inopportune moments. Hal had been the undisputed king of black humour and his platoon often had the rest of the company in stitches. Stan could only imagine what the Japanese defenders must have thought. The men who would soon be attacking them were cackling with laughter as they honed their bayonets and re-loaded Thompson magazines with newly cleaned shells.

'Right, we may as well get on with it,' said Nye. Last cigarettes were smoked, tin hats were donned at rakish angles and the men turned and sauntered down to the start line. The thickly wooded land sloped slightly downwards to the south from where the Australians were forming up. The track to brigade headquarters ran down a flat-topped spur, which was about 250 metres wide before it dropped steeply away. Nye's men shook out in an extended line over a frontage of 100 metres to the west of the track, and away to the left the two 2/16th companies did the same.

'Company …' boomed Nye, the first time anyone had raised their voice in preparation for this attack, 'fix … bayonets.' The men dropped to one knee and the sound of sixty troops dragging sixty bayonets out of sixty scabbards must have been an unnerving experience for all concerned. In this thickly wooded country, the bolt-action .303s were too slow and unwieldy for close-quarter combat and the only way the track could be cleared was with automatic fire from Brens and Tompsons, grenades, and — most importantly — with bayonets. For any soldier there was nothing quite so daunting as fixing bayonets for an attack, but B Company was better prepared than most. Hal, when he had been the company's sergeant major at Puckapunyal, had made bayonet drills one of the company's major concerns and the men had spent hours training in mock combat so that now all could wield the foot-long Lee-Enfield bayonets with deadly effect. Doubtless they realised that the Japanese could do the same with their weapons.

At the predetermined time, the companies set off from their start line down the broad saddle. The men were only half a dozen metres apart and they moved forward at a brisk walk, each man covering his partner and taking advantage of the cover afforded to them. In a few moments they were lost from the view of Stan and Phil, waiting with Lieutenant Colonel Caro behind the start line, and seconds later the saddle erupted with gunfire. Stan was startled to recognise the chatter of the Juki machine-guns; amazed that the enemy had been able to drag such weapons up the slope during the night.

The men who had set off for the attack may have feigned high spirits but Stan and Phil sat quietly, almost forlornly, and listened to the sound of the engagement. Neither man spoke — there was nothing to say. The chances of success for Nye's men had been slim from the outset but Stan could tell from the first few seconds of the battle, by sound alone, that the Australians were being mauled. The enemy machine-guns had opened up with such a synchronised roar there could be no doubt that B Company had walked into a well-planned killing field, crisscrossed by multiple Jukis at the range of only a few metres.

The noise of the fading battle then told Stan and Phil, just as clearly, that the next sad chapter of events was unfolding. Just as suddenly as it had begun, the fire ceased. There was still the occasional crack of a .303 or the thump of a Mills grenade, but the bulk of the company had been wiped out in only a matter of moments. Stan saw 'Blue' Steward, the medical officer of the 2/16th, rush forward from behind B Company's advance. For the next few hours, Steward and his team brought back a score of badly wounded men. The remainder of the company had been killed.

Unbeknown to Phil and Stan at that point, some elements of the 2/16th companies on the eastern flank led by Lieutenant Bill Grayden had in fact broken through to brigade headquarters. The track, however, remained firmly in Japanese hands.

Stan and the rest of the 2/14th helped Steward and the others treat those wounded men who could be dragged back from the saddle. The volume of medical supplies available to the Australians during the campaign had always been slim, but after a month in the jungle the situation was dire. Stan and Roy saw Steward drag a West Australian, Keith Norrish, out of the fight and prop him up against a tree. The young man had a gaping wound in his chest. Steward took three oral sulphonamide tablets from his pocket, the only form of antiseptic he had left, and crushed the tablets up in the palm of his hand before pushing them into the wound. Out of the other pocket he took a roll of sticking plaster, tore off several strips and slapped them as best he could over the wound. 'Alright Norrish,' he said to the barely conscious lad who was being supported by two comrades, 'Port Moresby's seven days walk up that trail. When you fall over, someone will pick you up. Now move.' Without another word Steward and his team set off in search of their next patient while Norrish turned and stumbled up the hill to the trailhead discovered by Roy the day before.

The day's action at Brigade Hill had cost the 2/14th twenty-six men. Among them was Hal's great mate, Charlie McCallum, who had won the Distinguished Conduct Medal at Isurava. The toll for the 2/16th was even worse: thirty-five killed and scores severely wounded. As night enveloped the ridgeline, Potts, who had effectively lost all contact with his brigade, set off for Menari along the main track from his brigade headquarters. The remnants of the 2/14th and 2/16th followed Roy's lead and plunged into the darkness on the southern side of the ridge in another desperate bid to outrun the Japanese.

Meanwhile, the 2/27th had suffered an equally fearful day at Mission Ridge. The Japanese had pressed them so closely it had been impossible to break contact and withdraw. It was only the bravery of Captains Arthur Lee and Justin Skipper that finally enabled them to do so. At five thirty in the afternoon, with their ammunition almost exhausted and with the dead and wounded lying about them unattended, it was clearly time for extreme measures. The two commanders jumped from their pits and called for their men to follow them in a wild rush at the enemy. They threw grenades and yelled and screamed abuse as they emptied the last of their magazines at the startled enemy, pushing them off the spur. The action earned Lee a bar to his Military Cross and Skipper was mentioned in despatches. The 2/27th's 'fighting war' in the ranges had lasted one whole day at a cost of thirty-nine killed and scores wounded. They were not to know it, but it was only the beginning of their ordeal. They too had to gather up their wounded and make their way to the ridgeline and follow the other two battalions into the darkened labyrinth.

Together with the remnants of the 2/14th and 2/16th, Stan slashed his way through the bush all night and reached Potts at Menari by daybreak. For the 400 men of the 2/27th, struggling with their stretcher cases, progress was much slower and by the time they came abreast of Menari the following day it was in the hands of the Japanese. It was the beginning of another extraordinary odyssey in the wilderness. They had to make their own way south, cutting a path parallel to the main track. After fourteen tortuous and foodless days they were met by Australian independent company commandos who had been sent to look for them. They were finally led to safety at Itiki, five kilometres from Owers' Corner, where they had their first proper meal for more than two weeks.

With the 2/27th officially listed as missing and the remainder of the brigade so depleted, the 2/14th and 2/16th were combined to form a composite battalion. At Menari they had received orders to continue their withdrawal to Ioribaiwa Ridge. They also received the heartening news that they would be met there by the Australian 25th Brigade which was advancing over the track from Moresby to join the campaign. An infantry brigade in the field normally numbers around 1800 men. Potts was now in command of 307, all ranks, evidence of an attrition rate unparalleled since the First World War. As for the 2/14th itself, it had left Port Moresby with nearly 600. That morning it paraded 121 officers and men for the march to Ioribaiwa.

The Australians filed over the steep Maguli Ranges and down a narrow and even steeper gorge into Ofi Creek. Stan and Caro immediately identified it as an excellent location for an ambush. Two trails ran down and then up the far side towards Ioribaiwa Ridge and the immediate approaches to the creek were devoid of cover. High on the opposite bank was a mass of boulders in the thick jungle where an ambushing force could remain undetected until it opened fire.

Caro and Rhoden ordered the battalion to dig in astride the main track and put forward standing patrols above the ambush points. There were light patrol clashes throughout the day and Stan spent his time visiting the forward patrols in an effort to appraise the situation. Then, on 11 September, they were met with a most astonishing sight. Advancing up the trail from the valley behind them were the 1800 fresh troops of the Australian 25th Brigade. The 2/14th and 2/16th now knew what they must have looked like when they first appeared out of the jungle at Isurava — strong, healthy and tanned, with clean weapons and gear and in seemingly impossible numbers. It was a welcome sight and the men, who had for weeks now resigned themselves to their fate, began to entertain the idea that they might survive this ordeal after all.

Prior to Brigadier Ken Eather of the 25th Brigade assuming overall command of the force on 14 September, Brigadier Selwyn Porter relieved Arnold Potts as commander of the composite battalion — all that was left of his 21st Brigade. Potts was told to return to Port Moresby to 'report to headquarters'. He should have anticipated a hero's welcome but he knew the world did not work that way. 'Fighting withdrawals' with 'heavy losses', irrespective of the odds against them, made lousy newspaper headlines and did nothing for career advancement. Besides, the staff officers' desks at Port Moresby and Canberra were already overflowing with experts who sported red collar flashes and gold-starred epaulettes. It was another of the great mockeries of war that those responsible for the woeful lack of supplies, the faulty intelligence and the failure to commit reserves in a timely manner would be the ones who, in time, received the credit for stemming the Japanese tide. As for those who actually fought in the field, there was nothing in store for them but rebuke and recrimination.

The exhausted composite battalion still had a role to play and Brigadier Eather told Caro and Phil Rhoden that their forces, however weak, would need to remain in the battle for the time being. Their troops were ordered to dig in astride the main track that led up to Ioribaiwa, sandwiched between the fresh 2/33rd Battalion and the 2/31st Battalion. Over the following days, Caro tasked Stan with taking various officers of the fresh brigade forward and putting them in the picture regarding the layout of the forward defences, the various trails and creek crossings, and the dispositions and patrolling actions of the Japanese, who were evidently massing on the far range for the next of their long series of attacks.

During this day, as Stan moved around the brigade's forward positions, the Japanese began to engage the Australian defences with their mountain gun. The same weapon that had caused such havoc at Isurava and Mission Ridge now began to pound their positions at Ioribaiwa. Sadly, it was in front of the defensive positions of the hugely depleted composite battalion that the Japanese had established their gun position. The Victorians and Western Australians of the 2/14th and 2/16th spent the following day crouching at the bottom of their meagre pits and slit trenches as the jungle erupted all around them.

Stan and Alan Avery were forward, briefing a group of 2/33rd Battalion officers, when their movement attracted the attention of the Japanese gun crew. Normally, artillery pieces like this were fired 'indirect', that is to say, the crews would be firing the weapon on a certain bearing and elevation without actually seeing their target. At Ioribaiwa, however, the mountain-gun position was so close to the Australian pits that it could fire line-of-sight, straight into the Australian positions, picking off individual pits and defences. The crew had evidently seen Stan, Alan and the other officers and a cascade of shells began to erupt all around them. Stan grabbed Alan and the pair half-dived and half-fell into the nearest Australian pit as they were buffeted by the shockwaves and reverberations of the shell-fire. The Japanese fired over forty rounds in rapid succession into the immediate vicinity.

Just as quickly as it had begun, the barrage subsided. Stan turned to talk to Alan but the ringing in his ears meant he could hear nothing, and it was obvious that Alan was in the same situation. The pair lay in the pit for a moment as their heart rates returned to normal and the ringing began to subside. 'Okay, let's move,' muttered Stan, and he reached out to the lip of the pit to heave himself out. He placed his hand on what he felt must be a section of root and heaved himself over the edge of the pit as Alan did the same. Stan lay prone for a moment to ensure that they had not been observed, but as he went to stand he saw that he was not grasping a tree-root as he had assumed, but an enormous and very much alive python. The snake, like the two soldiers, must have been temporarily stunned by the barrage but it and Stan seemed to realise their predicament almost at the same moment. Stan froze involuntarily, then without even thinking let out a bellow of shock. Thankfully the snake was only too keen to seek refuge from the man-made anarchy that had descended on its otherwise peaceful habitat.

This might have provided a moment of light-hearted relief except for the carnage around them. Only ten metres away, a pit had taken a direct hit and there was little left of its occupants other than scarlet-smeared earth and shreds of khaki. Stan followed the heart-wrenching but necessary procedure of recording their details and officially disabling their already shattered weapons. This set the pattern for the next four days. There were some heavy patrol clashes but most of the casualties sustained by the 2/14th were from the Japanese mountain gun.

On paper, the Australian situation now looked quite solid. After a month of desperate fighting withdrawals conducted by a handful of exhausted men, the Australians had over an entire brigade of fresh troops strung out over a two kilometre front at Ioribaiwa, with another brigade on its way to the front. Stan knew that in reality the position on the ridge itself was fast becoming untenable. It was the best defensive position the Australians had occupied throughout the whole campaign — a long, broad feature where a whole brigade could spread out and limit enemy outflanking movements. The problem was that the forward troops were so close to the Japanese they were in danger of being wiped out by the mountain guns and heavy machine-guns that hammered the Australian pits day and night.

In addition to the dangers of the Japanese mountain gun, enemy attacks had been wreaking havoc on the Australians. On 15 September, the Japanese pushed the 2/14th's forward men back out of their positions except for a few who were encircled by the advancing enemy. Private Les 'Pappy' Ransom — the redoubtable veteran of the Great War, who at fifty years of age was still serving with the unit after having been wounded on the first morning of the Lebanon Campaign — was cut off from the battalion for a day and surrounded by Japanese before fighting his way back. Other Japanese patrols had crossed the stream unseen during the night and lodged themselves in pockets inside the perimeter of the 3rd Militia Battalion, which was supporting the 25th Brigade.

On the morning of 16 September the Japanese again attacked over the stream. It was the weary composite battalion that once more bore the brunt of the onslaught. After a month of jungle fighting, weakened by malaria and dysentery, it finally looked like the men were going to be broken. Even the best soldiers in Stan's battalion were starting to show signs of physical and, more importantly, emotional breakdown. Blue Steward, the composite unit's medical officer, ordered three or four individuals to the rear, all of whom were suffering complete nervous breakdowns.

Australian General Thomas Blamey had visited Port Moresby for the first time on 12 September and confidently announced to the press that the Japanese would be held at Ioribaiwa. He said that the feature itself was as defendable as any in the ranges. The Australian supply lines had been shortened and secured and 1800 men of the fresh 16th Brigade were disembarking in Port Moresby at that very moment. The Japanese, on the other hand, had reached a 'culmination point' where their advance had exceeded the limits of their logistical support.

Frustratingly, events on the ground failed to follow Blamey's script. To abandon Ioribaiwa would represent an early reversal for the new commander on the ridge, Ken Eather, and a massive loss of face for Blamey. Eather explained his position to General Arthur Allen in Port Moresby over a weak and spluttering telephone line on the morning of 16 September: if the Australians fell back to the next ridgeline, Imita, they could call on artillery support for the first time; the 16th Brigade would be ready for deployment and it would ultimately extend the Japanese to near breaking point. All of this was true, but sound logic and strategic thinking would never be sufficient to prevent howls of criticism emanating from the Cabinet Room in Canberra. Nor would it prevent the derisive communiqués issued by the Supreme Commander, US General Douglas MacArthur, who was enduring the rigours of the war in his suite at Lennon's Hotel, Brisbane, under the dutiful care of his wife Jean. 'There won't be any withdrawal from the Imita position,' Allen insisted to Eather. 'You'll die there if necessary. You understand that?' Eather understood, and the permission was begrudgingly granted.

Two days before this decision to withdraw was made, the 2/14th and 2/16th were finally relieved and the two units regained their own identity. Over the four days that they had occupied the ridge, seven of their men were killed and another twelve seriously wounded. Stan personally oversaw the burial of these Victorians. Facing the loss of companions was always traumatic. Sometimes, in the heat of battle, the dead had to be abandoned and there was no time to reflect, but there was something about the services on Ioribaiwa that left Stan inconsolably distraught. Perhaps it was the fact that they were so close to safety, and that they sensed that the Japanese advance had exhausted itself. This was the hardest part to face. They had come all this way and now these men had to die in the last days of the battle. After the burials, only seventy-three members of the 600-strong unit were able to parade.

CHAPTER EIGHT

Run Rabbit

On 26 September 1942, the remnants of the once robust 2/14th headed for a camp on the overgrown fields of the Sefton family's Koitaki Plantation, eight kilometres from Owers' Corner and only a few days march from the battle that still raged in the Owen Stanley Range. They passed the 25-pounder guns of the 14th Field Regiment at Owers' Corner conducting fire mission after fire mission, pounding the Japanese who now occupied Ioribaiwa Ridge. The Australian forces had withdrawn to Imita Ridge, but this was to be their last withdrawal. The Japanese were a spent force.

Stan and Phil led their men along a trail that wound through neat rows of rubber trees — the source of the territory's and the planters' wealth. The grounds of the Koitaki rubber estate resembled a tent city, a temporary base for the brigade as well as an annex of the 46th Camp Hospital. As Stan passed the estate's sprawling work sheds and its homestead he found it difficult to reconcile how quickly he had passed from the jaws of hell back into the world of the living. It was as if the intersection of the jungle and the road-head, a few kilometres back, demarcated two separate universes.

In the few weeks they had been at the front, the army's rear echelon in New Guinea had transformed the road between the Koitaki plantation and Port Moresby into one extended army base, far more complex than anything they had seen at Puckapunyal, Singleton or Liverpool. There were units of every type, from signals' camps to field hospitals, from mechanics' yards to supply depots, from the army newspaper unit to a cavalry squadron tasked with capturing and breaking wild horses for the transport corps. One young soldier remarked to Stan that he had no idea the army even had that many support units, let alone the ability to re-establish them in New Guinea in just six weeks. Liberty ships crammed Fairfax Harbour and there was a constant drone of allied aircraft shuttling men and equipment into the Seven Mile airstrip and Ward's Drome.

Few men were aware of the existence of Australian General Thomas Blamey's private retreat in the pass that led down from the plateau, half-way to the coast. It was described as a luxuriously appointed country club in a botanical garden setting. One person who saw it was Doctor Geoffrey Vernon, the self-appointed medical officer for the Fuzzy Wuzzy carriers. Setting aside its undoubted beauty, he wondered how many thousands of pounds and how much native labour were expended in its construction. It was incredible that Blamey could live in such luxury while his men were enduring such hardships only a few kilometres away in the ranges.

Meanwhile, Stan and Phil led the battalion's remaining seventy-three officers and men into the tent-lines at Koitaki. As for the other 500, they were either lying dead beside the track, still lost in the jungle, or hospitalised through wounds, illness or disease. By all external appearances the battalion presented a vastly different image to the one recorded by Australian journalists when they had first entered the ranges. Many of these once-bronzed Anzac faces were now drawn and thin. Their skin had an unnatural, waxy pallor and their eyes had that thousand-yard stare, typical of men exhausted by battle. Their muscles were now sinewy and taunt under skin absolutely devoid of fat. The green dye had long been leeched from their ragged shorts and shirts, which were now stained with mud and blood. The full story of their struggle will never be told, as so many deeds were enacted by men who fought and died unseen by others, shrouded by a wall of green. The few who later returned to Australia were told to get on with their lives. So much had happened throughout the world on such a grand scale. Would anyone want to listen to their stories? Would anyone want to read about them? How can you accurately relate the horrors of war to someone who has no concept of the reality?

Of course, no one talked like this at the time. For many, life was reduced to the absolute basics: food, sleep, washing, going to the latrines, shaving in hot water, groaning with pangs of dysentery and sweating through the nights with the flu-like symptoms of the onset of malaria. After all this, Stan could just about manage the more advanced tasks of cleaning weapons and sorting gear. Only then could he face doing what he knew he had to do, but had already put off for too long — write a letter home. How would he start? What lies would he be compelled to tell? 'Dear Mum and Dad, I am writing to tell you that Hal did not suffer ...'

On 4 October Stan made the first of many trips to Port Moresby to deliver the battalion's mail, to visit the sick and wounded, and then report on the battalion's condition at New Guinea Force Headquarters based at Four Mile — all the localities along the main road having been named after their distance from the harbour. Stan could not help but reflect on the difference between the Middle East and the Pacific when it came to the facilities available during times in reserve. The cities in Lebanon and Palestine were alive with bars and restaurants, all serving exotic food and wine, and the region abounded with historic sites. Here, there was nothing but the sprawling military encampments while Port Moresby itself was devoid of character, with the few habitable houses and hotels used as billets and storerooms. The surrounding area was drab and dusty, its scant covering of brown, dry grass interspersed with the odd native species of eucalypt.

When Stan returned to Koitaki on 6 October he was informed that he had been promoted to adjutant. He was now the senior captain and would be the battalion commander's personal staff officer, responsible for all organisational, administrative and disciplinary duties. This role, however, was not just a backroom one. When in combat, the adjutant actually controlled the battle, carrying out the lieutenant colonel's commands in the field. As such, the adjutant was considered a man of great significance and influence. Phil Rhoden was now a major and still in temporary command of the battalion.

On 23 October Stan was informed that the brigade commander, Arnold Potts, was being relieved and sent to Darwin. Earlier that month, on the 4th, they had been paraded and addressed by Major General Arthur Allen and he had congratulated the battalion on its 'fine performance' over the previous month and made special mention of Potts. Allen described Potts as 'a cool, lion-hearted commander' who 'had saved Port Moresby from invasion'. Potts' banishment to the backwater of Port Darwin seemed an odd reward for such an achievement.

Late in the afternoon of 8 November Stan received word that the Commander-in-Chief of Allied Land Forces, South-West Pacific Area, General Thomas Blamey, would address the brigade. The site of the parade would be the cricket pitch of the Koitaki plantation, adjacent to the 2/14th Battalion's camp. Obviously Blamey wanted to add his congratulations to those of Major General Allen. The battalion diary's entry for the following day was 'weather fine and warm'. It was something of an understatement. It was stiflingly humid and the tropical sun shone fiercely in an unblemished cobalt sky. After some early morning training, the remainder of the day was spent in preparation for the parade. The troops stood proudly to attention as Blamey mounted his podium to address them at precisely 1545 hours.

It was one of the greatest shocks Stan has ever received. Blamey was speaking from a wooden platform in a strong voice only twenty or thirty metres away. One of the first things he said was that the Australians had been defeated by inferior troops in inferior numbers. Then he made the infamous remark to the effect that 'the rabbit that runs away was the rabbit that gets shot'. Everyone was outraged. There were loud jeers, right throughout the ranks. Some men advanced menacingly towards the podium and had to be wrestled to the ground by their sergeants. Others actually raised and cocked their rifles.

'Shoot the frigging bastard,' someone yelled.

Of all the things that angered Stan in his life, this address stood out above all others. It enraged him. How could one possibly explain such provocative, insensitive and ill-informed comments? Blamey was known to be fiercely protective of his position of power as head of the Allied Land Forces. He stood uncomfortably in the hierarchy, answerable to the unsupportive Allied Supreme Commander, Douglas MacArthur, and subject to the whims of an inexperienced and jittery Australian War Cabinet. MacArthur had goaded Blamey throughout the campaign, telling him that Australian troops were poor fighters lacking aggression. On MacArthur's insistence, and against Blamey's own wishes, Blamey had been ordered by the Prime Minister, John Curtin, to go to New Guinea and personally take charge of the campaign to 'energise the situation'. Blamey's arrival put the New Guinea commander, General Sidney Rowell, off-side as he interpreted Blamey's presence as a slight on his own performance. Rowell would soon be dismissed by Blamey for his refusal to cooperate. In the meantime, Rowell kept Blamey woefully uninformed about what was happening on the ground. It was pure coincidence that Blamey happened to arrive in New Guinea in September 1942, only days before the Japanese forces were halted at Ioribaiwa Ridge and began their agonising retreat over the Owen Stanley Range.

Run Rabbit

Opinions abound as to Blamey's character, but one thing was certain — he made no attempt to build a rapport with either his junior officers or with the troops under his command. Ralph Honner could attest to this. On recounting his meeting with Blamey prior to the Koitaki parade, Honner said Blamey did not know his name, even though Ralph held the rank of lieutenant colonel, and when introduced made no enquiry as to Ralph's background or experiences in the battles on the Kokoda Track. Such indifference and evident lack of briefing on the part of a commanding officer is beyond belief.

There is another possible explanation for Blamey's extraordinary address to the 21st Brigade. In 1980, Norman Carlyon published a book entitled *I Remember Blamey*. Carlyon, who was Blamey's aide-de-camp and personal assistant throughout the war, kept a diary of events. In the chapter where he talks about the Koitaki address he makes a clear error. He says Blamey addressed the 21st Brigade (true, of course) but the campaign actions Carlyon attributes to that brigade are clearly wrong. He confuses the 21st Brigade with the 25th. To quote from page 110 of Carlyon's book, he writes (the italics are mine):

> I well remember Blamey's *close attention to the performance of his fighting men*. It concerned the 21st Brigade, *after a setback in their thrust forward from Ioribaiwa Ridge* [it was the 25th that went forward from Ioribaiwa and suffered a setback, not the 21st]. This brigade, which had a fine record in the Middle East [true for both the 21st and the 25th] *was fighting its first jungle action* [false for the 21st, true for the 25th]. *When its flanks were infiltrated by the enemy the brigade made a limited retirement* [false for the 21st, true for the 25th]. This was a successful operation in which very few casualties were suffered. However, this check displeased Blamey. He ordered that the entire brigade be paraded at Koitaki so that he could address them.

Clearly, Blamey's personal assistant confused the two brigades at the time of the Koitaki address. One's first reaction to this might be that it can't be true. However, the fact remains that Carlyon *did get it wrong* and what is more extraordinary, neither he nor his editor, nor any other historian (to my knowledge) has subsequently drawn attention to this error.

Elsewhere in the book, Carlyon recounts how he spent twenty-four hours a day, every day, with Blamey. They slept in the same tent and read all the same reports. If Blamey's own assistant was confused then there is every reason to believe that Blamey himself was confused. Of course, Blamey should not have addressed any of his troops in the manner in which he spoke at Koitaki. However, confusing the 21st Brigade with the 25th might help explain the otherwise inexplicable. Earlier sections of Carlyon's book refer to Blamey's displeasure with the 25th Brigade commander, Ken Eather, when he requested to withdraw from Ioribaiwa to Imita Ridge on 16 September 1942. This withdrawal panicked the Australian Cabinet badly and precipitated Curtin and MacArthur sending Blamey to New Guinea — a move that greatly displeased Blamey.

Blamey subsequently addressed the 25th Brigade at Donadabu Rest Camp on 24 December. His tone was completely different to the one he had adopted at Koitaki. He said: 'I am frequently asked how the old [First World War] AIF measured up to the new AIF. I say, "Never was the original AIF called to perform so difficult a task as the one you have accomplished so splendidly." I bring to you from the Prime Minister the thanks of the nation for what you have done. You deserve, and you have, the highest praise of the nation. Your deeds will remain to your eternal credit.' Given that Blamey had made no secret of the fact that he was displeased with the 25th Brigade, why would he praise them in this later speech while earlier disparaging the 21st Brigade at Koitaki? Was he still confused, or did he realise he had made a mistake at Koitaki and then tried to make amends at Donadabu? Either way, he had lost the confidence and respect of all Australian forces and his address at Donadabu did nothing to salvage his reputation. After his Koitaki address, Blamey was openly jeered and booed by Australian troops wherever he went. When he visited the wounded in hospital, for example, the men refused to address him and simply munched on the lettuce leaves they had smuggled into the wards.

When asked about Blamey and his speech at Koitaki, Stan still refers to an article written by Ralph Honner entitled 'The Koitaki Factor'. According to Honner, Blamey's address led directly to the unnecessary death of many men in the brigade, most particularly when they next went into action at Gona. The men were consumed with an intense sense of bitterness towards Blamey and stunned by the obvious lack of support from the government and other commanders. Now that their reputation had been slurred, Honner felt that many men threw themselves at the enemy with almost suicidal abandon. One thousand, three hundred and ninety Australians were killed in the following two months of the campaign on the northern beaches of Papua, pursuing mass type attacks against entrenched rifle and machine-gun positions. The blame for these outmoded tactics and the excessive death rate that was incurred must be laid squarely at the feet of Blamey.

By late 1942, while there was general acceptance that the war would drag on for some time, there was also a growing belief that Japan's military dominance had reached its apogee. Japanese naval forces retained a degree of ascendency, but the continual build-up of the US 5th Air Force in New Guinea meant that there was near parity in the air. American marines were locked in a titanic struggle for control of Guadalcanal in the Solomon Islands. Meanwhile, the vital shipping lanes across the Pacific remained open, facilitating an increasing flow of supplies, armaments and manpower into Australia so that by November 1942, US troops were ready for deployment in Papua and New Guinea for the first time.

The Japanese force that had been routed from the Owen Stanley Range by the Australians had fallen back to the north coast of Papua and was concentrated in three strongholds: Buna, Sanananda and Gona. The Buna sector was initially given over to the Americans while the Australians concentrated on Sanananda and Gona.

Allied intelligence in the lead-up to these battles was faulty in three key areas. Firstly, the number of Japanese defenders, put at 2000, was a gross underestimation; their actual number was closer to 6000. Secondly, it was believed that the coastal swamps and marshes would render the construction of substantial Japanese defences impossible. On the contrary, their beachheads were protected by a series of bunkers, machine-gun posts and interlocking trench-works that made them almost impregnable. Indeed, many of these bunkers remain intact to this day. Thirdly, it was believed that the Japanese could be easily reinforced once the battles had commenced, hence the perceived urgency of ill-prepared attacks. From November onwards, however, repeated attempts to land large bodies of enemy troops by sea were thwarted by air raids.

In addition, there was political pressure for a quick allied victory. MacArthur was vying with the US Navy's Chester Nimitz for overall command of American forces in the Pacific and was desperate for a land victory as soon as possible to enhance his claims.

The correct strategy for the northern beaches campaign would have been to isolate and starve out the Japanese garrisons while subjecting them to sustained bombing from the air and land. Instead, high command called for hasty, ill-coordinated infantry attacks. As a consequence, the Australians were exposed to lethal fire and battle conditions not seen since the First World War.

On 25 November the 2/14th Battalion, made up of three half-strength rifle companies, enplaned at Seven Mile airstrip and was landed at Popondetta, thirty kilometres from Gona. They camped at Soputa on the 26th and the following day's march proved to be one of the unit's toughest. The first half of the trail wound through deep swamps with brackish water up to the men's waists, a haven for swarms of mosquitoes and sandflies. Once past the tiny village of Jumbora, the track alternated between thickly wooded copses and open kunai that steamed in the tropical sun. Just as they emerged into the open, a flight of thirteen Mitsubishi Zero fighter-bombers roared over their heads and everyone dived for cover. They needn't have bothered. This time, the Zeros were hunting for a softer target.

The Australian Army headquarters on the northern beaches had been established at Soputa. Nearby, there was an American Clearing Hospital and the Australian 2/4th Field Ambulance Medical Dressing Station. All of the medical tents were clearly marked with red crosses. The Zeros climbed and banked and then roared down in waves, firing their 20 mm cannons and unleashing 60 kilograms of bombs. Twenty-two Australians were killed, including two beloved medical officers, Ian Vickery and Hec McDonald, both of whom had done such outstanding work in the campaign over the Owen Stanley Range. Such was the nature of the Japanese war machine.

As the battalion moved closer to the coast it turned away to the right, making for the small village of East Gona, the unit's immediate objective. Their new commander, Lieutenant Colonel Hugh Challen, received orders that they were to begin their attacks that night. When Challen told Stan this he could not believe what he was hearing. In Stan's view it was always imperative that a unit put in several days of close reconnaissance before any attack. Small patrols needed to closely map the enemy's defensive perimeter, pinpointing their bunkers and machine-gun nests, sniper positions and weapon pits. Forward artillery observers needed to be snuck forward to mark these positions for accurate indirect supporting fire. The infantry platoon commanders needed to be briefed as to the location of every gun pit and nest along the enemy position so that their section commanders could plan how to best manoeuvre their advancing teams and how break-through and then fight-through plans could be implemented. Challen, however, refused to listen to Stan's complaints, telling him Brigadier Ivan Dougherty insisted that the attack be put in that night.

'Well tell him it's impossible,' replied Stan. The Japs had months to prepare these defences and Stan wanted at least to recce them in daylight. Despite Stan's requests, Challen refused to challenge the Brigadier's order to go straight into the attack.

The battalion was now laying up at a designated map reference called 'Point Y' on the Australians' maps. It was from here that they would advance on the Japanese defences at East Gona. It was terrible country, oppressively humid and teeming with insects and bugs. It was clearly a malarial area but it was the scrub typhus that everyone feared most. This disease was transmitted by trombiculid mites — Stan referred to them as 'chiggers' — that could crawl onto a man's skin whenever or wherever he lay down. Anyone who was bitten was covered in characteristic black scabs. According to Stan, these were called the 'black wound' and it was almost a kiss of death as there was a 90 percent fatality rate for anyone who was infected.

Immediately north of the battalion's laying up point was a brackish swamp, up to waist deep in parts. Then the land rose to a drier section of thick jungle before opening onto the black sand of Gona beach. The advancing 2/14th would need to cross the swamp and enter the jungle, then swing to the left and attack. It was Challen's intention that the battalion creep forward that night and attack the Japanese defences in the early hours of the next morning.

The battalion officers had a brief orders-group meeting and Lieutenant Bob Dougherty was tasked to go forward with a patrol and find the best route through to the Japanese positions. Bob was one of Stan's and Phil Rhoden's old Power House friends. He was a tough, nuggetty man who possessed immense physical and emotional strength. With his curly fair hair and broad grin, Bob was to set himself apart over the coming days as one of the most

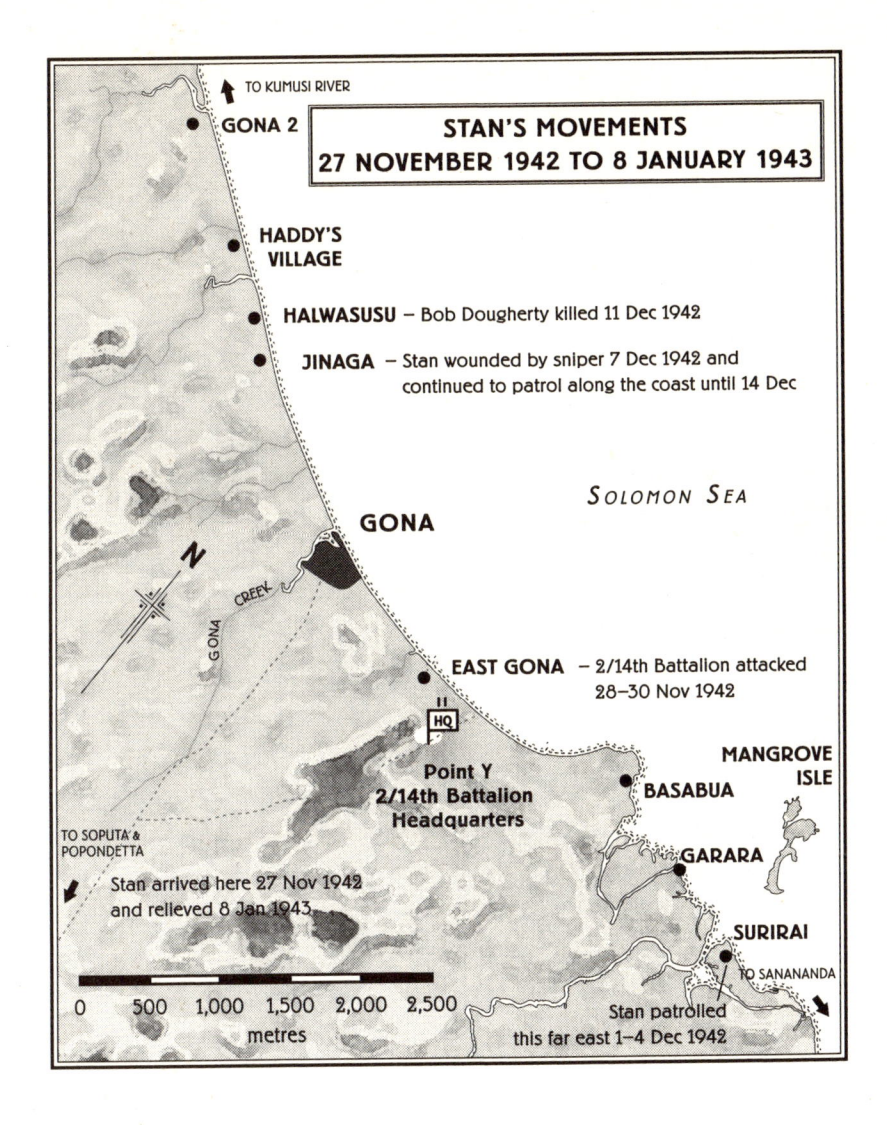

STAN'S MOVEMENTS 27 NOVEMBER 1942 TO 8 JANUARY 1943

- TO KUMUSI RIVER
- GONA 2
- HADDY'S VILLAGE
- HALWASUSU – Bob Dougherty killed 11 Dec 1942
- JINAGA – Stan wounded by sniper 7 Dec 1942 and continued to patrol along the coast until 14 Dec
- GONA
- GONA CREEK
- SOLOMON SEA
- EAST GONA – 2/14th Battalion attacked 28–30 Nov 1942
- HQ
- Point Y 2/14th Battalion Headquarters
- BASABUA
- MANGROVE ISLE
- GARARA
- SURIRAI
- TO SOPUTA & POPONDETTA
- Stan arrived here 27 Nov 1942 and relieved 8 Jan 1943
- TO SANANANDA
- Stan patrolled this far east 1–4 Dec 1942

0 500 1,000 1,500 2,000 2,500 metres

courageous men Stan and the rest of the 2/14th had ever known. Major Bill Russell summed Bob up poignantly to the others in the unit soon afterwards. 'Bob has got to be in the front rank of Australia's war heroes,' he mused. 'When the spirits of the brave meet in conference, the spirit of Bob Dougherty will not be far from Albert Jacka.' Bill had always been eloquent in his descriptions, but in this war of the citizen-soldier it was no great shock to come across men of Bob's calibre.

Bob set off with his 11 Platoon at 3 p.m. but by 5.30 the unit had received no word from him and Challen decided to commit the battalion to the advance. Alan McGavin's B Company set out first, wading the deep swamp in the gathering darkness. As his men pushed on through the jungle to the beach they were engaged by the Japanese. The enemy had dug bunkers deep underground and camouflaged them with dense, live foliage. Built of thick palm trunks and earth-filled oil drums, they were impervious to rifle or machine-gun fire and invisible to the Australian attackers. Suddenly, and seemingly from nowhere, Al's men found themselves caught in enfilading fire from the invisible enemy. Challen immediately deployed Charlie Butler's C Company on a wide flanking move to the west through the swamp and Stan rushed forward to see what was happening. It soon became apparent that the attack was failing and Australian casualties were mounting. The screams of the dying could be heard and the first wounded started dragging themselves back to the start line at Point Y. Five of the six officers leading the attack had been killed or wounded and the troops were so heavily engaged they could neither advance nor retreat.

Stan dashed back to battalion headquarters to try to convince Challen to order a withdrawal. Headquarters, like the forward positions, was in chaos. The regimental aid post staff rushed about attempting to deal with the tide of wounded soldiers who had been carried or crawled back through the swamp. Stan tried to find Challen in the darkness. He eventually found him, astonishingly, not controlling the unit's engagement but sitting behind a log taking no part in proceedings.

Stan grabbed the commanding officer by the shoulder, but Challen would not respond. 'Hugh!' Stan persisted over the roar of gunfire, but Challen had gone to water. He sat with his head in his hands, totally unresponsive. The carnage of the battle was too much for him. Stan was astonished. Stan had been the one who had so persistently complained about the flawed build-up to the assault, and now that it was floundering Challen had completely disengaged with his subordinates.

'What the hell's going on?' Stan asked Phil Rhoden, who was now the unit's second-in-command. Rhoden didn't know, other than that Challen wouldn't listen to him. Charlie and Al's companies must have been getting mauled up there but he couldn't communicate with them. No runners could get back through the swamp.

Stan and Phil paused for a moment in the darkness, both deep in thought. Even after their two long years of almost ceaseless war, this was the worst position in which the pair had found their unit and they were momentarily taken aback at the apparent hopelessness of the situation. They both knew, however, that immediate action needed to be taken if the two forward companies were to avoid destruction.

Then, making a snap decision, Stan found the signals sergeant Bob Thompson and commandeered two signalmen and a roll of field telephone cable. 'I'm going to try to get to B Company,' he explained to Phil. 'I'll try to give you a "sit-rep" as soon as we get forward. Considering the circumstances, you'll need to stay here.' Phil hated staying behind in the relative safety of battalion headquarters but he knew that Stan was right; it was vital that he be ready to assist with the coordination of the unit's operations.

Stan and the small team of signallers set out across the dark swamp, taking cover from the heavy Japanese Juki fire while they payed out the coil of signal wire so that they could communicate with Phil back at the start line. After what seemed like an eternity of slithering around in the tepid waters, the trio finally crawled up onto the patch of jungle hinterland that ran between the beach and the swamplands. Captain McGavin's company had swung to the west once they reached here, Stan explained to the young signalmen, pointing through the jungle to their left, and attacked into the village. Their conscientious efforts to maintain their orientation in the darkness were somewhat unnecessary as the rattle of Brens and Jukis and the crump of grenades left the party in little doubt as to the location of the engagement.

When Stan arrived at the forward edge of B Company's faltering advance, just beside the beach, the situation was absolutely chaotic. The commander had been killed and the attacking troops were pinned down by intense fire from Japanese heavy machine-guns. So thick was the enemy fire that the surviving troops could neither advance nor retreat. As Stan crept forward the last few yards to where the men were pinned down, he passed through the carnage of dead and wounded hit in the first few moments of the contact. He grabbed the first body he crawled past and rolled the man on to his back to see if he was still alive. He was shocked to see the bloody face of his old friend, Alan McGavin. He didn't even need to check a pulse. Al was dead. As he moved further forward under the roar of battle he passed more bodies, all of whom he recognised. Hec McDonald, the redoubtable centre-forward from Stan's and Hal's football team at Puckapunyal, was the next battered corpse. Stan crawled further towards the front and then came upon Captain Charlie Butler. He had sustained a horrific bullet wound to the eye but, shockingly, was still alive.

After this traumatic ordeal, Stan found it difficult to fully assess the unit's situation. He looked around in the dark jungle for an officer or NCO. Eventually he found Sergeant Bill Bartlett and asked him what was going on.

Stan had known Bartlett since Lebanon and was aware that he was a brave and conscientious soldier, but Bill had been severely injured in the Middle East when a shell had landed on the lip of his foxhole. Since then he had suffered occasional physical fits as a result of shell-shock. The roar of the enemy fire had initiated one such fit and Stan had no alternative but to grab Bill by the lapels, heave him off the ground and belt him in the face with the back of his hand. The slap had the desired effect. Al was dead, Bill told him, but Jimmy Coy was still alive.

'Right,' said Stan, desperately looking for Jim in the darkness. Stan grabbed Charlie Butler, heaved him up and shoved the blinded soldier towards Bill. 'I've got a job for you mate! Get him bloody-well out of here.' Stan led Bill to the signal wire that he could follow to the rear and Bill carried the badly wounded officer back out of the fighting.

Stan crept forward and soon found Sergeant Jim Coy with one of the wounded officers, Lieutenant Russ Clarke. Within a few moments of arriving at the front of the attack Stan made a decision that the assault would need to be abandoned and all efforts put into trying to get the wounded men to safety across the swamp. He quickly outlined his plan to Jim. Once the decision was made to pull back the instincts of most soldiers would have been to break contact as soon as possible, but it was imperative that the remainder of the company stay in the fight long enough to allow the wounded to be extracted. Stan, Jim and the remainder of the company's NCOs organised the survivors into a strong line and began to put down as much fire as they could muster on the Japanese positions while the wounded were dragged back to safety. Stan cranked the field telephone he had brought forward and coordinated the evacuation of B Company's casualties with Phil, still back at battalion headquarters. Even as the wounded were extracted, Stan refused to retire and asked Coy exactly where the pillboxes were. It was important for the unit to gain as much intelligence on the Japanese fortress as possible. Despite the carnage around him, Coy needed no second bidding to help Stan and the pair crawled out into the night, far ahead of the last Australians, and Jim pointed out one by one the Japanese machine-gun nests and pillboxes that had cut such a swathe through B Company.

The Japanese defences lay in the thick hinterland on the narrow strip of land between sea and swamp, immediately in front of

East Gona. This village formed the easternmost point of the huge Japanese lodgement that stretched 700 metres along the coastline to Gona Creek in the west. As Coy pointed out the heavily fortified and camouflaged pits, Stan realised how mammoth a task lay ahead of the Australians. The bunkers were all but invisible in the jungle night and their tiny fire-slits meant that no rifle or machine-gun fire would do them any damage. They would need to be cleared by 'posting', a technique whereby a soldier would crawl all the way to the lip of a bunker and physically shove a Mills grenade through the machine-gun fire-slit. Other than a direct hit by a 25-pounder artillery shell, there was no other way to dispatch the well dug-in enemy.

As the pair finally crawled back to the last remaining B Company troops waiting to break off the engagement, Stan realised that he had not encountered Ken Evans' 12 Platoon, which had been the first to attack through the village. Coy said he knew where the men were and Stan sent him off to tell them they were all pulling back.

As Jim bounded off into the darkness and gunfire, Stan, with Lieutenant Russ Clarke and the survivors of B Company, finally broke contact with the Japanese.

It was 2 a.m. by the time Stan and the survivors of the assault dragged themselves back to their start line. Phil Rhoden was waiting for them at Point Y. The full toll of the night's fighting soon became known. The unit had lost eleven men killed and over twenty wounded. Soon after their return a medical orderly told Stan that Jim Coy had been wounded and wanted to speak to him.

Stan dashed over to the aid post and found Jim covered in blood. 'Why hasn't this man been seen to?' Stan demanded angrily, only to be told he had refused any treatment until he'd debriefed Stan. Although it was a wonder he was alive let alone capable of speaking, Coy insisted on giving Stan as battalion adjutant the details of his recent sortie. He had found Ken Evans' missing 12 Platoon still in East Gona village and although they had taken heavy casualties they were going to be able to pull back to Point Y. Stan was furiously recording Jim's information in his notebook, and the second the sergeant finished his debriefing he keeled over, lapsing into unconsciousness from shock and loss of blood.

Eyewitnesses said that Jim Coy had been next to Alan McGavin when he was killed. Jim crawled forward and dispatched the enemy sniper responsible, then silenced two machine-gun posts with grenades. He had then assisted Stan to establish the holding line and continued to work throughout the night bringing in the wounded under constant harassing fire. He was awarded the Military Medal in recognition of his courage.

As for Stan, according to accounts compiled in preparation for his subsequent citation, his work in extricating the battalion from its position and the evacuation of the wounded saved the lives of scores of men. Official recognition of his deeds would not be long in coming.

The battle for East Gona continued until the evening of the third day when, with the assistance of a heavy artillery and mortar barrage, the battalion finally achieved its objective. Twenty-five men were killed and thirty were severely wounded. In a ceremony even more depressing and emotional than the one they had held at Ioribaiwa, the battalion's dead were laid to rest in a small cemetery near the beach. Native carriers brought bright-leaved shrubs to ornament the graves. The hymn they chose was from the repertoire of St Margaret's Church choir, 'Lead Kindly Light':

So long Thy power hath blest me, sure it still will lead me on.
O'er moor and fen, o'er crag and torrent, till the night is gone,
and with the morn those angel faces smile, which I have loved
long since and lost awhile.

Gona, Papua, December 1942. Stan with Ed Cortis (left) and Bill Russell (right).

The 2/14th's padre, Keith Dowding, who conducted the service, was so distraught at the waste of men's lives that he resigned his chaplaincy. He re-enlisted as a private and in its special way of saying thank-you for services rendered, the army posted him to another battalion.

The assault on the main Gona Mission was now left to the other units in the brigade. In a late vindication of Stan's initial wishes, the 2/14th was now instructed to take up reconnaissance duties. Brigade headquarters put Stan in active command of A Company and directed him to lead operations from the front. The company ranged along the coast to the south-east and established standing patrols to alert the brigade of any enemy movement from that direction.

They were then instructed to swing around to cut off a possible enemy thrust from the north-west. As Stan closed-in on a small coastal village he received word from a runner that a patrol ahead

Run Rabbit

of them, led by Stan's mate from the 2/16th, Allan Haddy, had been attacked and that Allan and half his small force had been killed. Allan's men had intercepted and checked the advance of 500 Japanese reinforcements. Stan wasn't the only one to be distressed at the loss of another friend. Haddy was idolised by his men for his courage, efficiency and engaging personality.

The tragic toll of losses continued. On 7 December, brigade headquarters ordered a patrol of fifty men to investigate the movement of these Japanese reinforcements. The job fell to another of Stan's mates, Bob Dougherty. Bob made contact with the enemy at what had now become known as 'Haddy's village'. Bob led his men in a skilful attack, and with the loss of only six wounded

Gona, Papua, 9 December 1942. Lieutenant Neville Young (left), Stan, and Lieutenant Bob Dougherty, who was killed in action two days later. Bob was a close friend of Stan's from the Power House club and one of the finest soldiers Stan ever knew.

235

inflicted ninety casualties on the enemy with Bob accounting for fourteen of them. Four days later he was killed while he led another patrol from the front.

Within a matter of days Jim Truscott, the brother of Stan's mate, Bluey Truscott, was killed in a similar fashion to Bob. Jim was a more reserved personality than his brother but his steadiness and courage were acknowledged by the whole unit. So few of Stan's original friends were left, it seemed as if the odds of survival were fading with each passing day. How long could a man's luck hold out in this deadly game of kill and be killed?

Standing patrols were now established to secure the area against encirclement and infiltration. Always outnumbered, Stan developed techniques to keep the enemy guessing. He and his men kept moving from one position to another to create the impression that their numbers were greater than they really were, and that they might attack at any time from any possible direction. Naturally they tried to take cover but the slightest movement invariably drew a hail of fire. Was Stan tempting fate? Was he being recklessly brave or did he simply possess some natural survival instinct that told him just how far he could push his luck? There was no rational answer.

On one occasion, towards evening, while Stan was taking aim at a target, an enemy sniper neatly removed part of his right eyebrow. As Stan then rolled into a depression, a burst of automatic fire tore away his left gaiter. Twice, within seconds, he was within millimetres of death. A photograph taken at the time shows him squatting, rifle in hand, with a bandage over his brow, smiling casually at the camera. One can only imagine what thoughts are shielded in that black-and-white image. Bill Russell wrote of Stan: 'The wonder was that they removed so little of him, for with his great physique he should have been an easy target as he constantly moved round directing, checking, observing, planning. The confidence inspired by his presence and his sound judgement and coolness under fire were vital factors in the success of the battalion throughout the campaign.'

Gona Mission finally fell on 9 December under the combined efforts of the 39th, 2/16th and 2/27th Battalions. 'Gona's Gone' was the cryptic message sent back to brigade by Ralph Honner. The scene of death and destruction at Gona beach will always be imprinted on the minds of those who fought there. The headless stumps of coconut and sago palms dotting the desolate moonscape of bomb craters filled with oily, putrid water were reminiscent of scenes from the First World War battlefields. The heavy monsoon rains were incapable of washing away the stench of death. Imagination gave the drinking water a flavour the chlorine tablets could not hide.

Nor will Stan ever forget the huge storm that blew in on the night before they were to leave the battlefield. When the heavy rains covered all vision of the ghastly scene and the crashing waves blotted out all other sound, it seemed that nature wished to cover her shame. Reality returned with the rising sun. When Stan looked about at first light, the wind and rain had uncovered scores of Japanese skeletons previously buried by the bombing. Standing sentinel over them was the white cross of the former Gona Mission chapel, the only thing, natural or man-made, to have survived the destruction.

The battalion moved inland a short distance to brigade headquarters, where they spent Christmas Day 1942. Stan remembers laughing at the circular from divisional headquarters advising him to warn his troops of the significance to the Japanese, of the New Year Week — a period when the enemy vowed to do great military and naval deeds, have haircuts and baths, and commit suicide. Stan hoped the emphasis for the enemy over the New Year would be on haircuts and suicides.

The enemy made no large-scale push towards the Gona area and it was thought they were moving further north-west to try to link up with their bases at Salamaua or Lae. Stan's men were still required to patrol the Gona area and on one occasion Jack 'Digger' Yates came across an unarmed, delirious Japanese, half-crazed from

Gona, Papua, December 1942. During an exchange of fire, Stan's right eyebrow was neatly removed by a Japanese sniper.

illness and starvation. When he was challenged, the Japanese lunged at Digger, latched onto his cheek with his teeth and ripped out a great lump of flesh. Digger was the only member of the battalion to be recorded as having been BIA — 'Bitten in Action'.

When the battalion was relieved at Gona on 8 January 1943, Stan was one of only twenty-one men still effectively deployed in action. Of the remainder, twelve were so weak they could only help out

Gona, Papua, December 1942.

at brigade headquarters while another twenty-five were in the care of the Field Ambulance. There were no other men alive to account for. Every one of these survivors was suffering from malaria except Stan who, amazingly, always seemed to be the one who was spared. Atebrin was not in use at that time and quinine was only a temporary suppressive. Only men with a temperature of over 104 degrees (40 degrees Celsius) could stand down. Scrub typhus was the main killer, and in the final week at Gona seven men succumbed to the disease before reaching hospital.

When those still standing reached Soputa on foot on 8 January, General George 'Bloody' Vasey came out to greet them and congratulated each and every one of them on a job well done. When Vasey had returned to Australia from the Middle East his service number had been changed from VX8 to just V8, indicating home service. The AIF service numbers all contained an 'X' to differentiate them from the militia. One of Stan's men had a Japanese flag as a souvenir and when he asked the general for an autograph, he signed it 'Vasey V8'. The wag looked at the number, then up at the general and said, 'Huh, a … Choco, eh?'

The battalion was trucked from Soputa to Popondetta where it rained non-stop for six days and nights, making the airstrip totally unusable. Airfields were springing up everywhere and so they were sent marching from one to another, according to the vagaries of the weather and the whims of the Field Engineers and Air Force controllers. When Stan was finally told they would have to march twenty-five kilometres back to Dobodura and enplane there, the air force dispatcher almost copped a straight left that would have made Weary Dunlop proud. For the fever-ridden battalion, the march was simply beyond their capabilities. Stan and Lindsay Schwind took off ahead of them and half jogged all the way. When they arrived at the massive American Air Force base they summonsed up a fleet of jeeps, drove back to meet the battalion and gave them a lift for the last ten kilometres. If the fleet of jeeps appeared like a mirage to the dazed men of the battalion, it was nothing compared with what the American forces had at their disposal. Not only was there a bewildering array of war-related equipment, their catering facilities had to be seen to be believed. They even had an ice-cream making machine. Best of all was the long, dry, dual-carriageway airstrip.

After a brief leave in Port Moresby the battalion embarked on the *Cannon Abbey* in Fairfax Harbour. After docking at Cairns in northern Queensland, Stan and his men travelled by train to Ravenshoe, eighty kilometres to the south-west, arriving on 25 January. The local people from Mareeba and Herberton met every train that passed by the towns and Stan can still recall the taste of their home-made cakes and scones with hot tea, fresh milk and sugar — they had never tasted so good. Two days later, Stan and Phil left for home leave in Melbourne. Stan's relief was tinged with the prospect of confronting his family. During the past few months, he had been so consumed with his own survival that he had managed to partially expunge the loss of Hal from his mind. As he waited to greet his parents, a surge of suppressed emotion overwhelmed him. Stan's brother, Noel, had also enlisted in the AIF and so the home he remembered, full of gaiety, music and song, seemed depressingly empty. What could he say to comfort his grieving parents? He was incapable of easing their loss by saying that Hal had died quickly without lingering in terrible pain. How could he possible convey the truth of what had actually happened, or find any means of lessening their suffering?

While in Melbourne Stan was informed that he had been Mentioned in Despatches (MID). A despatch is an official report from a commanding officer detailing the conduct of military operations and being Mentioned in Despatches is a military award for commendable service. While the recipients are not awarded a medal, they do receive a certificate and are entitled to wear a bronze oak leaf on their campaign medal. Stan's citation reads: 'His Majesty the King has been graciously pleased to approve that Captain S.Y. Bisset be mentioned for having rendered gallant and distinguished service in the South-West Pacific area.'

CHAPTER NINE

Captain Bisset Military Cross

I n 1943 the travelling time by train from north Queensland to Melbourne was seven days. Given the need to reorganise the battalion, leave was restricted to a fortnight. The main topic of conversation between Stan and Phil Rhoden on the trip back to Queensland was the rumour that the 6th and 7th Divisions would have to be combined due to the horrific rate of attrition in New Guinea. When Stan alighted from the train at Ravenshoe on 28 February the battalion's commander, Hugh Challen, immediately scotched this idea.

In early March, Phil was sent to NSW to command the brigade's training battalion, a move recognised as an immediate stepping stone to the rank of lieutenant colonel and subsequent command of a battalion. The following months at Ravenshoe were spent incorporating reinforcements and easing the returning sick and wounded back into the ranks. When Stan did a final tally, he calculated that of the thousand men who had embarked for the Middle East in 1940, only 180 were still with the unit. By April, Stan was consumed by the organisation of a return to full-scale training.

Rumours of a move to New Guinea came and went. The weeks passed quickly. On 9 July Stan was informed of a change in battalion command. Hugh Challen was seconded to a senior staff appointment and none other than Ralph Honner arrived to take his place. There was no doubting Honner's credentials. He had commanded the 2/11th in the Middle East and had endured an incredible campaign in Greece, where he won the Military Cross. He had then commanded the 39th Battalion in their darkest hours in the Owen Stanley Range and he was awarded the Distinguished Service Order. Stan welcomed him as an old friend. There was a mutual confidence between the men that was essential for efficient command and esprit de corps.

The battalion finally embarked for Port Moresby for the second time in two echelons. The first left Townsville with Honner on the *Duntroon* on 31 July. Stan left with Major Bill Landale, the newly appointed second-in-command, on the *Taroona* on 6 August. On 8 September, at camp at Bootless Bay near Moresby's Seven Mile airstrip, Stan was issued with masses of maps, photographs and pamphlets as well as swathes of documents on the equipment that would be flown with them on their next campaign. Stan prepared sand-table models of Lae, Nadzab and the Markham-Ramu valley region for a series of detailed briefings. Perhaps the army had learned the need for thorough preparation after all.

Stan put the battalion on twelve hours' notice to move. He should have known better. When the order to emplane finally came at 9.30 p.m. on 14 September, he was only given four hours notice. This meant dispatching military police to the usual hang-outs — American movie shows, Australian two-up schools and the sly-grog 'jungle juice' depots Stan knew existed but to which he had turned a blind eye. At exactly 0630 hours on 15 September, the first plane left the newly laid bitumen strip of Ward's Drome bound for Nadzab, near Lae, in the Markham valley.

The battalion was to take part in a series of actions along the coast and hinterland north-west of Lae. During 1942 the Japanese had established major bases at Lae and the smaller ports of Salamaua to the south and Finschhafen to the east. These towns had been major staging posts for Japanese troops en route to Kokoda and they still operated as major enemy supply bases. A combined Australian and US force of 30,000 men was to recapture them. This involved a landing by sea followed by a thrust along the coast to the north. At the same time, one of the largest insertions of allied forces by parachute was carried out around the airstrip at Nadzab. Once the strip had been secured the remainder of the allied force, including the 2/14th, was landed by plane.

Some of the enemy withdrew along the coast but the majority, estimated at 20,000, moved north-west following an inland walking track. This main enemy line of communication initially followed the Markham-Ramu River valley and then crossed the precipitous Finisterre Ranges en route to Madang. The job given to the Australians was to pursue the Japanese along this route and, if possible, cut off their line of retreat and hunt them down.

The valley itself was a natural curiosity. It was a broad, grassy plain, up to fifteen kilometres wide and covered in tall kunai grass broken by occasional outcrops of trees and palms along the tributary creeks or around small villages. Steep jungle-covered ranges towered above each side of the valley. The Markham River ran south-east towards the sea near Lae. Inland, at its headwaters, tributaries flowed into the Ramu, which ran to the sea in the opposite direction. From the village of Dumpu, 130 kilometres up the valley, the track swung right and headed up into the jagged peaks of the 2000-metre high Finisterre Ranges. One of the highest sections became known as Shaggy Ridge, named after Lieutenant Bob 'Shaggy' Clampett of the 2/27th Battalion who was at that moment leading the advance. The track then made its way down to the coast, just south of Madang.

Before departing Nadzab, Stan again briefed the troops. They would be following the 2/27th Battalion, which was several days ahead of them, so their advance up the valley would be as rapid as possible. It would be about 'a hundred miles as the crow flies' to Dumpu he explained, to which a new recruit asked, 'How far would it be if the crow had to wear my ... army boots?' Ralph Honner was a genuine athlete and he and Stan, no doubt wanting to impress the younger men, set an absolutely cracking pace. Each of them had been allotted a native carrier and this meant they had greater freedom of movement and more energy for planning and coordination. As the unit headed out in single file, the men were strung out over one and a half kilometres.

When they reached the headwaters of the Markham River, several of the tributaries marked as perennial proved to be dry and the drinking water situation became serious. Stan was placed in charge of the battalion headquarters and C Company, and he settled them into a secure defensive position. Honner sent the other three companies in different directions in search of the enemy and water. They found some enemy but no water. It was at this point that Ralph decided to move out with four men in the direction of A Company on his own recce. Stan was dead against this, and told him so. The enemy was all about them and patrols should be no less than platoon size. The relationship between the two men was such that they could challenge one another without offence being taken, but Ralph insisted and set off with Tom Pryor and two other men.

After several kilometres, Ralph saw troops moving around in a banana plantation. He assumed they were A Company men but as he closed to within one hundred metres, Japanese rifle and automatic fire opened up from the front and right flanks. Ralph was seriously wounded in the thigh, and even though Tom was hit in the face and chest he was able to run back for help. Ralph could only crawl with difficulty. He was joined by Bill Bennett and together they had to hide in the kunai grass as the Japanese sent

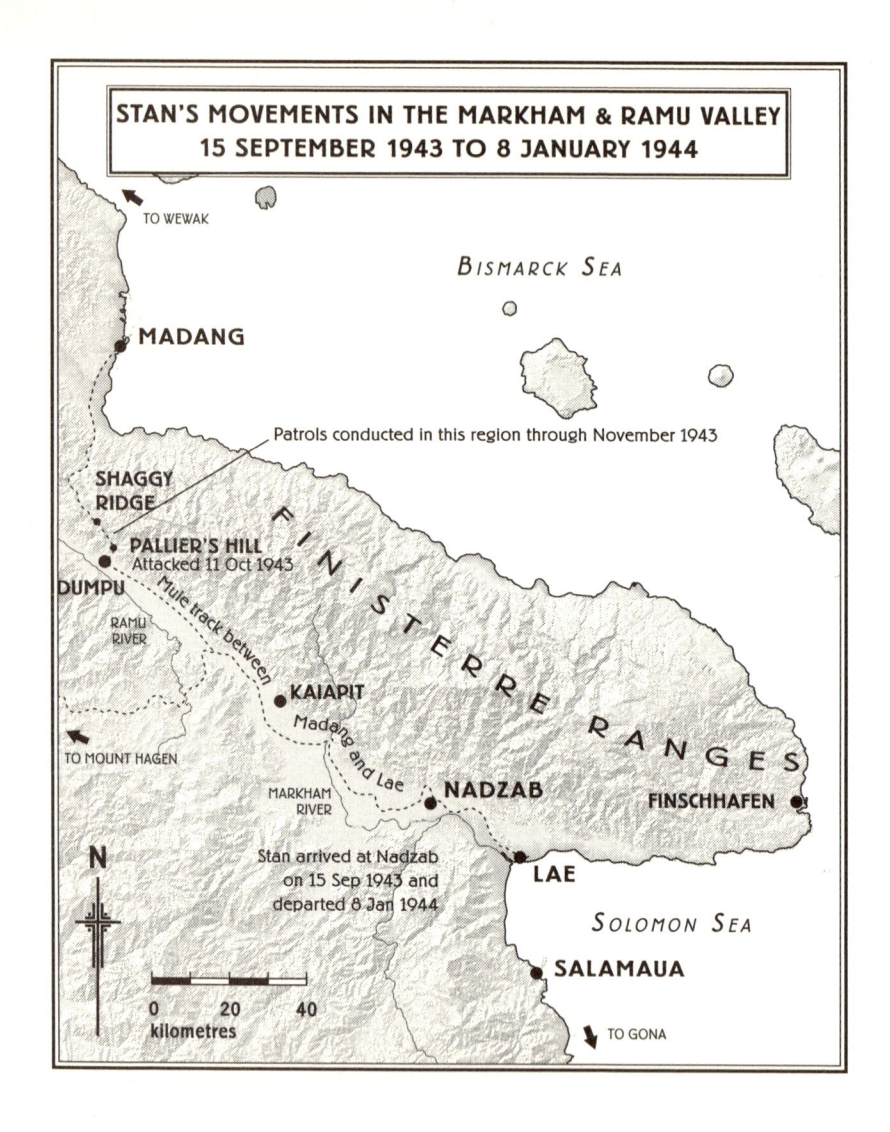

**STAN'S MOVEMENTS IN THE MARKHAM & RAMU VALLEY
15 SEPTEMBER 1943 TO 8 JANUARY 1944**

out patrols to find them. When an enemy patrol had passed, Alan Avery managed to crawl forward with several men and find Ralph, bringing with him a 536 wireless set. Alan radioed for further assistance and Stan directed a four-platoon attack that cleared the enemy from the area. He then had a stretcher party go forward to administer first aid and bring Honner back to safety.

Several days later, the unit headed towards the foothills of the ranges. They paused about five kilometres south of Shaggy Ridge where the 2/27th was known to be engaged. All that day they had been passed by native stretcher-bearers, guarded by armed men from the battalion, bringing the 2/27th wounded back along the track. Stan formed a holding position for the battalion, just off the track, down in the valley next to a river.

The track ahead led up the spine of a spur to a peak called King's Hill, then dipped before climbing up to the crest of what came to be known as Pallier's Hill. Both crests were visible from the unit's position in the valley. Two platoons were sent up ahead to establish standing patrols and to ensure the track stayed open. It was the only supply line for the 2/27th and the only way to extricate their wounded. The first patrol was that of 9 Platoon led by Lieutenant Nolan 'Noel' Pallier, who was to take up a position atop King's Hill. The second patrol under the command of Alan Avery was to move several kilometres further ahead.

Early the next morning, one of the young headquarters staff asked Stan if 9 Platoon had already taken up its position on that second crest. Stan followed the young private's gaze. Quite clearly, silhouetted against the sky, Stan could see figures hastily digging in on Pallier's Hill. They weren't meant to move that far forward, Stan explained. As Stan considered dispatching a runner to establish what had happened, he received instant clarification. The morning air was split by a volley of rifle fire from Pallier's Hill. 'They're bloody Japs,' someone yelled. As Stan looked on, the enemy began to pour volleys of heavy fire back along the narrow track and in the direction of the battalion's position.

Major Bill Landale, who had assumed command after Ralph's evacuation, ordered the battalion's Vickers gun section to engage the Japanese positions. As Stan and Landale conferred, Jack Barnard, crouching behind his Vickers only a few paces from where they stood talking, was hit and killed. Obviously the Japanese had to be attacked, but how? All approaches to the enemy position seemed to be totally exposed and Landale appeared to be devoid of any constructive ideas. With precious minutes ticking by Stan made a snap decision. He snatched a wireless set from the signals section, moved out of hearing range, and radioed brigade headquarters. He explained in clear and certain terms the seriousness of the situation. Such was Stan's reputation at brigade that immediate changes were put into effect. Major Arthur 'Mert' Lee would come forward to take over command. Lee was the 2/27th officer who had led the attack on Mission Ridge during the withdrawal over the Owen Stanley Range. He was known to be a brilliant and courageous officer who had since received a bar to his Military Cross. He would leave immediately and arrive later that day. Taking his wireless with him, Stan plunged alone into the tributary river beside their position and headed towards a feature called The Pimple.

It was a long, hard climb of over 300 metres and while the lower slopes were thickly wooded, the upper part was open grass that shimmered in the fierce tropical sun. When he arrived alone at the grassy summit after a tough hour of climbing Stan sat for a few moments to catch his breath, then took up his field glasses and surveyed the Japanese positions on the adjacent ridge. It was only 400 metres across from where he crouched. In the valley below, he and Landale had only been able to see the edge of the enemy position. From his new vantage point, the situation became much clearer. The Japanese had managed to infiltrate a full company of troops from the jungle beyond the ridge and slip them through between Stan's and Noel's patrols. The hill on which they were now digging in was an excellent defensive position. One side was a sheer cliff of several hundred metres and the other, which overlooked the Australian's supply lines and the rearmost units of the 2/14th, was a steep, open grassy hillside up which an attack would be virtually impossible.

Stan was momentarily stumped. He remained where he was and sat motionless for almost half an hour, scanning the enemy positions with his binoculars. Eventually, he saw a possible way up. A narrow razorback ridge ran at an angle to the one upon which he sat, and it led up to the rear of the enemy positions. One side of the ridge was in clear view of the Japanese, but the reverse slope was hidden from them. This reverse slope, however, was bordered by an almost vertical drop, but it levelled out slightly just before the summit. One man at a time, if he was lucky, could make his way along this ridge hidden from view. It was a terrifying prospect. Troops would need to traverse several hundred metres during which any single wrong step would bring death from a cliff-fall in one direction, or from the enemy in the other, as raising one's head above a crouch would attract fatal attention. The troops would have to form up for an attack only fifteen metres from the Japanese company.

It was a daunting undertaking, but if the Japanese were to be pushed off the hill then this was the only way it could be done. Noel Pallier's 9 Platoon, already up on King's Hill, would be the obvious choice to mount the attack. It would mean that one platoon of thirty men would be attacking an enemy force of around 120. Defensive forces invariably hold innumerable advantages over their attackers including elevated positions and protective pits, as was the case here. Stan, therefore, would have liked to have mounted an attack with a full battalion but the ridge the attacking troops needed to traverse, and the tiny knoll on which they would have to form up to attack, were so small and narrow that using any force larger than a platoon would be near impossible.

Stan radioed Bill Landale in the valley below and outlined his plan to him. Landale remained unconvinced and explained all the flaws in the plan that Stan himself had already identified, but Stan refused to give up on the prospect. 'It's the *only* way we can do it,' he insisted, 'and it's *got* to be done. That track has got to be opened or we'll get destroyed at the front.'

When Landale hesitated yet again Stan lost all patience with him. Men were going to be killed if he didn't act immediately, and the major was refusing to take the initiative required.

Stan asked that the Vickers section and the mortar observers be sent up to him, then pondered how to circumvent Landale's indecisiveness. The problem was soon solved for him. The next time he called battalion headquarters on the radio it was answered by

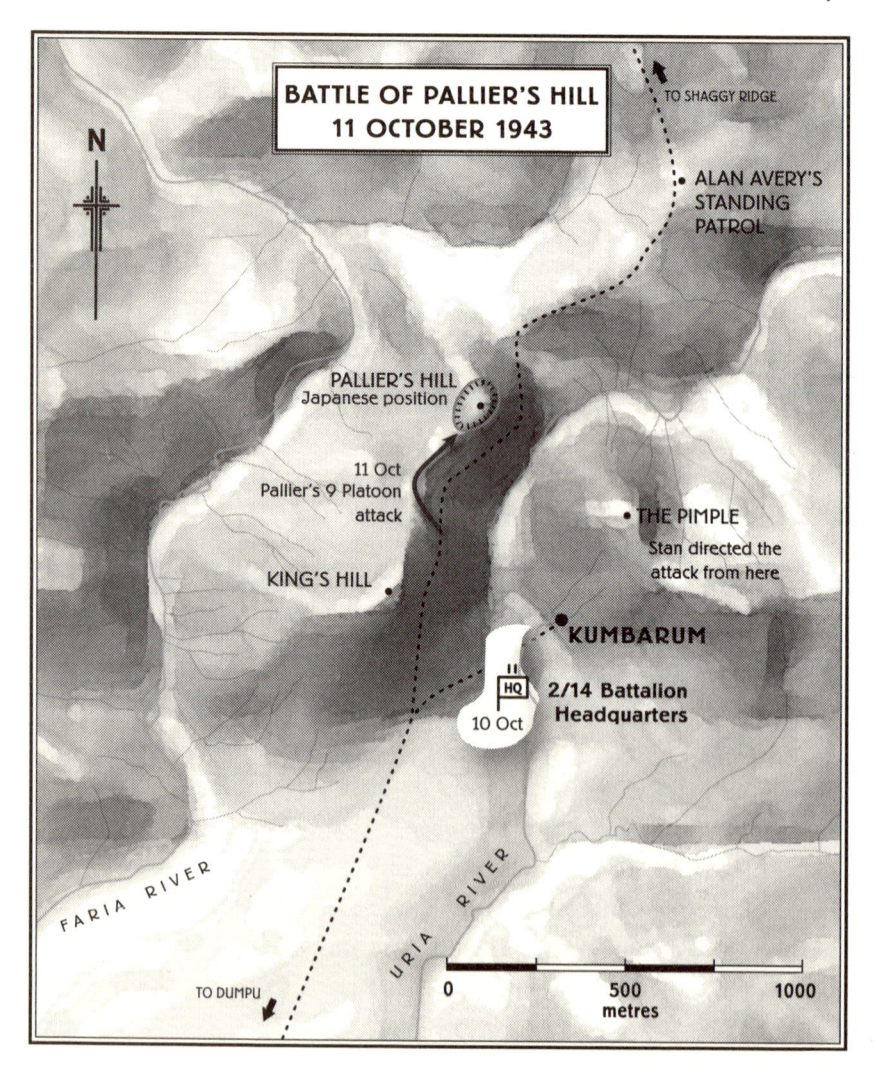

Mert Lee, the brigade major. Someone else was obviously as fed up with Landale as Stan was. It was a relief to have some understanding and cooperation from below. 'What do you need, Stan? We'll get it.'

Stan immediately began to outline a plan for the assault. Over the past half hour he had been carefully planning the best way to mount the attack with the relatively small volume of resources he had at his disposal. He asked again for the Vickers gun section and some mortar observers to be sent up to him, plus a full rifle platoon to bolster the supporting fire. Lee promised him 18 Platoon.

Over the following hours, Stan's vigil on The Pimple became anything but lonely. The unit's two Vickers machine-gun sections, under the command of Sergeant Doug Chrisp, carried their heavy weapons, sustained-fire tripods and a huge volume of .303 ammunition belts up the steep slopes and deployed their weapons. Chrisp's gunners were soon joined by Don McEwan and a mortar observation team whose role was to control and coordinate the battalion's mortar teams in the valley, which would be firing blind towards the Japanese positions. Eighteen Platoon of D Company also reported to Stan after their own exhausting climb and he deployed them along the narrow summit so that they could direct harassing area fire onto the enemy positions. Stan was also lucky enough to get a forward artillery observer up onto The Pimple, who would direct fire for the brigade's 25-pounder guns.

Once his various fire support elements were in place, Stan explained to Lee the details of how he wanted the assault to progress. He would engage the Japanese defences with Vickers gun and mortar fire from his present location in an attempt to force the Japanese to take cover while Noel Pallier's 9 Platoon made the hazardous traverse along the ridge to their small form-up point on the enemy ridge. Although a platoon would usually be considered too small for such an attack, Stan was confident Pallier had enough 'force multipliers' on his side. The attackers had the benefit of well-coordinated supporting fire and the Australians had

251

the element of surprise—if they could traverse the ridge unseen they would be able to burst completely unannounced over the lip of the hill right into the midst of the enemy foxholes. In addition, Stan was confident that the Australians were simply better soldiers. They were physically bigger and fitter than the enemy and their level of training and experience was second to none.

9 Platoon had more experience and had seen more action than almost any platoon in the AIF. Their sergeant at this point was the legendary Lindsay 'Teddy' Bear DCM MM, who had earned his Military Medal at Isurava in the same action in which Bruce Kingsbury had won his Victoria Cross, and their senior platoon commander was Ted 'Heigh-Ho' Silver. Bear and Silver, as well as others like Alan Avery MM, had served through the most vicious actions in Lebanon and then throughout the Kokoda Track Campaign. In fact, by the end of the war, 7 Section, 9 Platoon was the most highly decorated section in the British Empire with one Victoria Cross, a Distinguished Conduct Medal and four Military Medals.

Stan and Mert Lee decided that the attack would need to be put in before nightfall and the word was passed via radio and runners to Noel Pallier on King's Hill. From The Pimple, Stan and his companions could observe the attack he had so meticulously planned and was about to put into action. At the appointed hour, Stan gave the nod to his fire-support officers and the supporting fire plan erupted into action. Chrisp's Vickers guns began to flay the enemy hill with heavy fire with a clear line of sight, and the mortar detachment of Lance Romaro began to 'walk' its rounds across the narrow feature, each strike erupting in a shower of shattered earth on the open hilltop. The brigade's 25-pounders also began to strike the summit with devastating effect.

With this hell breaking loose on the enemy position, Pallier gave his men the order to begin their move towards their form-up point. From The Pimple, Stan could clearly see Silver stealthily leading his men in Indian file along the narrow ridge. The men made painfully slow progress on the edge of the ravine, but Stan's supporting-fire program was devastatingly effective and the Japanese were too busy to spot the Australians traversing the narrow ridge. Nonetheless, Stan had his heart in his mouth as the men clambered and crept along the razorback. Just one man slipping there could spell the end of the attack before it had even begun.

Stan need not have worried. In the afternoon sun he could clearly see Silver clamber up onto the tiny knoll where the platoon would be forming up for the attack. One by one, as they crept across the narrow spur-line, the remainder of 9 Platoon joined him. Just over the lip of the tiny knoll, less than fifteen metres from where they crouched, were more than one hundred well-entrenched Japanese. From his vantage-points, Stan could clearly see both the thirty Australians huddled on the knoll and the Japanese position. Once 9 Platoon was complete at the form-up point, he yelled to Chrisp for his gunners to increase their rate of fire. 'One minute rapid!' he boomed over the clamour of machine-gun fire, and Chrisp's gunners and Lieutenant Tom Simmons' 18 Platoon began rapid fire with their weapons sweeping along Pallier's Hill. As 9 Platoon approached the enemy pits, the supporting fire from The Pimple was eased so as not to endanger their own men. Stan and the fire-support teams immediately came under concentrated light machine-gun fire and Stan had to crawl as he moved around coordinating the fire.

Stan saw Bear and Silver leap to their feet and dash the last few metres to the lip of the hill, but as they did so the Japanese in their foxholes must have either heard or seen them as Stan could see a dozen Japanese grenades being tossed over the knoll into the attacking Australians. The 9 Platoon men all dived for cover in various directions while at the same time kicking and flailing at the grenades, ensuring that all but one rolled over the edge of the cliff before exploding harmlessly in the air below them. That single grenade detonated in the midst of the platoon and a man was thrown bodily towards the edge of the cliff by the impact but, astonishingly, he was able to stop himself careering over the precipice and no one else appeared to have been injured.

Stan saw Bear and Silver again fling themselves to their feet and charge the last few metres over the knoll towards the Japanese position. Just as the two men clambered over the last crest they confronted a Japanese soldier coming out of his fox-hole and all three of them opened fire at once. Nothing happened. They had already emptied their magazines. Bear lunged at the soldier with his bayonet and hurled him over the cliff. At such close proximity the bolt-action Lee-Enfields the Australians carried were of little use and the heavily outnumbered platoon went to work with their bayonets. Stan was screaming at the Vickers gunners now, telling them to shift their fire forward to keep it in front of the advancing Australians, and he turned back to the battle in time to see Bear tossing Japanese troops off either side of the escarpment with his bayonet, just as a man might toss sheaves of wheat off a cart.

Despite their overwhelming strength in numbers, the Japanese had evidently suffered heavily under Stan's supporting fire and the Australian bayonet attack appeared to be too much for them. Although still outnumbering their attackers, many of the Japanese simply dropped their weapons and fled. Stan saw at least a dozen enemy leap out of their trenches and run, screaming, down the escarpment with such momentum that several of them lost control and plunged over the edge of the cliff. It still took Pallier's platoon half an hour to eliminate the remaining Japanese. Finally, those Japanese who had not been killed managed to slip away into the jungle and 9 Platoon sat alone on the summit of the ridge dominating the now-clear trail to the 2/27th's forward positions.

Overall it had been an astonishing action. One platoon of Australians had routed a Japanese force of over 120 after having to advance over the most difficult terrain conceivable. The destruction of this lodgement of Japanese was acknowledged by the Australian High Command as, in many ways, a turning point in the entire campaign.

Consequently, several decorations were awarded for the outstanding attack. Lindsay Bear was awarded a Distinguished Conduct Medal for his inspiring leadership and bravery and Ted Silver and John Whitechurch were awarded Military Medals. Ernie 'Lofty' Back was mentioned in despatches. Given the nature of the terrain and the well-entrenched enemy position, the casualties sustained by the Australians could have been much higher had the action not been so well-planned and executed.

Stan was recommended for the Military Cross after this action, but his role in the attack on Pallier's Hill formed only part of his citation. The Military Cross was created in 1914 to recognise gallantry in the field. It is reserved for officers while the equivalent Military Medal is awarded to other ranks. This award ranks second only to the Victoria Cross for action in the field. While the Distinguished Service Order is technically of a higher ranking, it is reserved for majors or above and rarely awarded for acts of personal gallantry.

Stan's tremendous leadership during his entire war service, his courage under fire and the huge responsibilities he had assumed during the Owen Stanley and Gona Campaigns were all acknowledged. His full citation makes impressive reading:

At Wampun on 4 October 1943 the Commanding Officer [C.O.] [Ralph Honner] was badly wounded. Captain Bisset directed operations in accordance with the wounded C.O.'s intentions until the new C.O. completely understood the situation. By then the operation in hand had been successful. On 11 October 1943 a party of Japanese cut the supply line of 2/27th Battalion by occupying the feature known as Pallier's Hill and this necessitated an attack by the 2/14th

Battalion in order to clear it. Prior to the arrival from another battalion of a new C.O. [Mert Lee], Captain Bisset as adjutant of the battalion made a personal reconnaissance and formed a plan of attack involving coordinated fire and movement by various parts of the battalion and supporting artillery and gave orders for the carrying out of the attack which was completely successful. At all other times Captain Bisset had been at hand and capable of carrying on temporarily should anything happen to his C.O. He has been untiring in his resourcefulness and in his visits to the battalion's forward posts when in contact with the enemy. He has never failed to get to know the country and the operational situation thoroughly at first-hand. Moving about among the forward troops and with his complete understanding of the situation he has done much to inspire the men with the confidence which has been a big factor in securing for us the sharp victory that we have won. In addition to having done such excellent work on the operational side Captain Bisset has always carried out his duties on the administrative side in the same efficient manner. He has always set an exceptionally high standard in all his work and for what he expects from others. During the Owen Stanley and Gona Campaigns of 1942, Captain Bisset as adjutant displayed the same high qualities of leadership always being unmindful of his own personal safety.

Major Bill Russell, one of the senior officers at the time of the formation of the 2/14th Battalion, had this to say about Stan: 'While he held his various posts his qualities of character, intellect and physique made him more a partner than a mouthpiece for the commanding officer. He teamed particularly well with Lieutenant Colonel Rhoden, their mutual confidence producing outstanding results both in action and between campaigns. His Military Cross had been earned several times over, as had his mention in despatches.'

CHAPTER TEN

Days in the Sun

During October 1943, despite constant attacks by the Japanese, the 2/27th Battalion held its position on the main track at Shaggy Ridge in the Finisterre Ranges. Having been thrown off Pallier's Hill by the 2/14th Battalion, the Japanese went on the defensive and withdrew by various alternative routes in the direction of Madang. Meanwhile, other Australian units had been advancing along the coast and they were now held up by the Japanese at Finschhafen. This meant that all the units in the area now held by the 2/14th were tied to a static policy since any further advance over the mountains had to be coordinated with the advance up the coast.

On 20 October 1943, Phil Rhoden returned to the battalion, taking over command from Mert Lee. Phil was promoted to lieutenant colonel and commanded the battalion until it was disbanded in February 1946. November 1943 was taken up with patrols of one to five days duration, varying from small reconnaissance or standing patrols to strong company patrols with artillery support. There were brief skirmishes with the Japanese along the Surinam and Faria River valleys near Shaggy Ridge at places named after their patrol commanders such as Young's Post, Levett's Post, Hamilton's Ridge, John's Knoll and Picken's Ridge.

On 15 December, the battalion was moved back into a reserve position and the Christmas period was spent in the Lakes District along the Markham River. On New Year's Day 1944, the men were back on active patrols, based along the Ioge and Evapia River areas. Stan did not know it at the time, but this was his last week of front-line combat. Orders were received for the unit to fall back to Dumpu, and on 8 January the battalion emplaned for Moresby. Apart from one plane turning upside down in mid-air and another diving towards the tree-tops, both actions occurring without apparent cause, the trip was free of incident.

Despite the fact they had been spared heavy casualties in battle, a staggering 958 men had been evacuated from the battalion during this campaign due to injury or illness, mostly dengue fever, scrub typhus and malaria. Two hundred and thirty reinforcements had been received. The River Valley was known to the locals as The Valley of Death. Its reputation for deadly diseases was such that natives who were brought in from the surrounding hills for interrogation literally trembled with fear at the thought of being held there.

At last it was over. On 25 February, 160 Queenslanders, all of whom had joined as reinforcements and who had been bed-ridden, were released from hospital and embarked on the *Canberra* and sailed for Brisbane. Stan was told he was to accompany them and by 20 March he was back in Melbourne for six weeks accumulated leave. Stan's only military obligation during this period was with the Victorian members of the battalion when they assembled at Watsonia in April and were inspected by General George Vasey before conducting a march through Melbourne to the rapturous applause of its citizens.

Several years earlier, at a Power House dance, Stan had met a beautiful young lady by the name of Shirley Joy Craig. They had communicated by letter after that, but given the uncertainties of the war neither Stan nor Shirley had been able to allow their relationship to develop. Now, with Stan aged thirty-two, having miraculously survived combat and having been spared from serious injury and illness, they permitted themselves to think that there could be a future to look forward to after all. After a whirlwind few weeks of social engagements, Shirley and Stan announced that they were to be married at St John's Anglican Church, Toorak, on 12 May 1944.

The six weeks leave passed ridiculously quickly and on 24 May Stan rejoined the unit at Strathpine on the northern outskirts of Brisbane. In July, several weeks were spent at the 7th Division's physical and recreational camp at Burleigh Heads combining

Watsonia, north-east Melbourne, 18 April 1944. General George Vasey, Commanding Officer 7th Division (in cap) addresses Stan. Brigadier Ivan Dougherty, Commander 21st Brigade, accompanies Vasey (far left of photo). Lieutenant Colonel Phil Rhoden, Commanding Officer 2/14th Battalion, walks behind Vasey. The Victorian-based members of the battalion paraded through central Melbourne the following day. AWM 065549

Melbourne, 1944. Captain Stan Bisset, Military Cross, Mentioned in Despatches.

commando training and beach landings, as it was expected that the battalion would next see action in the Philippines. It was at Burleigh Heads that Stan finally succumbed to malaria. He probably contracted the disease in Gona twenty months earlier and was reinfected in the Ramu Valley. His body had fought against the parasites for so long, but now its normally high resistance had succumbed. Fortunately the introduction of the Australian-produced drug Atebrin meant that the disease could be relatively well controlled.

Stan rejoined the battalion for their move to the Atherton Tableland in August 1944. Several British Royal Marines together with the two Royal Navy landing ships that had taken part in the D-Day landings cooperated in amphibious training at Trinity Beach near Cairns. By December, the battalion was ready for any task that might be allotted to it, but it was now clear that they were going to be overlooked for the month-old Philippine Campaign. At the time, newspapers suggested that the main reason for this was that the unexpectedly rapid success of the Americans meant that no allied support was necessary. Privately, however, the main reason was believed to be that General Douglas MacArthur would gain great domestic political advantage from an all-American victory.

In early 1945 Stan was seconded to the 1st Australian Corps Headquarters. Shortly thereafter, Phil Rhoden received news that the 2/14th Battalion would be taking part in the landings at Borneo. Phil requested that Stan rejoin the battalion and Stan paraded himself to Lieutenant General Leslie Morshead to press his case, but the request was refused. It was evident that Morshead felt that Stan has seen more than his fair share of frontline action and that he would make a valuable contribution to headquarters' planning. Consequently, Stan was immediately flown to Morotai, in Indonesia's Maluku Islands. MacArthur had selected it as the location for air and naval bases to support the US liberation of the Philippines. Aircraft of the US Thirteenth Air Force and the

Toorak, Melbourne, 12 May 1944. Stan married Shirley Joy Craig at St John's Anglican Church. The couple had four children, Thomas Harold, Holly Ann, Sally Joy and James Stanley.

Trinity Beach, Cairns, August 1944. Stan (standing) addresses Australian troops at the conclusion of an amphibious landing exercise. A US Navy vessel stands by to take the men to Green Island for refreshments as reward for their hard and efficient work.

Australian First Tactical Air Force were based there and attacked targets in the Netherlands East Indies and southern Philippines until the end of the war.

From April 1945, Morotai Island was used by the 1st Australian Corps to plan and mount the Borneo Campaign and Australian Army engineers expanded the base facilities to support this operation. Stan threw himself into preparations for the Australian amphibious landings planned for Tarakan on 1 May, code-named Operation Oboe One, and then at Balikpapan in Borneo on 1 July.

Following the dramatic atomic bombings of Hiroshima and Nagasaki on 6 and 9 August 1945, on 15 August Emperor Hirohito announced the nation's unconditional capitulation. On 9 September General Thomas Blamey accepted the surrender of the Japanese

City Hall, Central Brisbane, 8 August 1944. The senior officers, Lieutenant Colonel Phil Rhoden, Regimental Sergeant Major Les Tipton, and Stan, the adjutant, lead the 2/14th Battalion as they parade through the city. On the saluting dais is the Queensland Governor Sir Lesley Wilson together with Generals Blamey, Morshead, Stevens, Milford and Vasey. AWM 068254

Second Army at a ceremony held on the 1st Corps' sports ground at Morotai. The US Army and Air Force were still using the island as a staging base and one night, on a pure whim, Stan's mate Bill Lynn talked the crew of a Liberator bomber into taking on board a few hitchhikers en route to Australia. Stan was feeling pretty smug about this great idea until the bomber reached its maximum cruising altitude and he and Bill, dressed in nothing but their tropical shirts and shorts, nearly froze to death.

Stan was officially discharged from the army on 17 October. The time had arrived to make the difficult adjustment to civilian life as a newly married man. There was no support structure in place for returning soldiers either in the form of medical assessment or pecuniary assistance. Most simply disembarked from ships and planes and were told to make their own way home and just get on with their lives. One can only imagine the difficulties this caused many ex-servicemen.

Stan had to find employment and corresponded with his former employer, William Angliss. He also considered investing in a motel but ultimately decided to join Norman J. Hurll & Co., a gas, furnace and kiln engineering company run by his brother-in-law, Bill Wight. It appeared to be an ideal choice for Stan, who worked in the company for the following twenty-four years, becoming a director and the company secretary.

On 10 August 1946, Shirley gave birth to Thomas Harold, the first of their four children. In order to make up financially for the years lost to war service, Stan supplemented his income by working part-time in a small engineering fabrication company, Wilby Engineering. Also, through his friendship with the Charles Brothers, saw-millers, at Woods Point in Victoria, he formed the Ash Flooring Company in partnership with Jim Kyffin and Jack Hedderman. Jim was a respected 2/14th officer who had won the Military Cross and Edward Medal and had lost an eye in Lebanon. Jack Hedderman was a veteran of the 2/6th Battalion who had been awarded the Distinguished Conduct Medal and Military Medal. Their small company specialised in supplying high quality alpine ash timber flooring at a time when alternative supplies were virtually unattainable.

Shirley and Stan's first daughter, Holly Ann, was born on Christmas Day 1947. Sally Joy was born on 3 September 1951 and then James Stanley on 17 February 1953. At this time the family was living at Waterloo Street, Camberwell, and it was obviously an incredibly busy period for both Shirley and Stan. In addition to caring for their young family, Stan was working six and sometimes seven days a week. The extra money he made from his part-time work was put to good use. The two boys attended Melbourne's Scotch College and the girls the Presbyterian Ladies' College. Stan and Shirley were also able to invest in a second home at Point Lonsdale, where the youngsters enjoyed many wonderful family holidays. Stan retained his association with the Lord Somers' Camp and successively took on the roles of canteen officer, maintenance officer and for fifteen years, games director.

The return to Somers' Camp was an extraordinarily emotional one for Stan as the club had been decimated by death and injury as a result of the war. Twenty-five members had lost their lives and their names are displayed on the club's Honour Board, a constant reminder of their sacrifice. The club found it difficult to field even one rugby team after the war, and while the game is still well supported today, Victorian rugby never regained its pre-war strength and popularity.

In 1967 Boral Limited, a large public company dealing in gas, quarries and building materials, bought a 50 per cent share in the Hurll company. This was intended to be a silent shareholding but it was a highly strategic move for Boral as Hurll & Co. had the exclusive agency for specialised gas plants developed in Europe and supplied to gasworks throughout Australia. However, being a family-owned and operated company, Hurll had a very different set of ethics and values to those of a public company like Boral and it wasn't long before disputes started to arise between the owners.

From the outset Stan was disenchanted with Boral's plans for the company. He had worked hard to build and develop it over the years but felt, strongly, that Boral would lead it in a direction he was not keen to follow. The conditions Boral offered the Hurll's staff, in particular, did not sit well with Stan. He had always placed his employees first, and they had responded in kind with diligence and loyalty. Stan didn't feel he could condone the pay and working conditions that Boral was offering. He stayed on for a year before offering his resignation.

So, at fifty-eight years of age, Stan now found himself looking for a new job. He was confident that suitable opportunities would present themselves but the new role he soon chose for himself was somewhat out of left field. Much to the surprise of almost everyone, Stan decided to acquire his own small engineering venture, a run-down and unprofitable little business in Clayton making household garbage incinerators. With all his management experience he could have sought a position at a leading engineering or fabrication firm but the concept of running his own private venture appealed to Stan, even at this age.

His new project, Alcon Incinerators, could not have been more different from Hurll & Co. Stan had only one employee in his new firm, a young man by the name of Gerry Basset, a boilermaker by trade but a skilled engineer and all-round fabricator. Gerry was an excellent offsider, who worked hard for both himself and for Stan. At Hurll & Co. Stan had managed the shop floor of the large fabrication plant, but at Alcon he and Gerry did all the manual work themselves. Stan spent his days heaving the concrete incinerator bases around the factory floor, welding the steel interior frames and distributing the loads of heatproof scoria rock used to make the incinerator's inner layers.

Stan was a skilled businessman and shop-floor manager and both of these attributes proved invaluable in the development of his business. Within a short period, by approaching the right individuals and making personal presentations, Stan secured a number of lucrative, long-term contracts, in particular with the Victorian Schools Department and the larger banks. Stan then turned to his shop-floor experience by converting the Alcon operation from one of slow and backbreaking manual labour into a streamlined and labour-efficient operation, increasing production at minimal cost and effort.

The factory was located in Clayton, just beyond Oakleigh, and the first step was to transform the interior. The building had a steel girder running the length of the roof and Stan used this as the basis for a gantry that could support dozens of incinerator bins in a production-line setup. Stan then acquired an old conveyer belt from the Carlton Brewery and connected the delivery platform to the mixing bins so the many tons of scoria rock that arrived weekly didn't have to be handled manually. A small, mobile hydraulic crane was purchased so that the heavy incinerators could be moved around the factory floor with ease. Outside, a conveyor belt was built through a small painting shed where the finished products were sprayed and made ready for delivery.

It took the best part of a year for all the changes to be made and it was a costly and time-consuming process. No outside contractors were used — Stan did most of the fabrication work and Gerry most of the welding. Within a year Alcon became an efficient and profitable small business with good long-term contracts and a seemingly bright future. Stan certainly felt more comfortable running his own operation rather than having to appease and conform to the management of a public company like Boral.

Running a business such as Alcon was not without its challenges, however. Now in his late fifties and after a decade in an executive-style role, Stan was obliged to do a huge amount of physical labour. At the end of each day he would drive home to Wattle Park in his baby Triumph, his overalls and hair covered in cement, paint and scoria dust. Alcon brought other, less tangible but still significant demands. As the owner and manager, Stan had sole responsibility for the business' profitability and this often drove him to work enormously long hours. At Hurll he often felt that he was just one cog in the wheel, but in his own business every little problem and issue had to be resolved by him and him alone.

As a result of these long hours and the mental strain that came with it, Stan began to sense that problems were developing at home.

He also detected a coolness on the part of Shirley's parents that he felt was the result of his change in vocation. This was the first time he had become aware of any form of rift developing. Over the preceding twenty years, the couple had been so selflessly dedicated to their family that there had never been any chance of this occurring. Stan had worked his two or three jobs and Shirley put in such long hours with the children that there was never a sense that their feelings might sour. They were committed to giving their children the happy childhood they deserved and anxious not to display any sense of discord. By the late 1960s though, with the children having grown-up and in the process of moving out of home, the relationship ceased to be as strong as it had previously been.

While Stan's personal life was on somewhat unsteady ground, it began to appear as if Alcon might also be facing an uncertain future. Forces beyond their control looked like conspiring against them. New environmental concerns were making the headlines and the Victorian government began to take steps to ban household incinerators. Clearly, the writing was on the wall for businesses like Alcon.

Stan had enjoyed his work immensely and it had given him the opportunity to exercise his considerable organisational talents, but in 1970 he made decision to dispose of the firm. At the same time, however, fate stepped in and another appealing offer was extended his way. One afternoon Stan bumped into an old friend, a former 2/14th lieutenant, Sandy Thompson, in the city and they caught up over a beer. Sandy was working as a director for a large fabrication firm, J.F. Thompson, which built and installed the huge oil and fuel tanks for the Shell and Caltex terminals throughout Victoria and Western Australia, and they were in desperate need of a new sales manager. With his varied background, Stan was obviously a standout candidate. This necessitated a move to Gladstone in Queensland where the company was based. Again Stan found himself confronted by a different set of cultures, not only in his dealings with management but also in what he regarded as the dubious work ethics of the employees.

This was very difficult situation for Stan. The attitude of the workers ran contrary to every fibre of his being. For the previous twenty years he had worked with men who were glad of the opportunity to work. Indeed, many of his workmates, especially those with whom he had served during the war, were grateful simply to have the opportunity to be alive and they threw themselves into each day's work with gusto. Throughout Stan's career he had felt that the role of a manager was to facilitate work, not to convince people to take up their tools.

As worker-management relationships deteriorated in Gladstone, Stan began to feel he would never understand this new generation of workers. Never in Hurll, in Alcon or in Ash Floors had there been a need to convince people to actually turn up for work. Stan remembered his first jobs at Nye's chemist shop and at the RACV and the feeling of how lucky he was just to have an opportunity to bring in any cash at all. He remembered how he had launched himself into sixty-hour weeks upon his return from the war in 1946, eternally grateful that he had the opportunity to go out and provide for his wife and family when there were others, like Hal, who would never be blessed with that opportunity.

Stan knew, as a result of all this, that work and pay were not a *right*, they were a privilege and a freedom that had to be fought for. What about Hal's right to work? His opportunity to raise a family? Hal would have given anything to have these privileges, but instead he had selflessly given his life so that others could have the opportunity to enjoy them in the country he loved … and now, how was his sacrifice being repaid?

Stan contacted the head of the union and organised a meeting to discuss a strike that had just been called. He also insisted that the entire sub-contracting force be present. There was obviously not going to be any work on site so there was no reason why the hundred boilermakers and fabricators couldn't turn up at the office to hear what Stan had to say. This was agreed to and Stan waited patiently in the ground floor office the next day while his workforce filed in, without tools or gear and in recreational clothes.

Stan stood in front of the assembled crowd. He had in his hands sheaves of copies of the union's demands as well as the responses from the Melbourne office. Doubtless the workers expected him either to propose a compromise or discuss the details of his communication with the head office. Instead, Stan unceremoniously dumped the papers on a desk and turned to the crowd.

'I'm sixty,' said Stan. 'When I was your age, in my twenties, I trained as a blacksmith. I wanted to work in fabrication, but I couldn't. After I finished my training I served for five years with an infantry battalion in the war.' There was silence on the floor now. Whatever the workers had expected to hear, this was certainly not it. 'I fought the French in Syria. I fought the Japanese on the Kokoda Track and on Shaggy Ridge. I saw more close friends die, before my eyes, than there are people in this room. I buried my own brother, and left him in a shallow grave in the jungle.' Stan told them about Hal. He told them about Mocca Tracey, about Claude Nye, about Bob Dougherty, about everything they had gone through together, when all they had ever wanted to do was work and play football. 'You only have these jobs, you only live in peace and in freedom, because of what these men did for you. They would have given *anything* for the opportunities you have, but they sacrificed their lives so that you could have them instead, and this is how you repay them.' Stan turned and glared at the British agitators from the Clydeside Shipworks, barely able to control his anger now. 'But then again, what would *you* know about that?' He turned to the rest of the workers, whose demeanour had changed significantly. Most weren't looking him in the eye, but staring self-consciously into space. 'Melbourne has approved your increase. I hope you're happy with yourselves. See you on Monday.' Stan stormed out without another word.

Several of the project's senior tradesmen, older men who had spent decades working in the industry, filed into Stan's office. 'We just wanted to say, sir,' one of them began, 'that we listened to what you had to say today and we agree with you. We didn't want these agitators here any more than you did, and we wanted to tell you that we're with you.' Stan smiled and thanked the men for their time and their support, but he knew that the support of these old hands would make little difference, even if they were the senior Australian workers on the site.

The 1970s continued to be one of the most unsettled periods of industrial relations in Australia's history, and Stan felt the behaviour of many employees both on and off site was nothing short of disgraceful. According to Stan, it approached near anarchy at times, and 'was worse than fighting a war'.

After nearly a year in Gladstone, Stan returned to the Melbourne office of J.F. Thompson. Unfortunately, Stan and Shirley had by this time decided on a separation. These years proved to be something of a watershed in their lives. Stan quit his job at Thompson's and decided to return to Queensland. At the age of sixty-one, he effectively began a new life. He had fond memories of his time on the Sunshine Coast during the war and so rented a house at Tewantin. He renewed his friendship with Gloria who had been a secretary at Thompson's office in Gladstone and together with Gloria's seven-year-old daughter Roslyn, they moved into an old 'Queenslander' home in Rectory Street, Pomona, about twenty kilometres inland from Noosa Heads. Subsequently they bought an old run-down newsagency in the town. Much blood, sweat and tears went into making their house liveable and building up the fledgling business, with Stan often putting in 120 hour weeks, beginning at 3.30 a.m. with the paper run. Gloria ran the house and cared for Roslyn while spending eighty hours a week at the shop herself. Christmas Day and Good Fridays were their only days off during the entire year.

Despite these hardships, Gloria says their relationship developed into a heart-warming experience, something that neither of them had previously felt.

Over the years, Stan expanded and re-fitted the shop and began to sell everything from children's toys and educational supplies to sporting goods and haberdashery. His idea was to keep the people of Pomona shopping in their own town.

Stan and Gloria talked often of these days: disasters brought on by floods, the pressure of the bank overdraft, being burgled, and Stan's occasional health problems — legacy of the rigours of his war service. They would recount how they had a constant stream of visitors when they had so little to offer them. Somehow, they found time to marry — in Brisbane, on 7 October 1978. Stan said these years at Pomona were also a life-changing experience. It was never easy, but the shared challenges helped both of them appreciate one another and weld their relationship even closer. 'It was a wonderful experience for both of us.'

Stan and Gloria finally sold the business in May 1980 and retired to Seaview Terrace, Sunshine Beach. They could now enjoy the simple pleasures of life: playing golf, fishing, walking in the national park and watching the whales frolic in the Pacific Ocean. In 1998 they moved to Noosa Springs, where Stan received badge No. 1 as the first member of the new golf course resort.

The days were never dull. In addition to golf there was the growing appreciation of Stan's war service. For several decades, the Second World War had faded from the nation's consciousness. The social revolution of the 1960s and the anti-Vietnam war movement made remembrances such as Anzac Day unfashionable. It is only in the last two decades that a new generation of Australians has shown a renewed interest in the country's history with a growing awareness and appreciation of the sacrifices made by Stan's generation.

For Stan, the memories never dimmed. He always played an active role in the 2/14th Battalion Association, regularly overseeing reunions of ex-servicemen and their kinfolk. One of Stan's visitors in 1995 was Graham Scott, an industrial psychologist from Brisbane who had been a surveyor in the army and who had spent time in New Guinea. Graham had recently trekked the Kokoda Track with his son's school group and he laid the seed of an idea with Stan that he should return to the Owen Stanleys with a group of veterans to say goodbye to the mates who had never returned. This eventually led to the hugely successful pilgrimage called The Last Parade in August 1998, which received the full support of the Australian Government, the Army, corporate bodies and the Returned Services League. It also sparked the search, led by John Rennie, to establish the exact location of the Isurava battlefield, as the rampant New Guinean jungle had covered all trace of it. Stan also successfully lobbied the Australian Government to fund the erection of the wonderful monument that now marks this most famous place on the Kokoda Track.

In June 2000 Stan was awarded the Medal of the Order of Australia (OAM), 'For the services to veterans, particularly through the 2/14th Battalion Association'. The Investiture ceremony took place at Government House, Brisbane, in September. In fact, Stan only relinquished responsibility for the Queensland Branch of the Association in 2006. He also gave valuable assistance to many historians recording the war. In addition to this biography, he contributed and reviewed many other books including Peter Brune's *Those Ragged Bloody Heroes*; Peter Dornan's *The Silent Men* and *Nicky Barr, An Australian Air Ace*; Patrick Lindsay's *The Spirit of Kokoda*; Peter FitzSimons' *Kokoda*; Paul Ham's *Kokoda* and Bill James' *Field Guide to the Kokoda Track*. He also contributed to many documentaries: Patrick Lindsay and George Friend's *Kokoda: the Bloody Track*, Chris Masters' *The Men Who Saved Australia*, the ABC's *Australians at War* series, 60 Minutes' *Courage Under Fire*, Shaun Gibbons and Stig Schnell's *Beyond Kokoda*, and Paul Coolahan and Brian Williams' *Men of Kokoda*.

The Cenotaph, Martin Place, Sydney, 2006. Stan talks with Ovuru Ndiki, one of the last remaining Fuzzy Wuzzy Angels from the Kokoda Track. Stan has fought to keep alive the memory of his brother and that of his fallen comrades.

In 2002, Stan, along with fellow members of the 1939 Second Wallabies, Andy Barr and Paul Collins, was a guest of the Australian Rugby Union at a match between the Wallabies and the South African Springboks at Brisbane's Gabba stadium. In an emotional ceremony, the Rugby Union awarded the three former internationals the cherished rugby caps they would have received for the test matches on the cancelled 1939 tour. These caps were awarded because the 'Australia XV' match they played against the Springboks in 1937 was given belated test status. In October 2006, Stan and Gloria moved to Peregian Springs on the Sunshine Coast.

Government House, Queensland 2000. Stan receives his Order of Australia Medal (OAM) from the Governor of Queensland, Major General Peter Arnison AC CVO.

Days in the Sun

*Peregian Springs, Queensland, April 2009,
Gloria and Stan.*

Epilogue

Stan passed away in a nursing home in Coolum, on the Sunshine Coast, on 5 October 2010 at the age of 98. I was working in Noosa so when Gloria called to tell me that Stan's health was failing rapidly, I quickly travelled down to visit him. Stan had celebrated his 98th birthday the month before and had been in good health and fantastic spirits, with visits and calls from former Wallabies and a small storm of press descending on the otherwise quiet nursing home. Indeed, only the week before his death he had been fit and healthy enough to listen to Gloria read him the entire final draft of this very book, which he enjoyed immensely. Throughout the writing process Stan had been both one of my most avid readers and one of my most accurate critics. He read all my drafts and sent enormous and detailed lists of corrections to my dates and facts.

By the time I arrived to visit him, however, his health was fading rapidly and he was slipping into unconsciousness. He died later that evening. Despite the sadness of his death, it was comforting to see someone who had always been so robust, energetic and powerful slip so quickly from this world to the next without lingering in a state unbefitting to such a great man

Stan's death was not a shock, but it was certainly sad to see the passing of someone I had come to love and respect so dearly. I had started research for this project in January 2007, when I had the privilege of spending several weeks with Stan and Gloria on the Sunshine Coast, doing daily interviews with Stan and chatting to

Epilogue

Gloria and Stan's son Jamie (who lived only half an hour away in Pomona.)

Throughout the whole experience I was stunned not only by Stan's kindness and willingness to help me with the project, but the vividness and precision of his memory. Stan, at the age of 95, could describe with clarity the events of a single day in the jungle or desert some 65 years ago. It was certainly an eerie experience: sitting in Stan and Gloria's living room in Peregian Springs with the kookaburras and currawongs making a racket in the bush outside, sipping tea and eating my lunch while Stan recounted the death of his brother or the attack at Alma Chaab. I was also stunned by the generosity of the family in assisting me in my research. I couldn't even afford to rent a car so Gloria made a point of picking me up at the station every morning, forcing lunch upon me every day and generally making me feel exceptionally welcome. I took the project on not only because I felt that Stan's story needed to be told but because I wanted the opportunity to get to know such a unique individual, and I'm now hugely grateful that I had the chance to do so.

This generosity is testament to Stan and Gloria's innate kindness, but it also reflects something deeper. Telling that story of the 2/14th Battalion, of the men who never came home, and of the 'Battle for Australia', was the single driving passion of Stan's later life. Stan, like many veterans of his unit, felt that to some extent their story had gone untold and took every opportunity to make sure that his friends — who had sacrificed so much — were remembered. In the last few years of his life Stan finally saw this goal being realised, and this was evident in our nation's growing relationship with the Kokoda Track.

At the time of the Last Parade in 1998 around one hundred trekkers made the effort to travel to New Guinea to walk the track every year, and several of the battle sites where so many Australians had died were still lost in the jungle. In 2009 over 6000

Australians walked the track, and now the biggest challenge facing those involved in the operation is not generating interest but simply managing such a vast number of pilgrims while still preserving the natural environment and supporting the local population. Organisations like the Kokoda Track Foundation, with which Stan was always closely associated, do an admirable job of this. In November 2010 I was lucky enough to attend the presentation of their inaugural 'Bisset Medal' to a young scholar from the Kokoda region, which included a grant enabling her to travel to Australia to study at university. Gloria was invited to Sydney to present the award and it was a touching moment for all present, as it seemed that all the goals Stan had worked towards over the last years of his life were finally being realised.

In 2004 my father, who has walked the track some twenty times as a researcher and guide, had the opportunity to take fourteen members of the Bisset family to Isurava to lay a plaque at the site of Hal's death. I've also been lucky enough to walk the track half a dozen times over the last few years as a guide for various groups. Some years ago I made a promise to Stan that every time I passed the plaque, I'd take the group off into the bush where Stan buried Hal and that we would all sing 'Danny Boy' and pause to say a prayer for Hal.

This is a practice I know has been adopted by a good number of other guides and trek operators, to the point that at any given day during the dry season one could probably bet that a group of Australians will make their way to the lonely clearing in the jungle in New Guinea where Hal died and say a quiet prayer for the Bisset brothers and sing 'Danny Boy'.

Index

Abuari, 1, 186
Alcon Incinerators, 267–9, 270
All Blacks, 48, 49, 54, 58
Allen, Major General Arthur, 214, 215, 219
Alma Chaab, 11, 119–126
Alola, 164, 166, 168, 169, 170, 185–7, 193
Amiens, 105
Anti-Comintern Pact, 141
Anzac Day, 273
Aquitania, 108, 117
army, discharge from, 265
Army rugby team, 104
Ash Flooring Company, 265, 270
atomic bombings, 263
Australian army militia, 101, 105
Australian Rules Football, 27–31, 108
Avery, Alan, 176, 212, 246, 247, 252

Back, Ernie 'Lofty', 255
Banzai charges, 172–3
Barnard, Jack, 247
Barr, Andy 'Nicky', 40, 67, 70, 71, 72, 73, 79, 81, 88, 92, 96, 276
Bartlett, Sergeant Bill, 230
Barton, Jimmy, 18, 54-5, 66
Basset, Gerry, 267, 268
Bastard, Ebbo, 53
Battle of Britain, 143
Bean, CEW, 105
Bear, Lindsay 'Teddy', 176, 194, 252–5
Beattie, Aaron, 54–5, 66, 81

Beaumaris, 8, 10
Beirut, 139
Bellcliffe, Mr, 33
Bennett, Bill, 245
Bisset, George Simpson, 5, 6, 7, 8, 11, 18
Bisset, Gloria (second wife of Stanley), 272–3, 276, 277, 278–9
    Roslyn, daughter of, 272
Bisset, Holly Ann, 265
Bisset, James Stanley, 265
Bisset, Jamie, 279
Bisset, Jean 'Jonnie', 5, 7, 8, 12
Bisset, Murray, 5, 9, 11, 12, 15
Bisset, Noel, 5, 10, 11, 13, 15, 16, 241
Bisset, Olive, 5, 6, 7, 8, 11, 18, 152
Bisset, Sally Joy, 265
Bisset, Stanley Young, 7, 9, 10, 13, 14, 16, 18, 20, 23, 28, 29, 49, 63, 71, 72, 73, 80, 107, 114, 120, 146, 148, 149, 156, 234, 235, 238, 239, 260, 262, 263, 264, 275, 276, 277
    adjutant, promotion to, 219
    army, discharge from, 265
    Australian Rules Football see Australian Rules Football
    Belgian baron, encounter with, 92–3
    birth, 5
    business venture, 267–9
    children of, 262, 265–6
    cultural pursuits, 18–21, 38, 47
    death, 278
    early years, 5–14

Bisset, Stanley Young, (cont'd)
    employment, 15, 16, 17, 265–73
    enlistment, 103–4
    family photograph, 20
    1st Australian Corps Headquarters, seconded to, 261
    intelligence officer, 142
    malaria, succumbed to, 261
    marriage, first, 259, 262, 265–6, 268–9
    marriage, second, 272–3
    marriage separation, 272
    Mentioned in Despatches (MID), 241, 260
    Military Cross, 255–6, 260
    nicknames, 79, 84
    Order of Australia, awarded Medal of, 274, 276
    Pomona, years at, 272–3
    Power House club see Power House club
    Queensland, move to, 269, 272
    retirement, 273
    school holidays, 11–12
    schooling, 8, 13, 25
    sport and fitness, 9–10, 12, 15, 17, 18, 22
    teetotaller, 36, 38, 43, 56, 89, 99
    war historians, assistance to, 274
Bisset, Thomas Harold 'Hal' or 'Butch', 3, 5, 8, 9, 10, 11, 12, 13, 14, 15, 16, 17, 40, 90, 101, 102, 103, 105, 106, 107, 112, 115, 135, 136, 137, 141, 158, 161, 170, 174, 175, 178–80, 184, 187, 206, 241, 271, 280
    death of, 178–80, 187
Bisset, Thomas Harold (son), 265
'Bisset Medal', 280
Bladen, Wing Commander Francis, 35
Blamey, General Thomas, 214, 217, 219–23, 263, 264
Blume, Col, 179
Blundell, Mo, 52
Bodyline series, 68
Bolitho, Murray, 179

Bombay XV, match against, 96–8
Boral Limited, 266–7
Borneo Campaign, 263
Bradman, Don, 68
Bray, Bill, 179
Bremner, Pop, 42, 64, 65, 67
Bridle, Owen, 41
Brigade Hill, Battle of, 177, 198, 204–9
'Brisbane Line' controversy, 149
British Distinguished Service Order, 128
Bruce, Stanley, 87
Buckingham Palace, visit to, 94–6
Buckler, Captain Ben, 194
Bullecourt, 105, 118
Burleigh Heads physical and recreational camp, 259–60
Butler, Charlie, 228–31

Cameron, Major Alan, 167
Campbell, Captain Sir Harold, 94
Canberra Cabinet Rooms, 211, 215
Cannon, Lieutenant Colonel Bill, 118, 131, 133, 147
Cannon Abbey, 240
Carlisle, 110
Carlyon, Norman, 221–2
Caro, Bert, 204, 205, 207, 210, 211
Carpenter, Gordon 'Max', 42, 66, 71, 72
Carrick, Des, 75, 95
Carter, George, 30
Caterpillar Club, 67
Cerruti, Bill 'Wild Bill', 56, 76, 77, 84
Challen, Lieutenant Colonel Hugh, 225–9, 242, 243
Chamberlain, Neville, 77, 85, 87, 100, 103
'chocolate soldiers', 105
Chrisp, Sergeant Doug, 251–3
Christie, W. J., 66
Churchill, Winston, 103, 145
City of Paris, 143, 145
Clampett, Lieutenant Bob 'Shaggy', 244
Clark, Ken, 195
Clarke, Lieutenant Russ, 231–2
Clover, Phil, 2

Index

Clover, Ross, 2, 3
Collins, Paul, 75, 276
Cooper, Lieutenant Colonel Geoffrey, 197, 200, 202
Coral Sea, Battle of the, 153
Cortis, Ed, 234
Cowper, Denis, 41, 66, 75–6
Coy, Jim, 231–3
Craig, Shirley Joy, 258, 262, 265–6, 268–9, 272
Crossing of the Line party, 79
Curtin, Prime Minister John, 144–5, 220, 222

Damour, Battle of, 136–9
"Danny Boy", 3, 4, 99, 161–2, 280
Darwin, bombing of, 144
Davis, C.V., 62
Day, Percy, 48
Dayan, Moshe, 128
de Courcy Gibbons, Eric 'Mike' or 'Squirt', 94–5
De Gaulle's Free French forces, 118, 130
Dickenson, Garry 'Gerry', 119, 121, 123, 124, 126, 169, 170, 174
Dillon, Cornelius, 137
Dilwana, 109–10, 111
Distinguished Conduct Medal, 177, 208, 252, 255, 265
Distinguished Service Order, 243, 255
Donadabu Rest Camp address, 222–3
Dorr, Ru, 66
Dougherty, Bob, 135, 226–8, 235, 236, 271
Dougherty, Brigadier Ivan, 226, 259
Dowding, Keith, 234
Duffy, Captain Don, 3, 178, 179, 180
Duke of York's camps, 24
Dumpu, 245, 258
Dunkirk, 103
Dunlop, Edward 'Weary', 41, 44–52, 58, 92, 240

Eather, Brigadier Ken, 211, 214, 215, 222

Ebury, Sue, 46
Edward Medal, 265
Efogi, 161, 162, 195, 196, 197, 199
Egypt see Middle East campaign
18 Platoon, 113, 114, 118, 119, 120, 129, 251, 253
enlistment, 100–12
Eora Creek, 164, 169, 170, 183, 187–90, 192
Evans, Ken, 232–3

Faber, Charles 'Tiny', 116
53rd Militia Battalion, 181, 182
Foreign Legion, 121, 123, 125, 126, 131–2, 134–5
14th Battalion, 102, 105
14th Field Regiment, 216
46th Camp Hospital, 216
Frank, Uncle, 11
French Army of the Levant, 140
Front Creek, 166, 169, 170

Gallipoli, 105, 119, 197
Geneva Convention, 1929, 173
German Rugby Federation, 70
German Wehrmacht, 102, 117
Germany declaration of war on US, 141
Gill, John, 204
'Golden Staircase', 160
Gona Campaign, 223–39
  Stan's movements 27 November 1942 to 8 January 1943, 227
Gowrie, Baron, Governor-General, 51
Grayden, Lieutenant Bill, 208
Greater East Asia Co-Prosperity Sphere, 151
Greenwood, Jock, 183
Grey, Sammy, 17, 18
Guam, 140, 153

Haddy, Allan, 128, 192–3, 235
'Haddy's village', 235
Half Moon Bay, 10
Hall, Tommy, 183
Hamilton's Ridge, 257

Hammon, John, 66
Hart, Fritz, 19
Hayes, 'Dooney', 56
Hedderman, Jack, 265
Hideki, Tojo, 152
Hippocratic Oath, 179
Hirohito, Emperor, 263
Hiroshima, 263
Hitler, 77, 78, 100, 102–3
Hodgson, Aub, 65, 66, 76, 82, 83, 84, 94
home leave, 145–7, 241, 258
Hong Kong, 141, 153
Honner, Lieutenant Colonel Ralph, 164, 165–8, 177, 180, 221, 223, 237, 243, 245, 246
Horii, Major General Tomitaro, 154, 199, 201
Houghton, Alan, 13
Houghton, Cecil, 13
Howe, Roy, 179

I Remember Blamey, 221
Ile de France, 143, 144
Imita Ridge, 160, 215, 216, 222
industrial relations, 270–2
Ioribaiwa, 157, 210–5, 216, 221, 222
Isakandaroun, raid on village of, 127–8
Isurava, 1, 2, 164–5, 166, 169, 170, 171, 173, 194, 195, 210, 212, 274, 280
Itiki Plantation, 154, 210

Jacka, Albert, 105
'Jacka's Mob', 105
James Fenimore Cooper, 150
Japanese
    Banzai charges, 172–3
    Buna, landing at, 167
    declaration of war on, 140–1, 150–3
    embargoes and sanctions on, 152
    Geneva Convention, not signatory to, 173
    incursion into China, 151
    invasion of Australia, debate as to, 153
    Juki 'woodpecker' heavy machine-guns, 168–9, 174, 207
    military discipline, 203
    night attacks, 172
    Pearl Harbor, 152–3
    2nd Battalion of 144th Regiment, 182
    surrender, 263–4
    vicious nature of, 173–4
Jardine, Douglas, 68–9
Java, 143
Jessep, Evan 'Ted', 44, 49, 58
Jewish communities, 118
Jezzine, Battle of, 133–6
John's Knoll, 257

Kalgoorlie Mob, 108
Kefar Gidon camp, 118
Kelly, Russell, 56
Key, Lieutenant Colonel Arthur, 147, 148, 155, 156, 157, 158, 161, 163, 175, 176, 177, 178, 180, 181, 183, 193, 194, 195
Kfar Matta, 139
Khamsin wind, 116
Kharatt, Mount, 133
'kiaps', 177
Kienzle, Bert, 162–3
King, Sydney, 53, 54, 63, 66
King George VI, 94–6
King's Hill, 247, 249, 252
Kingsbury, Bruce, 176, 252
Kittyhawk fighters, 201
Koitaki address, 219–2
'Koitaki Factor, The', 223
Koitaki Plantation, 216, 217, 219
Kokoda Track, 154–80, 184
    Kokoda Track Foundation, 280
    Last Parade, The, 274, 279–80
    monument, 274
    retreat, 181–215
    return to, 1–4
    Stan's movements 12 August – 21 September 1942, 157
Kyffin, Jim, 127, 128, 265

Index

Lae, 237, 244
Landale, Major Bill, 243, 247–51
Lane, Bert, 158
Lang, Cliff 'Haggis', 47–52, 62, 64, 66, 104
Lansdowne Club, 92
Last Parade, The, 274
Late Arrivals Club, The, 67
Lavarack's 7th Division, General, 118
Lawley, Ray 'Snowy', 119, 122, 125, 126
Lawton, Tommy, 61
'Lead Kindly Light', 233
Lebanese campaign see Middle East campaign
Lee, Corporal Gil 'Bluey', 123
Lee, Major Arthur 'Mert', 209, 248–52, 257
Legionnaires see Foreign Legion
Levant, French Army of the see French Army of the Levant
Levett's Post, 257
Litani River, 126, 128, 129
Long, Colin, 17
Long, Maurice, 17
Lord Somers' Camps, 25–7, 28–9, 34, 37, 67, 96, 266
Louw, Matthys Michael 'Boy', 48, 77
Louw, Stephanus 'Fannie', 48, 77
Luff, Roy, 22, 23, 26
Lynn, Bill, 183, 184, 188, 190, 191, 192, 203, 264

McAdam, Doctor Cecil Gordon, 24, 25, 34, 35, 38, 73, 78, 90, 106, 141
McAllester, Jim, 106, 140
MacArthur, Jean, 215
MacArthur, US General Douglas, 149, 215, 220, 222, 224, 261
Macdhui, 150
McCallum, Charlie, 177, 208
McDonald, Hec, 201, 225, 230
McDonald, Percy, 154
McEwan, Don, 251
McGavin, Alan, 135, 197, 200, 202, 228–30, 233

McLean, Bill, 64–5
'Mad Mile, The', 133
'Mad Minute, The', 133
Madang, 244, 257
Maguli Ranges, 210
Malaya, 141, 153
Malone, John 'Steak', 57, 58, 79, 88
Markham-Ramu River valley, 168, 244, 245, 258
   Stan's movements 15 September 1943 to 8 January 1944, 246
Maroubra Force, 165
Marsh, Jim, 137
Marshall-Hall, George, 19
Mason, Lieutenant Lindsay, 184
Matsuoka, Foreign Minister Yosuke, 151
Matthews, Doctor Wally, 75, 79–80, 90, 95
Mauretania, 108
Melba, Dame Nellie, 19
Melbourne, 6, 7, 8
   parade through, 258, 259
Melbourne Amateur Football Association (MAFA), 28
Melbourne Conservatorium of Music, 19, 21
Melbourne Cricket Ground, 28
Melbourne Sydney Orchestra, 18–19
Menari, 200, 203, 209, 210
Mentioned in Despatches (MID), 241
Menzies, Prime Minister, 87
Mersa (Port) Matruh, 114–16, 117
Middle East campaign, 109, 113–43
   Stan's movements 7–16 June 1941, 127
   Stan's movements 17 June–12 July 1941, 129
Middle East Intelligence School, 140
Middleton, Mr, 19
Milford, General, 264
Military Cross, 128, 209, 248, 255–6, 265
Military Medal, 176, 233, 252, 255, 265
militia, 101–2
Mission Ridge, 196, 198, 201, 203, 205, 209, 212–15
Molotov-Ribbentrop Pact, 103

Mooltan, 68, 71, 72, 73, 74, 78, 80, 82, 84, 86, 96
Moore, Albert, 116, 135–6, 155, 156
Moore, Lieutenant George, 175, 184
Moran, Doctor Herbert 'Paddy', 60
Morotai Island, 261, 263, 264
Morshead, Lieutenant General Leslie, 261, 264
"Mountains of Mourne", 3, 161
Munich Agreement, 77
Myola, 162, 163, 164, 193, 195, 196

Nadzab, 243, 244, 245
Nagasaki, 263
Nagumo, Admiral Chuichi, 144
Ndiki, Ovuru, 275
Nel, Philip, 50
New Guinea see Papua New Guinea
Nicholas, Alfred, 37
Nicholas, George, 35, 37
Nimitz, Chester, 224
9 Platoon, 176, 247, 249, 251–4
1939 rugby tour, 69–99, 276
    acrimony towards Victorians, 74–84
    Bombay XV, match against, 96–8
    Buckingham Palace, visit to, 94–6
    cancellation, 87, 100
    departure for, 71–3
    farewell programme, 69
    itinerary, 69
    London, time in, 90–6
    physical training, 81–4
    return to Australia, 96–9
    sandbagging, helping with, 88–90
    selection for, 61–9
    team photographs, 86, 91
Noonan, Captain Brendan 'Steve' or 'Uncle Diddy', 113, 116, 119, 121, 131, 139
Norman J Hurll & Co, 265–7, 270
Norrish, Keith, 208
Noseda, Jeff, 80, 81, 90, 95
Nye, Captain Claude, 157, 170, 184, 205–7, 271
Nye's chemist shop, 15, 270

Obolensky, Prince Serge, 93
O'Brien, Frank 'Fob', 58
Officer Cadet Training Unit (OCTU), 111–12, 135
    Middle East, 110, 111
    rugby team, 110, 112
Orcades, 144
Order of Australia (OAM), Medal of the, 274, 276
O'Reilly, Bill, 68
Oxenham, Brian, 95
Owen, Bill, 167, 168
Owen Stanley Range, 1, 108, 150, 154, 156, 190, 216, 221, 224
Owen sub-machine gun, 149
Owers' Corner, 155, 156, 194, 210, 216
Oxlade, Boyd, 81

Palestine see Middle East campaign
Pallier, Lieutenant Nolan 'Noel', 247, 249, 251, 252
Pallier's Hill, Battle of, 247–57
Papua New Guinea
    arrival, 150, 154
Parker, Arthur Cyril, 53
Pearl Harbor, 140, 152–3
Pearson, George, 66, 71
Percival, Lieutenant General Arthur, 143
Perrin, Tom, 48, 49
Philippines, 141, 153, 261
Picken's Ridge, 257
Pocock, Hilda, 8
Pocock, Millie, 8
Popondetta, 224, 240
Port Moresby, 150, 154, 196, 211, 218, 243
Port Phillip Bay, 8, 11
Porter, Brigadier Selwyn, 211
Potts, Brigadier Arnold, 154, 163, 164, 166, 168, 169, 170, 178, 196, 197, 200, 203, 204, 205, 209, 210, 211, 219
Power House club, 22, 24–6, 36–8, 40, 141
    C Company, formation of, 102
    1936 rugby team photo, 40

Index

rugby team, 34–6, 38–47, 52, 55, 58–9, 61, 66, 71, 72, 73, 74
Poziéres, 105, 118, 197
Prince Albert, Duke of York, 24
Prince of Wales, sinking of, 153
Pryor, Tom, 125, 131, 245
Puckapunyal army camp, 104, 106, 107, 111

Queen Elizabeth, 94–6
Queen Mary, 108

Rankin, Ron, 81
Ransom, Les 'Pappy', 118, 126, 214
Ravenshoe, 241, 242
Rennie, John, 2, 3, 274
Repulse, sinking of, 153
'rest house' area, 177, 181
Rhoden, Phil, 102, 142, 194, 196, 200, 201, 204, 205, 207, 208, 210, 211, 216, 217, 219, 226, 229, 232, 242, 256, 257, 259, 261, 264
Righetti, Alistair, 17
Ring, Mrs 'Mum', 9
Rofe, Esther, 18
Romaro, Lance, 252
Rommel, Field Marshal Erwin, 113, 114, 147, 173
Roosevelt, US President, 145
Ross, Alec, 75, 84
Rowell, General Sidney, 220
Royal Australian Air Force, 35, 67, 81
Royal Automobile Club of Victoria (RACV), 17, 100, 101, 270
Royal Military Academy Sandhurst, 111
Royal Military College Duntroon, 35, 66, 111
rugby, 24, 30–59
   All Blacks see All Blacks
   amateur code, 32
   Australian XV, 52–3, 64, 276
   Australian Rugby Union, 43, 276
   Australian Rules, contrast with, 31–2
   cap, award of, 276

   interstate series, 62
   Melbourne University Club, 32, 44–5
   New South Wales, 52, 56–8, 60, 61, 62
   1939 domestic season, 60–9
   1937 Springbok tour, 43, 47–54
   Power House, 34–6, 38–43, 45–7, 61, 66
   Queensland, 62
   South Australian, 42
   Springboks see Springboks
   team numbering, 47
   'The Lucky 29', 61, 65
   'The Second Wallabies', 60–1, 276
   Victorian state team, 41, 42–3, 44, 48–52, 55–8, 62
   Wallabies see Wallabies
Russell, Bill, 236
Russell, Major Bill, 147, 227, 234, 256

Salamaua base, 237
Sandringham, 8, 10
Schultz, Allen 'Al', 119, 121, 123
Schwind, Lindsay, 240
Scott, Graham, 274
2/14th Battalion, 2, 103, 104, 105, 107, 108, 109, 111, 113, 114, 117, 118, 128, 129, 145, 147, 148, 149, 164, 169, 170, 174, 175, 181, 182, 183, 193, 194, 195, 201, 202, 203, 204, 205, 208, 209, 210, 212, 213, 215, 216, 219, 224, 226, 234, 244, 248, 258, 259, 261, 264, 269, 273
   physical training, 109, 118
2/16th Battalion, 108, 109, 117, 126, 128, 189, 192, 193, 195, 203, 204, 205, 208, 209, 210, 212, 215, 234, 237
2/31st Battalion, 133, 211
2/33rd Battalion, 211, 212
2/27th Battalion, 108, 128, 129, 130, 132, 197, 199, 201, 202, 205, 209, 210, 237, 244, 245, 247, 254, 257
17 Platoon, 119, 121, 123
7th Division, 102, 103, 130, 242
Shaggy Ridge, 244, 247, 257

287

Sheffield Shield Cricket, 42
Sidon, 128, 130, 132
Silver, Ted 'Heigh-Ho', 252–5
Simmons, Lieutenant Tom, 253
Simonson, Don, 170
Singapore, fall of, 143–5, 153
16 Platoon, 119, 123, 125
6th Division, 102, 242
Skipper, Captain Justin, 209
soldier-settlement land-grants, 15
Somers, Lord (Arthur Herbert Tennyson), 22–7, 35
Somers' Camps, 25–7, 28–9, 34, 37, 67
Soputa, 224–5, 240
South Seas Detachment, 166
Springbank training camp, 146
Springboks
    1937 tour, 43, 47–54
Stanton, cousin, 11, 12
Stevens, Brigadier Jack, 110, 111, 137, 138, 139, 264
Steward, 'Blue', 208, 214
Stokes, Johnny, 117
Stone, Alby, 67
Strathmore, 96, 98
Suez Canal, 111
Sutcliffe, Joseph, 102
Sword, Bob, 170
Syrian campaign see Middle East campaign

Talbot, Reg, 40, 58
Templeton, Captain Sam, 164, 167
Templeton's Crossing, 164, 188, 190, 191, 192, 193, 194
10 Platoon, 3, 158, 170, 175, 178, 179
Thai-Burma railway, 44, 144
"The House That Jack Built", 5, 6
3rd Militia Battalion, 214
39th Battalion, 164, 166, 167, 168, 169, 170, 172, 173, 174, 175, 181, 195, 196, 197, 237
Thompson, J F, 269–72
Thompson, Sandy, 269
Thompson, Sergeant Bob, 176, 229

Timsah, Lake, 111
Tipton, Company Sergeant Major Les, 117, 183, 184, 186, 187, 189, 190, 191, 194, 264
Tobruk, 114, 116
Towers, Cyril, 52, 53, 58, 74–6, 77, 80, 81
Tracey, Lieutenant Maurice MC 'Mocca', 184, 271
triage nursing, 179
Trinity Beach landing exercise, 263
Tripoli, 140
Truscott, Jim, 236
Truscott, Keith 'Bluey', 30, 103, 236
Tsukomoto, Colonel, 175
25th Brigade, 210, 211, 214, 221–3
21st Brigade, 108, 118, 143, 166, 211, 221–3
Twickenham, 93, 95
Tyre, 127, 128

Uberi, 156, 160
Ulysses, 132–3
US Air Force, 163, 223, 240, 261

Vafiopolous, Con 'Vappy', 2, 3, 135, 178
Valley of Death, The, 258
van den Berg, Mauritz, 50, 51
Vasey, General George 'Bloody', 240, 258, 259, 264
Verdi's Aida, 21
Vernon, Doctor Geoffrey, 217
Vichy forces, 130
Vickery, Ian, 225
Victoria Cross, 105, 176, 252, 255
Victorian Football League (VFL), 28
    Coulter Law, 32
Victorian 2/4th Field Regiment, 130
Vietnam War, 273

Wake Island, 140, 153
Wakefield, 'Wink', 125, 126
Wallabies, 32, 43, 54
    naming of, 60–1
    1939 tour see 1939 rugby tour

288

Index

1933 South African tour, 68, 75, 76
   playing colours, 43
Wallace, Johnny, 81
Ward, Eddie, 149
Ward, Fred, 42
Watson, Lance Corporal Roy, 142, 169, 194, 199, 200, 209
Watson, Reg, 42
Wehrmacht see German Wehrmacht
Whelan, Padre, 116
Whitechurch, John, 255
Whiteman, Bevan, 92
Wight, Bill, 30, 265
Wilby Engineering, 265
William Angliss and Co, 103, 265
William Webb Ellis, 34
Williams, Ralph Vaughan, 19
Wilson, General, 119
Wilson, Sir Lesley (Queensland Governor), 264
Wilson, Vay, 80, 81, 83
Wintour, Dickie, 125
Woodley, Sergeant Geoff, 142, 159
Woodward, George, 3, 178, 179
World War I, 7, 8, 15, 24, 105, 111
World War II, 273
   declaration of, 85, 100
   lead up to, 77–8, 84–5
wounds, rotting, 191–2
Wright, Captain George, 189, 190, 191

Yandina camp, 146–7
Yates, Jack 'Digger', 237
Young, Lieutenant Neville, 235
Young's Post, 257